Studies in Renaissance Literature

Volume 4

KING JAMES I AND THE RELIGIOUS CULTURE
OF ENGLAND

Although James I was more interested in religious matters than in any other aspect of English culture at the time, this topic has received little attention in recent literary scholarship, which this book aims to redress. It studies his influence, both direct and indirect, on aspects of religious life, and particularly his hitherto neglected writings. Beginning with an examination of the roots of his religious thinking in the Protestant understanding of biblical monarchy, and his own experiences as king of Scotland, it moves to his reign in England, bringing together literary, religious and political history to consider such subjects as the poetic response to his accession, prophetic poetry at court, and the politics of conversion. Going beyond the usual critical attention to the short devotional lyric, the study draws on such forms as religious narrative, philosophical or theological verse, works of religious satire and controversy, liturgical verse and sermons, by both well and lesser-known writers. James' own attempt to provide a new English versification of the Psalms is examined in particular depth.

JAMES DOELMAN teaches in the Department of English at McMaster University.

Studies in Renaissance Literature

ISSN 1465–6310

Founding editor
John T. Shawcross

General Editor
Graham Parry

Editorial board
Helen E. Wilcox
John N. King
Graham Parry

Studies in Renaissance Literature offers investigations of topics both span-
ning the sixteenth and seventeenth centuries and growing out of medieval
concerns, up to the Restoration period. Particularly encouraged are new
examinations of the interplay between the literature of the English
Renaissance and its cultural history.

Proposals or queries may be sent directly to the editors at the addresses
given below; all submissions will receive prompt and informed consideration.

Professor Graham Parry, Department of English, University of York,
Heslington, York YO1 5DD, UK

Professor Helen E. Wilcox, Rijksuniversiteit Groningen, Broerstraat 5, POB
72,9700 AB, Groningen, The Netherlands

Dr John N. King, Department of English, Ohio State University, Columbus,
Ohio 43210, USA

KING JAMES I AND THE RELIGIOUS
CULTURE OF ENGLAND

James Doelman

D. S. BREWER

First published 2000
D. S. Brewer, Cambridge

ISBN 0 85991 593 X

D. S. Brewer is an imprint of Boydell & Brewer Ltd
PO Box 9, Woodbridge, Suffolk IP12 3DF, UK
and of Boydell & Brewer Inc.
PO Box 41026, Rochester, NY 14604–4126, USA
website: http://www.boydell.co.uk

A catalogue record for this book is available
from the British Library

Library of Congress Cataloging-in-Publication Data
Doelman, James, 1963–
  King James I and the religious culture of England / James Doelman.
    p. cm. – (Studies in Renaissance literature, ISSN 1465-6310; v. 4)
  Includes bibliographical references and index.
  ISBN 0-85991-593-X (hardcover: alk. paper)
    1. England – Religious life and customs. 2. James I, King of
England, 1566–1625 – Influence. 3. James I, King of England, 1566–1625
– Religion. 4. James I, King of England, 1566–1625 – In literature.
5. Christian literature, English – England – History and criticism.
6. England – Church history – 16th century. 7. England – Church
history – 17th century. I. Title: King James the First and the religious
culture of England. II. Title. III. Studies in Renaissance literature
(Woodbridge, Suffolk, England); v. 4.
BR757.D64   2000
274.2'06–dc21   00–036094

This publication is printed on acid-free paper

Typeset by Joshua Associates Ltd, Oxford
Printed in Great Britain by
St Edmundsbury Press Ltd, Bury St Edmunds, Suffolk

CONTENTS

ACKNOWLEDGEMENTS

The early work for this book was made possible by an SSHRRC post-graduate fellowship. Thanks are due to Konrad Eisenbichler, Germaine Warkentin and David Galbraith of the Centre for Reformation and Renaissance Studies in Toronto, where I held the fellowship. Graham Roebuck, Chauncey Wood and Jim Dale of McMaster have been encouraging and helpful since the beginning of this work; John Shawcross and Graham Parry provided numerous helpful suggestions when the book was approaching its final form.

Chapter 2, "The Accession of King James I and English Religious Poetry", first appeared under that title in *Studies in English Literature* 34 (1994): 19–40, and is reprinted by permission of the Johns Hopkins University Press. Portions of chapter 7 appeared in an earlier form in "George Wither, the Stationers Company, and the English Psalter", *Studies in Philology* 90 (1993): 74–82. A revised version of this chapter will appear in *Royal Subjects: Essays on the Writings of James VI and I*, edited by Daniel Fischlin and Mark Fortier, Wayne State University Press, 2001.

Special thanks must go to my wife Nancy, who saved me from numerous instances of ghastly sentence structure and was supportive through the many years of work on this project. This book is dedicated to her and our three daughters, Sarah, Esther and Elizabeth.

LIST OF ABBREVIATIONS

CSPD	*Calendar of State Papers, Domestic*
CSP, Ireland	*Calendar of State Papers, Ireland*
CSP, Scotland	*Calendar of State Papers Relating to Scotland*
CSPV	*Calendar of State Papers, Venetian*
DNB	*Dictionary of National Biography*
ELR	*English Literary Renaissance*
HLQ	*Huntington Library Quarterly*
HMC	*Historical Manuscripts Commission*
JMRS	*Journal of Medieval and Renaissance Studies*
MP	*Modern Philology*
PBSA	*Papers. Bibliographical Society of America*
RSCHS	*Records. Scottish Church History Society*
SB	*Studies in Bibliography*
SQ	*Shakespeare Quarterly*
STC	*Short-Title Catalogue of English Books, 1475–1640.* Eds Pollard and Redgrave
SP	State Papers, Public Record Office, London, England

Unless otherwise noted, all quotations are from the Authorized (King James) translation of the Bible.

PREFACE

On the morning of 27 March 1625, in the full knowledge that King James I lay dying, Daniel Price preached on the significance of a monarch for the cultural flavour of a nation:

> For, as all in Alexanders time, did affect Chivalry, because hee was a Souldier; and Poetry in Augustus time, because hee loved Poets; and Musicke in Nero's time, because hee was a Musitian; and Fencing in Commodus time, because hee delighted in Fencers; so all were forward in Christianity in Constantine's time, because hee loved Christians.[1]

Price is comparing James with Constantine, and while contemporaries joked about their king's love of hunting, it was James' religious interests that had the greatest effect on England. This understanding of the cultural influence of a monarch lies behind the present study.[2] Malcolm Smuts suggests that "The King's tastes and cultural interests need to be studied more carefully, but it seems unlikely that he will emerge as a major trendsetter even in many fields in which he took some interest."[3] This book is an attempt to assess the role of James in that aspect of English culture, religion, which most attracted his interest. I suggest that in this area James was a "major trendsetter", or perhaps it is better to say that he was that "North Star" from which the religious culture of the period took its bearings.

During his English reign King James was frequently hailed as the "nutritius" (nursing father) of the church, an image that he himself had

---

[1] *A Heartie Prayer* (1625), pp. 18–19.
[2] In the sixteenth and seventeenth centuries monarchial change did have a tremendous effect on culture generally and religious life in particular. Each of the later Tudors, of course, serves to illustrate this, as does French history. The reign of Charles I also illustrates it, if we follow Julian Davies in arguing that the marked changes in the English church began already with Charles' accession, and not just the rise to influence of William Laud (Julian Davies, *The Caroline Captivity of the Church*, pp. 24 and 299). For an insightful consideration of James' manifold if often indirect influence on English culture, see Curtis Perry's introduction to *The Making of Jacobean Culture: James I and the Renegotiation of Elizabethan Literary Practice* (Cambridge: CUP, 1997), esp. pp. 6–8. Unfortunately, Perry's work appeared too late to have the influence on the present study that it deserves.
[3] "Cultural Diversity and Cultural Change at the Court of James I", *The Mental World of the Jacobean Court*, ed. Linda Levy Peck (Cambridge: CUP, 1991), p. 301n.

1

used in *Basilikon Doron* and *The Trew Law of Free Monarchies*.[4] This striking image, which had its roots in Isaiah 49:23 ("kings shall be thy nursing fathers"), summarizes well the role that James envisioned for himself, not just in reference to the church, but for the religious life of the nation in general. In this book I have set out to consider a number of the ways in which James influenced what I have broadly termed the "religious culture" of England. While James is the starting point for this study, frequently attention comes to rest more firmly on his subjects and their response to his perceived interests and views.

The religious culture of the Jacobean period has been relatively neglected for a number of reasons. James' accession marked the first since that of Henry VIII where the new reign did not coincide with a manifestly new direction in religion. There was no equivalent to the "Elizabethan settlement" for James; the theology and church government remained largely the same with his accession.[5] As a result, church historians have given the church of his reign short shrift, even though, unlike Elizabeth, James was vitally interested in a wide range of religious matters.[6] In recent years this lacuna has begun to be rectified by Nicholas Tyacke and Peter White on the theological developments and disputes of the time, the work of Kenneth Fincham on the Jacobean episcopate, William Patterson on James' ecumenism, and, most recently, Peter McCullough on the court sermons of the period.[7] While heavily indebted to these scholars my own work concerns not church history so much as the broader religious culture of the time. I hope, in this book, to do justice to what Julian Davies has called "the remarkable institution that was the Jacobean Church", an institution that owed more to James than simply its name. However, this study is not primarily one of church history or history of theology; "religious culture" includes, but also extends beyond, the church. James' influence reached beyond the boundaries of the church proper – to the areas of religious poetry, scholarship, and personal religious commitment – and it is these matters that are the central concern of this

---

[4] For further examples of James as "nutritius", see Richard Eedes, "Princes too bee Nurces of the Church", in *Six Learned and Godly Sermons* (1604), and John King, *A Sermon at Paules Crosse* (1620), p. 42.

[5] The beginning of his reign was marked by the Hampton Court Conference (1604), but this assembly largely confirmed the direction of the late Elizabethan church.

[6] Leo F. Solt, *Church and State in Early Modern England* (Oxford: OUP, 1990), p. 163.

[7] Nicholas Tyacke, *Anti-Calvinists: the Rise of English Arminianism ca.1590–1640* (Oxford: Clarendon Press, 1987); Peter White, *Predestination, Policy and Polemic: Conflict and Consensus in the English Church from the Reformation to the Civil War* (Cambridge and New York: CUP, 1992); Kenneth Fincham, *Prelate as Pastor: the Episcopate of James I* (Oxford: Clarendon Press, 1990); William B. Patterson, *King James VI and I and the Reunion of Christendom* (Cambridge and New York: CUP, 1997); Peter E. McCullough, *Sermons at Court: Politics and Religion in Elizabethan and Jacobean Preaching* (Cambridge and New York: CUP, 1998). See also the seminal article on James and the church, Kenneth Fincham and Peter Lake, "The Ecclesiastical Policy of King James I", *Journal of British Studies* 24 (1985): 169–207.

book. The king's influence and role extended into all these areas, and James was willing to countenance a religious culture that lived beyond the church, if never in opposition to that church. It must also be remembered how thoroughly the religious and political spheres overlapped; Kevin Sharpe notes that "James's tracts, speeches, and letters contain constant applications of scripture to issues and problems of state. Scripture for him was a text of state because the Christian and political realms were one and shared a discourse."[8] This aspect is most pronounced in Chapter 6 where I consider the biblical roots of James' peacemaking stance.

I approach the subject as a literary scholar, and it is the shortcomings in this field that have inspired my work. Literary scholars have most often focussed on short devotional poetry of the period and particularly the holy sonnets of John Donne,[9] but such literary forms as religious narrative, philosophical or theological verse, liturgical verse, and controversial or satiric writings on religious subjects have been neglected. Sermons, apart from those of Donne and possibly of Lancelot Andrewes, need to be much further considered; both in their oral and printed forms they were the most popular and contentious of cultural forms.[10] It is with these relatively neglected areas that the present study concerns itself.

Religious culture of the Caroline era has received more recent attention than that of the Jacobean; typical is Malcolm Smuts' *Court Culture and the Origins of a Royalist Tradition in Early Stuart England*, which devotes a chapter to religious culture in the reign of Charles, but not one to James on the same subject.[11] I would argue that James' religious culture is less accessible for the modern scholar because of James' emphasis on the written word, rather than visual symbolism, and the neo-Latin vehicle of so much of this written culture. Our relative ignorance of neo-Latin writings has cut us off from a good part of the higher culture of the time, and that in which James was most interested.[12] The emphasis on the verbal over the visual was a

---

[8] John Morrill *et al.*, eds, *Public Duty and Private Conscience in Seventeenth-Century England: Essays Presented to G. E. Aylmer* (Oxford: Clarendon Press, 1993), p. 90.

[9] Such scholarship has been very insightful and helpful; see particularly Barbara K. Lewalski's broad-ranging *Protestant Poetics and the Seventeenth-Century Religious Lyric* (Princeton: Princeton UP, 1979).

[10] My very unscientific counting of references in contemporary letters finds that there are approximately twenty references to controversial sermons for every one to a controversial play. See also McCullough, pp. 101 and 125, on the relative significance of sermons and drama.

[11] His essay, "The Political Failure of Stuart Cultural Patronage", *Patronage in the Renaissance*, eds Guy F. Lytle and Stephen Orgel (Princeton: Princeton UP, 1981), also gives much more attention to Charles than James.

[12] The preface to *Northerne Poems Congratulating the Kings Majesties entrance to the crown* (1604) (*STC* 14427) states that "I wrote them [the poems] in Latine for the King, in English for the Queene" (sig. A2r). This suggests that even early in his English reign, it was noted that the better way to address the king was in Latin.

general trend in Protestantism, especially in the years between 1580 and 1630, but it was heightened by James' personal interests and abilities. Hence, this study as well is primarily concerned with written religious culture.

The religious iconography applied to James during his English reign is also of central concern to this study. Recent scholarship has tended to focus on the iconography of classical figures that were applied to James. Jonathan Goldberg, for example, suggests that while Elizabeth was widely celebrated as a latter-day Deborah, with James "classical allusions dominated".[13] Such a quantitative statement is difficult to sustain or refute, but Goldberg certainly overlooks the wealth of biblical figures and later Christian emperors and kings to whom James was compared. The distortions in Goldberg's book may be due partly to his emphasis on drama and masque, genres not readily open to biblical or Christian subject matter because of the Blasphemy Act of 1605.[14] In addition, Malcolm Smuts notes that "Our understanding of that history [of James's court] has been coloured, however, by a preoccupation with two major figures – Ben Jonson and Inigo Jones – and by a tendency to interpret developments in James's reign as a prelude to the 'artistic renaissance' that occurred under Charles I."[15] Considerations of the iconography of James must move beyond the limited visual worlds of the theatre, architecture and art, to consider a wide variety of prose and poetry.[16]

This book takes James as its starting point, but in doing so I am not suggesting that he was by any means the only significant factor in the development of the Jacobean church or Jacobean religious culture. The English church had been instituted by king and parliament, and the respective roles of church, king, parliament and people were to be disputed throughout the period, and play a large role in the outbreak of the civil war.[17] Patrick Collinson has demonstrated how in late sixteenth- and early seventeenth-century England, personal and private commitment to the faith encouraged men to feel that they should play a significant role in shaping how that faith was publicly expressed.[18] Thus, it is the interaction of James' ideas of religious life with that of his subjects that provides the material for this study. For, as James brought certain desires forward, they were met with expectations and models of the clergy and people themselves, expectations derived from scripture and the history of the church, and particularly the Protestant church. Thus an area of negotiation emerged, and frequently this study

---

[13] *James I and the Politics of Literature* (Stanford: Stanford UP, 1989), p. 33.

[14] Collinson, *Birthpangs of Protestant England* (New York: St Martin's Press, 1988), p. 113.

[15] "Cultural Diversity and Cultural Change at the Court of James I", p. 99.

[16] If Leeds Barroll is correct in arguing that James ultimately cared little for the drama staged in his reign, this adds still further to the argument not to over-emphasize its role in developing a royal iconography ("A New History for Shakespeare and His Time", *SQ* 39 (1988): 441–64).

[17] Davies, *Caroline Captivity*, pp. 313–18.

[18] Patrick Collinson, *The Religion of Protestants: the Church in English Society, 1559–1625* (Oxford: Clarendon Press, 1982), pp. 467–99.

concerns itself with the failure of James to match the expectations of his people, or, to put it another way, the failure of the religious culture to allow itself to be shaped. In considering the relative role of James, my study comes close to that of Curtis Perry, who suggests that while James' "influence on literature and culture was manifold", it was "mediated in practice by a wide variety of local agendas and contingencies".[19]

Any study such as this must confront also the difficulty of distinguishing between the views and actions of James himself, and those immediately below him who were responsible for putting his ideas into practice, but who also had ideas and influence of their own. While James' writings circulated much more widely and have survived to a much greater extent than most early modern monarchs', most of the day-to-day influence was through such figures as the archbishop of Canterbury, the secretary of state, and particularly in later years, the duke of Buckingham. In reference to James' writings, D. H. Willson argued that the majority of James' works were in fact largely the work of his "literary assistants"; in response Robert Peters suggested that it might be better to describe these figures as "scholarly research workers", and that at the very least there existed a "Jacobean school of theology".[20] While I am broadly in agreement with Peters' view, I would qualify it by noting the tension that frequently existed between James and those bishops with whom he worked most closely, or James and such theologians as Casaubon and du Moulin, and that any "school of theology" or vision of religious culture was in a constant state of change, and responded to both continental and domestic developments. A shared vision of one year might be replaced by unarticulated or open struggle in the next.

James Stuart was king of Scotland, England, Ireland, and recognized by many Britons and other Europeans as the leader of Protestantism. Hence there are three different venues or contexts for James' religious program: Scotland, England and Europe; and at points I will consider James' experiences with the church in Scotland in the years up to 1603, and his desire to play a significant role in the Christianity of all of Europe.[21] However, this study takes the religious life of England from 1603 to 1625 as its major focus.

The religious culture of Jacobean England is a topic of such breadth that this study is by necessity merely a limited consideration of selected aspects. I have deliberately focussed on those matters, which seem to have "fallen between the stools" of church history and literary study. The book bypasses,

---

[19] *The Making of Jacobean Culture*, p. 6.

[20] Robert Peters, "The Notion of *the Church* in the Writings attributed to Kings James VI and I", *Studies in Church History* 3 (1966): 223; D. H. Willson, "James I's Literary Assistants", *HLQ* 8 (1944–5): 35–57.

[21] James took greater interest in Irish matters than many in England at the time, but seems to have been content to leave the religious situation there as it was. See Jenny Wormald, "James VI, James I and the Identity of Britain", *The British Problem, c. 1534–1707*, eds B. Bradshaw and J. Morrill (New York: St Martin's Press, 1996), pp. 166–70.

for example, the best known and most enduring legacy of James' religious interests, that translation of the Bible completed in 1611, which in North America goes by the name of the "King James" version. The role of James in encouraging this work and its success is known even by the non-specialist, and I would have little to add to what has been written by earlier scholars.[22] James' reign coincided with an increased interest in church music and the restoration of organs;[23] and such remarkable composers as Tomkins, Byrd, Gibbons and Bull were at work during his reign. While all these were in some way connected with the Chapel Royal during their careers, and thus functioned as part of James' court, there is little indication of his interest in music. However, they certainly also wrote works in his honour, such as "Be Strong and of Courage" by Tomkins[24] for his coronation, but such things will remain beyond the scope of this work. Similarly, the liturgical and architectural developments in the royal chapels will only be glanced at occasionally in passing. This is an area that deserves far closer examination than it has received to this point.[25]

---

[22] A. W. Pollard, *Records of the English Bible 1525–1611* (Oxford: OUP, 1911); David Daiches, *The King James Version of the English Bible* (Chicago: U of Chicago P, 1941); Olga Opfell, *The King James Bible Translators* (Jefferson and London: McFarland, 1982).

[23] Peter Le Huray, *The Music and Reformation in England, 1549–1660* (New York: OUP, 1967), pp. 45–7.

[24] Published in *Musica deo Sacra & Ecclesiae Anglicanae* (1668).

[25] Liturgy in James' reign tends to get lost between the Reformational developments of the Elizabethan period and high-church Laudianism under Charles. Peter Le Huray comments in reference to the developments at the Chapel Royal: "As to the King's own views, there are contradictory reports" (p. 47). See McCullough's excellent chapter on the architecture and seating arrangements of the chapels royal (pp. 11–49). Further work needs to be done on the liturgy of these chapels.

Chapter 1

BEGINNINGS: THE ROOTS OF JAMES' ROLE IN RELIGIOUS CULTURE

JAMES Stuart arrived in England in 1603 with a well-developed under-standing of the role of a king in the religious life of his kingdom. This understanding had two prime sources: the Protestant understanding of the Bible as it related to kingship, and his experiences as a young king of Scotland. The Scottish reign not only affected James' own view of his role, it also developed expectations among the English, as they looked to the church and court of Scotland for a model of what they themselves might expect in 1603.

In his opening speech to the Hampton Court Conference of 1604, James said "It is no novel device, but according to the example of all Christian princes, for kings to take the first course for the establishing of the church, both in doctrine and policy. To this the very Heathen related in their proverb, *A Jove principium.*"[1] This motto sums up well his understanding of the king's role in religious life.[2] This, however, was only one strand of thought within Christendom: in the fourth century Donatus had rhetorically asked: "What has the Emperor to do with the Church?", and many since had answered, "nothing". British Christians of the early seventeenth century might look to a number of different eras for a model of the relation between a ruler and the religious life of the state: Old Testament Israel, the early church under the Roman emperors, and the customs of the medieval church. A king such as James would find none of these models completely satisfactory: as an heir of the Reformation he would look to biblical and early church patterns, although neither of these fits his high view of the monarch's role. Neither the medieval and counter-Reformation model, with its emphasis on the Donation of Constantine, and the subsequent removal of royal or imperial authority from the religious domain,[3] nor the Calvinist model, which in

---

[1] Qtd. in Fuller, *Church History of Britain* (London, 1868), vol. 4, p. 193. See also Thomas Cogswell, *The Blessed Revolution: English Politics and the Coming of War, 1621–24* (Cambridge: CUP, 1989), p. 311.

[2] Cogswell, *The Blessed Revolution*, p. 311.

[3] While Valla's scholarship on the Donation of Constantine had discredited it in the fifteenth century, the Protestant use of this scholarship led to a reaction in the counter-Reformation, as some within the Catholic church turned once again to the Donation in their defence of papal

James' view threatened to create a pope in every parish, was satisfactory. Thus, James needed to develop an ideology of royal leadership in religious life that was drawn from a variety of sources, and thus wrestled with the biblical institution of kingship as well as the various paradigms evolving in Protestant nations.

THE BIBLE, PROTESTANTISM AND KINGSHIP

Those Protestants of the sixteenth and seventeenth centuries who turned to the Bible, and particularly the Old Testament books that dealt with the era of the kings in Israel and Judah, for a model, found something far short of *jure divino* support for monarchy. The fullest description of the institution of monarchy in Israel is presented in I Samuel 8, where Israel's stubbornness and envy of other nations leads to the anointing of Saul as king. If Israel wanted a king, God would grant them one, but they would also suffer because of this desire:

> 10 And Samuel told all the words of the Lord unto the people that asked of him a king.
>
> 11 And he said, This will be the manner of the king that shall reign over you: He will take your sons, and appoint them for himself, for his chariots, and to be his horsemen; and some shall run before his chariots.
>
> 12 And he will appoint him captains over thousands, and captains over fifties; and will set them to ear his ground, and to reap his harvest, and to make his instruments of war, and instruments of his chariots.
>
> 13 And he will take your daughters to be confectionaries, and to be cooks, and to be bakers.
>
> 14 And he will take your fields, and your vineyards, and your oliveyards, even the best of them, and give them to his servants.
>
> 15 And he will take the tenth of your seed, and of your vineyards, and give to his officers, and to his servants.
>
> 16 And he will take your menservants, and your maidservants, and your goodliest young men, and your asses, and put them to his work.
>
> 17 He will take the tenth of your sheep: and ye shall be his servants.
>
> 18 And ye shall cry out in that day because of your king which ye shall have chosen you; and the Lord will not hear you in that day. (I Samuel 8:11–18).

That monarchy came to Israel in this fashion was to plague the kings of Christendom for centuries. According to this passage kingship was not looked upon favourably by God as a means of governing his people: it was brought in

power. See Christopher Bush, *Constantine the Great and Christianity* (New York: Columbia, 1914), pp. 203–5.

due to the sheer stubbornness of the people. In demanding a king they were denying God as their king (I Samuel 8:7). Earlier, the people of Israel had offered to make Gideon their king, but he had refused: "I will not rule over you, neither shall my son rule over you: the Lord shall rule over you" (Judges 8:23). In spite of this and other anti-monarchial passages in the Old Testament, kingship in Christendom developed in such a way that monarchy and the church were closely related, especially in the state-churches of the Reformation. Monarchy was no longer seen as incompatible with the worship of God: in extreme cases the King was seen as God's representative or deputy on earth, unassailable and unquestionable in affairs both civil and religious.

James tackled the passage from I Samuel 8 directly in his *True Law of Free Monarchies*, finding in it not a warning against the institution of monarchy, but a prohibition of any later resistance to kingship or an individual king: "And will ye consider the very words of the text in order as they are set down, it shall plainly declare the obedience that the people owe to their king in all respects".[4] This is followed by an extended commentary on the particulars of Samuel's speech to the people. Frequently, James' later writings on the Oath of Allegiance draw upon this same set of assumptions – that royal authority was instituted by God – and included both the civil and religious realms.

Today's biblical scholars recognize two strands within the Old Testament literature, the monarchial and the anti-monarchial. In opposition to the tradition expressed in the story of Samuel, we find a strong monarchial tradition in much of the Wisdom literature. In the reigns of David and Solomon the worship of Israel's God and divine wisdom become directly associated with the king and court. Reformation proponents of monarchial leadership of religious life drew upon those texts which are now recognized as firmly within the monarchial tradition, and carefully avoided those which presented the throne as being opposed to the will of God. The reigns of David and Solomon were particularly important for developing the idea of a godly king, in whose court the worship of Israel's God is encouraged.

The New Testament added little to the understanding of kingship and the worship of God. While Christ is metaphorically referred to as a king, actual kings do anything but promote the kingdom of God. At the same time, Jesus had said, "Render therefore unto Caesar the things which are Caesar's; and unto God the things that are God's" (Matthew 22:21), without spelling out what belonged to Caesar and what belonged to God; and the apostle Paul had appealed to Caesar for justice when he was persecuted by the high priests in Jerusalem (Acts 24:11).

Through its first three centuries the church was a subcultural movement, frequently persecuted by the Roman emperor. Only with the conversion of Constantine in AD 312 did the emperor/king assume a place of leadership

[4] *The True Law of Free Monarchies* and *Basilikon Doron*, eds D. Fischlin and M. Fortier (Toronto: CRRS, 1996), p. 60.

within the Christian church. From that point, the emperor was the secular head of Christendom, a counterpart to the sacred head of the pope. Through the centuries their roles varied depending on circumstance and the personalities of the figures involved. Until 1530 emperors continued to be crowned by the pope.

Through these centuries the role of the national kings in religious life varied from state to state, and age to age. In some the king held the power of making senior ecclesiastical appointments, and churchmen were ministers of state and councillors – in others his influence was minimal. Throughout all, however, religious life and religious culture continued to be centred in the Catholic church and its officials, especially the pope.[5] The religious painting, poetry, music and architecture produced was expressed through and in the centres of power within the church. The national court played little role in this area. With the Reformation this was to change drastically: for as princes became the heads of national churches, national religious cultures developed as well. The way in which an English poet expressed the faith might now be significantly different from the way in which it was expressed by an Italian or even a Dutch poet.

In Protestant countries there was no longer a clear separation between the spiritual and secular realms; in all matters the monarch was governor of both clergy and laity, and responsible for both the physical and spiritual needs of his people. Some historians have described the Reformation as largely a rebellion of princes against the central authority of the pope, while others have seen them harnessing and directing an otherwise potentially radical movement. Luther appealed to Frederick, elector of Saxony, for support in 1518, soon after he had begun to openly criticize the church. Later the support of Frederick's son John was to be essential to the success of the movement.[6] While Frederick passively supported the Reformation, John actively worked to establish a non-Roman church. Henry VIII was proclaimed "supreme head of the church in England" in 1534, a title later rejected by his daughter Elizabeth, who argued that such a title could be applied only to Christ.[7] Much more so than Henry or James, Elizabeth conceded that some others shared in her governing of the church.[8]

The early Reformers did not set out to establish a monarchial church: while they turned to monarchs for assistance they did not expect that this would

---

[5] See Felicity Heal and Rosemary O'Day, eds, "Introduction" in *Church and Society in England: Henry VIII to James I* (Hamden, Conn.: Archon, 1977).

[6] Euan Cameron, *The European Reformation* (Oxford: Clarendon Press, 1991), pp. 267–8. See pp. 267–91 for a worthwhile overview of how various princes participated in the furthering of the Reformation.

[7] The 1559 Act of Supremacy recognized her only as "the supreme governor" of the church. See Claire Cross, "Churchmen and the Royal Supremacy", *Church and Society in England*, eds Felicity Heal and Rosemary O'Day, p. 24.

[8] Cross, pp. 23–4.

translate into continued monarchial headship. Claire Cross writes of the English Reformation: "Tyndale and his fellow theologians turned to the godly prince as the agent for the introduction of true religion into England but also assumed that once papal dominion had been renounced the king and kingdom would be ruled by the word of God as interpreted by God's ministers."[9] The 1550s saw many Protestant exiles from England and Scotland in Geneva, and when they returned in the late 1550s and early 1560s, they brought with them a Calvinism that put great limits on royal authority in matters of faith. They also brought with them the Geneva Bible, the marginalia of which frequently includes negative comments on kingship. For example, beside the passage from I Samuel quoted above there is the following comment: "Not y^t Kings have this authoritie by their office, but that suche as reigne in Gods wrath shulde usurpe this over their brethren contrary to the Law". In the Scandinavian countries Reformation came from above, and given James' Scandinavian links this likely had some influence on his own conception of monarch/church relations. James was to present the top-down institution of the Protestant church to be the better way in contrasting Scotland with England. At the same time, states, both Protestant and Catholic, in the sixteenth century came to have a greater internal coherence, a development which increased the authority and influence of the king.[10]

In England, the Reformation greatly disturbed the existing cultural scene. The high culture of learning, art and architecture was disrupted by the dissolving of the religious houses in 1539 and the loss of the church as patron. Pre-Reformation provincial culture was largely religious, and such traditional cultural activities as the mystery plays slowly became victims to the times as well.[11] The dissolution of the religious houses increased the wealth of the crown and laity, and increased their importance as patrons of art and education. At the same time, emergent Protestantism encouraged active participation by the laity in the shaping of religious life. What developed then was strictly controlled by neither clergy nor monarch.[12] The iconoclasm of Elizabethan Protestantism has often been stressed, but while it certainly eroded one set of cultural forms it built another in their place. Recent studies have gone a long way toward dispelling the notion that Puritanism was simply "anti-culture" generally.[13] The centrality of the Bible for cultural life became

[9] Cross, p. 16.
[10] See Geoffrey Elton, *Reformation Europe, 1517–1589* (New York: Harper and Row, 1963), p. 298.
[11] Imogen Luxton, "The Reformation and Popular Culture", *Church and Society in England: Henry VIII to James I*, eds Felicity Heal and Rosemary O'Day (Hamden, Conn.: Archon, 1977), p. 59.
[12] This avoids the controversy over "slow" or "fast" reformation, and whether from "above" or "below"; my main point is that the Elizabethan settlement created a situation for James where all parts of society might expect to play a role in the shaping of religious life.
[13] See especially, Patrick Collinson, *Birthpangs of Protestant England*; for more particular studies of drama and Puritanism, see Ritchie D. Kendall, *The Drama of Dissent: The Radical Poetics of*

pronounced in this period, and the particular culture of psalmody under James I will be examined in Chapter 8. Another significant legacy of the Tudor Protestantism for Jacobean England was the clearer separation between secular and sacred culture that it encouraged.[14]

Although James' interest in theology was frequently noted, and he is usually described as a Calvinist, it is fruitless to try to precisely pin down James' theological views in isolation from his political views and his role as king. Any theology or theory of church government which questioned the hierarchy as he understood it would not be tolerated.[15] For James, the political and religious could not be separated. He could be suspicious of *de jure* arguments for both episcopalianism and Presbyterianism, for in both he saw a threat to the king's prerogative. In governing the church the king was to be above faction, to be a "universal king", bringing together the diversity of theological and ecclesiastical opinion in his land.[16] A "universal king" would overcome the self-interests of men to ensure that God was worshipped aright and the unity of the church preserved. Such was the rationale behind James' conducting of the Hampton Court Conference in January 1604, where he listened to the arguments of the bishops and the Puritans from a position of lofty wisdom.[17] James' published writings would seem to offer a perspective on his religious views, but they are limited in that most deal with the question of authority in church and state rather than theology or faith per se, and largely emerged from the particular debate surrounding the Oath of Allegiance.

JAMES IN SCOTLAND

Any discussion of James' influence on English religious life cannot begin with his accession of 1603; for James' understanding of kingship and Christianity took shape through the experience of his Scottish reign.[18] In 1572, when

Nonconformity, 1380–1590 (Chapel Hill: U of North Carolina P, 1986), Margot Heinemann, *Puritanism and Theatre* (Cambridge: CUP, 1980), and Huston Diehl, *Staging Reform, Reforming the Stage: Protestantism and Popular Theater in Early Modern England* (Ithaca: Cornell UP, 1997).

14 Collinson, *Birthpangs of Protestant England*, p. 98.
15 See Johann P. Sommerville, "James I and the Divine Right of Kings: English Politics and Continental Theory", *The Mental World of the Jacobean Court*, ed. Linda Levy Peck (Cambridge: CUP, 1991), pp. 55–70.
16 Gordon Donaldson, "The Scottish Church, 1567–1625", *The Reign of James VI and I*, ed. Alan G. R. Smith (New York: St Martin's Press, 1973), p. 49. See also Kenneth Fincham and Peter Lake, "The Ecclesiastical Policy of James I", pp. 169–207.
17 See Mark Curtis, "The Hampton Court Conference and its Aftermath", *History* 46 (1961): 1–16; and Frederick Shriver, "Hampton Court Re-visited: James I and the Puritans", *Journal of Ecclesiastical History* 33 (1982): 48–71.
18 On the connections and continuity between Scottish and English reigns, see Jenny Wormald, "James VI and I: Two Kings or One?", *History* 68 (1983): 187–209. See also the Epilogue to her *Court, Kirk and Community: Scotland 1470–1625* (Toronto: U of Toronto P, 1981), pp. 191–4.

James was six years old, the Oath of Supremacy demanded of all Scottish clergy that they recognize him as the "onlie lawfull and supreme governour of this realme, als weill in things temporall as in the conservatioun and purgatioun of religioun".[19] However, through the first part of his Scottish reign James' position as king, as well as his place in the religious life of the nation, was problematic; the throne had become his, not through any clear application of divine right and inheritance, but through the struggle that overthrew his mother and placed him on the throne as an infant. If a monarch was instituted only by God, what did that say about James' own hold on the crown while his mother was alive?

The young boy-king slowly grew into an understanding of his role, an understanding based partly on the instruction of his tutors George Buchanan and Peter Young. Buchanan was chosen as chief tutor largely for his Protestantism and antagonism towards Queen Mary. Many in Protestant Europe and Scotland hoped that James would be raised as a "godly prince" (a phrase that will be explored later in this chapter), but Buchanan's instruction was more firmly within the long tradition of the classical and humanist virtuous prince. While Buchanan may have nurtured in James the concept of a virtuous prince and a love of learning, from early on there was evidence of tension between the boy and his tutor, and ultimately the tutor's justification of elective monarchy, and hence tyrannicide, was to turn his pupil/prince violently against him.[20] In his English reign, disparagement of Buchanan would continue to be a strategy of choice for those attempting to attract the king's favour.

From an early age, James demonstrated great intelligence, and he was frequently perceived as a sort of scholar-king. In 1603 the Venetian secretary in England referred to James's Scottish reign as "his almost private and studious days in Scotland".[21] As a young king James adopted theology as an area of special interest. However, in a nation where the monarch had little central control, and where the church was firmly held by the Presbyterian clergy, there was small scope for using this theological interest to direct religious culture. In Scotland James frequently found himself not directing church policy, but serving merely as a passive pawn for competing factions. In 1582 he was kidnapped from Esmé Stuart by a group of Presbyterians in what came to be known as the Ruthven Raid. After his rescue, a backlash against the Raiders and their clerical supporters set in, culminating in the "Black

---

[19] *Source Book of Scottish History*, eds W. Croft Dickinson and Gordon Donaldson, 3 vols (London: Nelson [1952–4]), vol. 3, p. 12.

[20] Roger A. Mason, "George Buchanan, James VI and the Presbyterians", *Scots and Britons: Scottish Political Thought and the Union of 1603*, ed. Roger A. Mason (Cambridge: CUP, 1994), pp. 112–37. On the relationship of James and Buchanan, see Caroline Bingham, *The Making of a King: the Early Years of James VI and I* (London: Collins, 1968), pp. 51–5 and 83–91; and I. D. McFarlane, *Buchanan* (London: Duckworth, 1981), pp. 445–50.

[21] *CSPV*, 1603–1610, p. 20, 8 May 1603.

Acts" of 1584, which established the supremacy of the monarch over the church. While in the years 1588 to 1591 James showed an increased willingness to accept Presbyterian ideas and church government, through the 1590s he became increasingly suspicious of participation by the laity in the affairs of the church; his princely role was circumscribed by the desires of the Scottish laity and clergy as expressed in the General Assemblies, which were called by James. The 1596 General Assembly was notorious for its direct criticism of the royal family and court.[22]

It was during these years of conflict and change that James began to articulate publicly his own conception of the kingly role in relation to the faith of the nation. In his earliest religious writings, *A Meditation upon the xxv, xxvi, xxvii, xxviii and xxix verses of the XV Chapter of the first Booke of the Chronicles of the Kings* (1589), and *Ane Fruitfull Meditation* (1588), he plays the role of the learned, godly prince patiently explaining scripture to his people. In both he follows a relatively militant Protestant line, portraying Scotland as the beleaguered church beset by enemies, most notably the Spanish, yet ever protected by God. Like King David dancing before the Ark of the Covenant, the godly prince is to lead the people in praising God for his many blessings. He is to be assisted by the various estates:

> a godly king findes, as his heart wisheth, godly estates concurring with him. Next, a godly king of his godly foresight in choosing good under-rulers, reapeth this profit and pleasure that as he goeth before, so they with zealous hearts doe follow.[23]

By the 1590s James was establishing more personal control, but still found himself threatened by the Catholic earls on the one side, and the intransigent Presbyterianism of Andrew Melville and his supporters on the other. Both threatened to place a clerical or ecclesiastical power over that of the monarch. The difference lay in that the Presbyterians could recognize the possibility of a godly prince leading the nation, and while they quarreled with James over such matters as liturgy and church government, they did not question his personal right to be the king of Scotland. A Presbyterian system that recognized him as the godly prince, rather than "God's sillie vassal" or "bot a member" of Christ's Church as Melville on different occasions called him, might be acceptable.[24] It was his actual experiences of the Presbyterian system in Scotland that led to his famous statement "No bishop, no king" and his later embracing of episcopacy in England. Realizing that such remnants of the Presbyterian system as the assemblies could not immediately be disposed of, James used and manipulated them to achieve his own vision of the church. With the 1601 Assembly he introduced his ideas of a revised Book of

---

[22] Wormald, *Court, Kirk and Community*, p. 127.

[23] *A Meditation upon . . . the XV Chapter of the first Booke of the Chronicles of the Kings*, in *Workes* (1616; Fasc. Rpt., New York: George Olms Verlag, 1971), p. 84.

[24] The latter quotation is cited in Wormald, *Court, Kirk, and Community*, p. 148.

Common Order and metrical Psalter. As works associated with the establishment of the Reformed faith in Scotland, these two volumes had a somewhat
sacrosanct reputation. This same assembly also decided to begin a correction
of the Geneva bible that had been traditionally used in Scotland.[25] Such plans
were diverted by James' accession in 1603.

If he were not present to direct the affairs of the General Assemblies, James
would rather they did not take place. The assemblies of 1604 and 1605 were
both postponed: a move that provoked some protest from Scottish churchmen. What was kept afoot was the establishment of episcopacy in the Church
of Scotland, formally concluded in 1610.[26] In 1615 the plans for liturgical
revisionism were resumed, and James began the push to introduce certain
measures regarding conformity in worship, which later came to be known as
Five Articles of Perth. These required kneeling at communion, the commem-
oration of Christmas, Good Friday and Easter, confirmation of the young by
bishops, and allowed for private communion and baptism in the case of
illness. These articles were the central reason behind his visit of 1617, for which
occasion drastic ceremonial changes were introduced into Holyrood Chapel.
When the General Assembly at St. Andrews failed to pass the articles in 1617,
they were reintroduced at the next year's assembly at Perth, where, after much
consternation on the part of the king, they were passed. While James was able
to force or persuade assemblies to approve such changes on paper, he could
not achieve their actual practice in the Scottish church, and seemed to
recognize that enforcement would totally destroy the peace of the church.[27]

In 1603 James must have looked forward to his reign in England where he
could expect a well-established episcopal system with the monarch in the
leading role, readily accepted as the defender of the faith, rather than "God's
sillie vassal".[28] However, James recognized that with episcopalianism there
could also be a threat to the royal prerogative. He was greatly offended by a
sermon of Richard Bancroft in 1589 where the divine asserted the *de jure
divino* nature of episcopacy and suggested that the king was at the mercy of the
Presybterians in Scotland.[29] The English bishops were actually apprehensive of

[25] William H. McMillan, *The Worship of the Scottish Reformed Church, 1550–1638* (London:
J. Clarke, 1931), p. 372.
[26] There has been scholarly disagreement about the Scottish attitude toward episcopacy in the
period; for a recent summary, see William B. Patterson, *King James VI and I and the Reunion
of Christendom* (Cambridge: CUP, 1997), pp. 12–13.
[27] Gordon Donaldson, *Scotland, James V to James VII* (Edinburgh and London: Oliver & Boyd,
1965), pp. 208–11.
[28] See Williamson, p. 42 and *Basilikon Doron*, eds Fischlin and Fortier, pp. 121–2, where James
contrasts the prince's role in the Church of England with the popular and clerical power in
Scotland.
[29] Claire Cross, "Churchmen and the Royal Supremacy", *Church and Society in England*, eds
Felicity Heal and Rosemary O'Day, p. 31. See also Gordon Donaldson, "The Attitude of
Whitgift and Bancroft to the Scottish Church", *Scottish Church History* (Edinburgh: Scottish
Academic Press, 1985), pp. 164–77.

James' accession, especially when he called the Hampton Court Conference to deal with the Millenary Petition, a Puritan call for further reform of liturgy.[30] The fears were somewhat assuaged by the conference itself, although it was not the unqualified episcopalian success that is traditionally thought.[31] Cross notes that toward the end of the sixteenth century the bishops recognized the crown as a potential ally against an increasingly demanding laity.[32] James in turn saw that if the crown were secured as the head of the church, the hierarchy inherent in the episcopal system could serve well. He would be, as Eusebius described Constantine, "a bishop of bishops, and universal bishop within his realme".[33] And as a ruler in the tradition of Constantine he would lead religious reform, using the power of the state.

James did find some of the same controversies in England that he had left behind in Scotland: there certainly was opposition to such things as kneeling at communion and liturgical revision, but for the English there was no avenue to express resistance. All power flowed down from the king: he had the power to name bishops, appoint members to the Court of High Commission, and through such institutions exert his will over the Church of England. James also eagerly anticipated the English throne in that it would make possible the fulfillment of his role as a "godly prince" or a new Constantine returning Christendom to the right path.[34] For as merely the king of Scotland he could do little, only as the king of the Britons would he be able to live out his apocalyptic significance.[35] Already in the works of the 1580s and 1590s he spoke to the whole island of Britain, and his fellow Scots followed him in this.[36]

JAMES AND RELIGIOUS POETRY IN SCOTLAND

In addition to theology, as king of Scotland James demonstrated a keen interest in poetry, particularly that of a religious nature. James published two volumes of verse, *The Essayes of a Prentise in the Divine Art of Poesie* (1584) and *His Maiesties Poeticall Exercises at Vacant Houres* (1591), an extraordinary step for a reigning monarch, which seemed to promise that poetry would be highly valued at his court. These volumes included sonnets, translations from Lucan

---

[30] Cross, p. 32. Among the practices that the Petitioners wanted done away with were bowing at the name of Jesus, the sign of the cross at baptism, and the use of the ring in the marriage service.

[31] See Curtis, "The Hampton Court Conference and its Aftermath", pp. 1–16.

[32] Cross, p. 15.

[33] Cited by Williamson, p. 44.

[34] Knox and many other Scottish reformers had looked forward to a union of the two nations for the same reason. Arthur H. Williamson traces these ideas back to the Marian exiles in Geneva and shows that they were shared by both episcopalians and Presbyterians (*Scottish National Consciousness in the Age of James VI* [Edinburgh: John Donald, 1979], p. 21).

[35] Williamson, *Scottish National Consciousness*, p. 42.

[36] See, for example, Andrew Melville's celebration of Prince Henry's birth in *Principis Scoti-Britannorum Natalia* (Edinburgh, 1594).

and the French poet du Bartas, a long poem on the Mediterranean naval battle Lepanto, and a treatise on Scottish poetry. As a poet, James saw himself playing the public and national role of exemplar: "it best becometh a king to purify and make famous his own tongue, and wherein he may go before all his subjects, as it setteth him well to do in all honest and lawful things".[37]

By the early 1580s James had surrounded himself with poets, an informal group occasionally referred to at the time as the "Castalian Band". This group included Thomas Hudson, Alexander Montgomerie, William Fowler (who may have functioned as a spy for the English)[38] and John Stewart of Baldynneis.[39] James' influence on the subjects and styles of these poets cannot be denied; R. D. S. Jack writes, "The Castalians might look to France for inspiration, but James/David gave clear guidelines on the authors he preferred. The result was a heavy bias towards religious and philosophical works."[40] James was most interested in poetry written in Scots-English, but in the close-knit circles of the church and court, neo-Latin poetry flourished in a way it never did in the English court of Elizabeth. James himself wrote in Scots-English while in Scotland, and advised his son that the writing of verse in the classical languages was not the task of kings and princes: "And I would also advise you to write in your own language, for there is nothing left to be said in Greek and Latin already; and ynew of poor scholars would match you in these languages."[41] Such Scottish courtier-poets as Robert Ayton, Sir David Murray, Sir William Alexander, and Robert Ker, earl of Ancrum, accompanied James to London in 1603, and in doing so contributed to the continuity between the poetic cultures of the two reigns. Their poetry, especially that in neo-Latin, has been largely ignored. Some of these men circulated between Edinburgh and London, others remained at the English court. Being deeply involved in neo-Latin literature, they served as a conduit between continental religious verse and that developing in England.

James' enthusiasm for religious verse was most clearly expressed in his appreciation for the epic religious works of the French poet, Guillaume Salluste du Bartas. James himself translated sections from the French poet, and encouraged other poets to make similar, and perhaps better, attempts. Later, this interest of the king encouraged English poets to attempt translations of du Bartas, or original poems in the style of du Bartas. The young King James received a copy of du Bartas' *La Sepmaine* in 1579, and he was moved

---

[37] *Basilikon Doron*, eds Fischlin and Fortier, p. 166.

[38] Bingham, p. 155.

[39] A substantial study of these poets has yet to be published. See Sandra J. Bell, "Poetry and Politics in the Scottish Renaissance", Ph. D., Queens, 1995.

[40] "Poetry under King James VI", *The History of Scottish Literature. Volume I: Origins to 1660*, ed. R. D. S. Jack (Aberdeen: Aberdeen UP, 1988), p. 133. See also Ian Ross, "Verse Translation at the Court of King James VI of Scotland", *Texas Studies in Language and Literature* 4 (1962/63): 252–67.

[41] *Basilikon Doron*, eds Fischlin and Fortier, p. 166.

to translate a section of that work entitled "Uranie". This was published in his first poetical publication *Essayes of a Prentise*, and a translation of the section entitled "The Furies" appeared in *His Majesties Poetical Exercises.*[42] The translation of "Uranie" is of special significance, for it was a "program poem" with which du Bartas had signalled his decision to write biblical verse.[43] In the poem the muse Urania appears to the poet and encourages him to write religious verse instead of secular. She goes so far as to suggest that such verse could lead the poet to laureate stature:

> O ye that wolde your browes with *Laurel* bind,
> What larger feild I pray you can you find,
> Then is his praise, who brydles heavens most cleare
> Makes mountaines tremble, and howest [sic] hells to feare?[44]

"Uranie" presents a moment of transition that was to be echoed frequently by poets when they began to write religious verse.[45] When Thomas Hudson of the "Castalian Band" published his translation of du Bartas' *Judith* (1584), James contributed a commendatory sonnet, the sort of gesture that would encourage other writers to attempt similar poetic exercises.[46] Such poets would have hoped that they might establish a relationship with the king like that enjoyed by du Bartas. In response to James's translation of "Uranie", du Bartas had translated James' "Lepanto" into French verse. Henry of Navarre sent the French poet to Scotland as his agent in 1587: discussion during the visit included not only poetry, but also the possible marriage of James to Henry's sister. At the end of the visit James tried without success to convince du Bartas to remain at the Scottish court.[47] These poetic activities of his

---

[42] A. L. Prescott, *French Poets and the English Renaissance* (New Haven and London: Yale UP, 1978), p. 177, notes that a further translation by James of a short section from the second day was not published.

[43] It was originally published in du Bartas' 1574 volume *La Muse Chrestiene*.

[44] "The Uranie", *Essayes of a Prentise*, sig. E4r. On the tension between its heavenly subject of "Uranie" and the worldly aspirations expressed in it, see Anne Lake Prescott, "Evil Tongues at the Court of Saul: The Renaissance David as a Slandered Courtier", *JMRS* 21 (1991): 184–5.

[45] On references to the figure of Urania in later English poetry see Prescott, *French Poets and the English Renaissance*, pp. 205–6, and John Steadman, "'Meaning' and 'Name': Some Renaissance Interpretations of Urania", *Neuphilologische mitteilungen* 64 (1963): 209–32.

[46] Rptd. in *New Poems by James I of England*, ed. Allan F. Westcott (New York: AMS, 1966), pp. 27–8. In the early 1590s the Dutch poet and scholar Adrian Damman was brought to Edinburgh University by James where he translated *La Sepmaine* into Latin verse. See James K. Cameron, "Some Continental Visitors to Scotland in the Late Sixteenth and Early Seventeenth Centuries", *Scotland and Europe, 1200–1850*, ed. T. C. Smout (Edinburgh: John Donald, 1986), p. 49.

[47] Urban Tigner Holmes, Jr., *Guillaume de Salluste Sieur du Bartas: A Biographical and Critical Study*, vol. 1 in *The Works of du Bartas*, eds John Coriden Lyons Holmes and Robert White Linker (Chapel Hill: U of North Carolina P, 1935), pp. 20–1.

Scottish reign established expectations for his English subjects; the effect of these hopes will be considered in the next chapter.

Both broader Reformational developments and James' specific experience in Scotland had ramifications for the development of religious culture in England during his reign. As the "godly prince" James was expected to foster church music, religious verse, church architecture. He would be perceived as the chief reader and patron of any religious work, whether in verse or prose. At the same time, the expectations were so high as to go inevitably unfulfilled: disgruntled poets turned their prophetic mode in the direction of criticism of the court and at times even James himself, or they began to look to Prince Henry or later Elector Frederick of the Palatine as the Constantinian "godly prince".

Chapter 2

THE ACCESSION OF KING JAMES I AND
ENGLISH RELIGIOUS POETRY

W HEN King James VI of Scotland became King James I of England in
1603, many English poets felt that the event marked the beginning of a
new cultural climate, one in which religious verse would be highly valued. His
accession encouraged some poets to switch from writing secular verse to
sacred or philosophical, and others to publish religious poetry that, while
written during the earlier reign, could now be published to a more receptive
climate. The result was an outpouring of religious verse in the years 1603–05.[1]
This chapter will focus on the optimism among writers that James would
patronise religious and philosophic verse as never before. We see such great
hope expressed in *Academiae Oxoniensis* (1603), a neo-Latin collection of
panegyrics; John Davies of Hereford's *Microcosmos* (1603); Joshua Sylvester's
translation of du Bartas' *Les Sepmaines,* William Leighton's *Vertue Triumphant* (1603) and in the writings of Sir John Harington. Although the hopes
of these poets were often frustrated, as James' patronage fell far short of
expectations, their poetry is worthy of notice for the way it reflects the
interaction between royal taste and national culture.

Queen Elizabeth died early on the morning of 24 March 1603; later the
same morning James was proclaimed king of England. Messengers sped to the
Scottish court at Edinburgh, and on 26 March James was informed by Robert
Carey, Lord Hunsdon, of his new position. Accompanying Carey was John
Davies, the author of *Nosce Teipsum.* According to Anthony à Wood, the

---

[1] The following is not a complete list of religious verse published in the years 1603–05: Edward
Wilkinson's *Isahacs inheritance* (1603); Drayton's *Moyses in a map of his miracles* (1603); John
Weever's *An agnus Dei* (1603); Thomas Winter's translation of du Bartas' *Third dayes creation*
(1604); John Bridges' *Sacro-sanctum Novum Testamentum* (1604); Nicholas Breton's *The
Soules Immortal Crowne* (1605); David Hume's *Lusus poetici* (1605), and "Ascelanus" in
Daphn-Amaryllis (1605). Also appearing were the anonymous works *Sain Marie Magdalen
conversion* (1603), and *Mary Magdalens Lamentations for the losse of her Maister Jesus* (1604).
Religious poetry continued to be published at Edinburgh during these years: Henry Dod's
Certaine Psalmes of David (1603); Alexander Montgomerie's *The mindes melodie* (1605);
James Cockburn's *Judas Kisse to the Sonne of Marie* (1605) and *Gabriels Salutation to Marie*
(1605).

king, having heard the name John Davies, "straitway asked, whether he was *Nosce Teipsum*? and being answered that he was the same, he graciously embraced him, and thenceforth had so great favor for him, that soon after he made him his solicitor and then his attorney-general in Ireland".[2] Whether Wood's account is completely accurate may be open to question; however, Davies was made a gentleman of the King's Chamber in April 1603,[3] and even the perception that he had been rewarded because of James' appreciation for his poetry would be enough to encourage other poets. Curiosity and the possibility of favour stirred many men to rush north to meet the new king. Among these were men with poetic inclinations: "the very poets with their idle pamphlets promise themselves great part in his favor", wrote John Chamberlain.[4] Early on, James confirmed his reputation for generosity, already knighting and bestowing offices on men on his progress down from Scotland.

Samuel Daniel described James' accession as "th'infancie of change",[5] but, as Jenny Wormald has pointed out, since that time the event of James' accession has become "so well known that its startling and dramatic nature is forgotten".[6] At the accession of James, many believed, or hoped, that religious change and renewal were imminent. There were rumours that James was to return England to Catholicism, or at least grant freedom of worship. On the other hand, in the Millenary Petition presented to James on his way down to London, a group of clergy expressed their hope for further reform of the church. Peter McCullough has demonstrated that the majority of court sermons in the spring of 1603 were encouraging James to maintain the status quo.[7] The beginning of James' reign also represented a cracking open of the closed shell of the English court: those outcast or ignored by Elizabeth looked for new opportunities. Men like Henry Wriothesley, Charles Blount, and the young Robert Devereux, who had fallen afoul of Elizabeth, were restored to prominence.[8] For nearly forty-five years, the country had been ruled by an unmarried queen who was frugal in her bestowing of gifts and who kept a meagre court. Elizabeth was replaced by a king in the prime of his life who quickly established a reputation for a lavishness that went beyond generosity. That there was now a royal family meant more opportunities for those seeking

[2] *Athenae Oxonienses*, 3rd edn (London, 1815), vol. 2, p. 401.
[3] *Poems*, ed. Robert Krueger (Oxford: Clarendon Press, 1975), p. xliv.
[4] John Chamberlain to Dudley Carleton, 12 April 1603, *Chamberlain Letters*, p. 192.
[5] *Panegyric Congratulatorie* (fasc. rpt. Menston: Scolar Press, 1969), sig. B2v.
[6] Jenny Wormald, "James VI and I: Two Kings or One?", *History* 68 (1983): 187–209.
[7] *Sermons at Court*, pp. 101–6.
[8] The connection of the new poetic and religious climate to the restoration of certain court figures is established by John Davies of Hereford in *Microcosmos*, *Complete Works*, 2 vols, ed. A. B. Grosart (1878; rpt. New York: AMS Press, 1967), p. 14. In an extra dedicatory poem later in the work, Davies presents James as the Christ-figure who has harrowed Hell and redeemed Wriothesley: "This *Hell* being harrowèd by his *substitute*/That harrowèd *Hell*, thou art brought forth from thence,/Into an Earthly *Heaven* absolute" (p. 97).

position at court: the queen would need chambermaids; the children, servants and tutors.[9] The spirit of new opportunities had its effect on poets as well, and as courtiers and poets perceived James' interest in the area of religious poetry, there was a marked increase in the number of volumes published.

Manifold written works greeted the new reign: indeed, through May the majority of works registered by the Stationers' Company concerned James's accession.[10] In these works James' poetic and scholarly interests were a recurring theme. Both universities produced collections of neo-Latin verse in honour of the new king: *Academiae Oxoniensis* by Oxford, and *Threno-thriambeuticon* by Cambridge. The Oxford collection in particular recognized James as a patron of the muses: he is "Musis vindex, pupillis tutor egenis".[11] A bringing together of James' roles as poet, king and earthly God/patron was frequent: Dr Richard Eedes, chaplain to Elizabeth and James, addresses him as "Divinus vates; divinus Rex; Deus alter/In terris, qui Rex atque poeta simul".[12] These Oxford poets were well aware of James' own poetic endeavours: "Transtulit in nostram Davidis carmina linguam,/Et multâ multos edidit arte libros".[13] Versifiers in English also alluded to James' interests in religious verse: Anthony Nixon argues that James deserved more fame than Caesar, for the Roman emperor had merely written of his own life, whereas James "sings *Iehovahs* acts".[14] Thomas Greene suggested that he who combined poetry and kingship "is equall with a Deitie".[15] The composers of these panegyrics did not overlook the implications of having a poet-king on the throne. Thomas Dekker wrote in this way about the new hope for poets: "The Scholler sings Hymnes now in honour of the Muses, assuring himselfe now that *Helicon* will be kept pure, because *Apollo* himselfe drinkes of it."[16] However, as Curtis Perry points out, the reign of a poet-king also created problems for the poet: he was "in danger of either seeming redundant . . . or presumptuous".[17]

[9] See Kevin Sharpe, *Politics and Ideas in Early Stuart England* (New York and London: Pinter, 1989), p. 57. On patronage in general at James' court see Linda Levy Peck, *Court Patronage and Corruption in Early Stuart England* (Boston: Unwin Hyman, 1990).

[10] On these works see Charles Bazerman, "Verses Occasioned by the Death of Queen Elizabeth I and the Accession of King James I", Ph. D., Brandeis, 1971. Some of the panegyrics have been collected in John Nichols, ed., *The Progresses of King James I*, 4 vols (London, 1828. Rpt. New York: Burt Franklin, 1964), vol. 1, and some in *Fugitive Poetical Tracts*, series 2 (1875).

[11] William Osborne, *Academiae Oxoniensis* (Oxford, 1603), p. 43. [He is protector of the muses, guardian of needy students.]

[12] *Academiae Oxoniensis*, p. 8. [Holy prophet; divine King; other God on earth, who is king and poet at the same time.]

[13] William Osborne, *Academiae Oxoniensis*, p. 44. [He has translated the songs of David into our tongue, and produced many books with great art.]

[14] *Eliziaes memoriall; King James his arrivall; and Romes downefall* (1603), sig. C4r.

[15] *A Poets Vision and a Princes Glory* (1603), sig. C1v.

[16] *The Wonderfull Yeare* (1603), p. 23.

[17] *The Making of Jacobean Culture*, p. 9.

II

As demonstrated above in Chapter 1, those English writers who expressed the hope that religious verse would be supported at the Jacobean court had a relatively sound basis for these hopes in the evidence of James' Scottish reign. Any English writers unaware of James' interests in religious verse would have had their hopes raised by the king's book *Basilikon Doron*, published in London immediately after the proclamation of James as the new English king.[18] That the work is so often referred to in the weeks after James's proclamation confirms that it was much turned to by those who desired to learn about the new king.[19] While the work primarily deals with the practice of kingship, in a section entitled "Of a Kings Behaviour in Indifferent Things", James instructs Prince Henry on the matter of poetry. He writes,

> If yee would write worthily, choose subjects worthie of you, that bee not full of vanitie, but of vertue; eschewing obscuritie, and delighting ever to bee plaine and sensible. And if yee write in verse, remember that it is not the principall part of a Poeme to rime right, and flowe well with many pretie wordes: but the chiefe commendation of a Poeme is, that when the verse shall bee shaken sundrie in prose, it shall bee found so rich in quicke inventions, and poeticke flowers, and in faire and pertinent comparisons; as it shall retaine the lustre of a Poeme, although in prose.[20]

I would argue that this passage, from the work to which Englishmen turned to learn about their new king, would have represented a prescription for their responses to his accession. Clearly, what the new reign required was a poetry of virtue, in which substance and invention took priority over prettiness of sound. Within three weeks two other works of James' were registered in the Stationers' Company Register for printing: *A True Law of free Monarchies* and the poem *Lepanto*. These works would also confirm for the English public that their new king was a man of high philosophical and poetic ambition.

---

[18] The work had originally been published in 1599, but only in Edinburgh. Stanley Rypins has shown that the printing of it was shared among a number of London printing shops in an effort to have it appear in sufficient numbers as quickly as possible ("The Printing of *Basilikon Doron*, 1603", *PBSA* 64 (1970): 393–417). James had been proclaimed on 24 March, and new copies printed at London were available on 30 March. John Manningham notes so in his diary (Rypins, p. 393); John Chamberlain writes to Carleton on the same date: "I know not whether you have seen the King's book but I sent it at all adventures, for it is new here" (*Chamberlain Letters*, p. 24). See also *CSPV*, 1603–7, p. 10, where the Venetian agent Scaramelli notes that it was "sent to press here within an hour of the Queen's death". The book was entered in the Stationers' Company Register on 28 March.

[19] See my article, "'A King of Thine Own Heart': The English Reception of King James VI and I's *Basilikon Doron*", *Seventeenth Century* 9 (1994): 1–9.

[20] *Political Works*, p. 48.

III

While poets anticipated an increase in the importance of religious verse at James' accession, such poetry certainly had been written and published in the latter decades of Elizabeth's reign as well. However, in that period it was generally not inspired by the culture of the court, nor did many religious poets hope their work would be patronized by the queen. There had been an increase in the writing of religious verse in the 1590s, as such works were presented as alternatives to the wantonness of Ovidean verse and Petrarchan sonnets. However, with these works there is no pattern of dedication to the queen. While Henry Lok dedicated his *Sundry Christian Sonnets* (1593) and verse paraphrase *Ecclesiastes* (1596) to Elizabeth (among many others), Barnabe Barnes dedicated his *Divine Centurie of Spirituall Sonnets* (1595) to Bishop Toby Matthew, and Thomas Middleton and Thomas Winter dedicated their works of religious verse to the earl of Essex in the late 1590s. Nicholas Breton and Abraham Fraunce dedicated their poetry to Mary Sidney, countess of Pembroke.[21] Yet with the accession of James such writers of religious verse had a new "north-star" to guide them, as they were likely to put it,[22] and from 1603 works of religious verse were most often dedicated to him.

This redirection of religious works is clear in the career of Nicholas Breton. Breton was a voluminous producer of religious verse, the majority of it in the 1590s being dedicated to Mary Sidney. He had a falling out with her in 1597, but by 1601 was back in her favour. In 1601 Breton dedicated *The Ravisht Soule, and the Blessed Weeper* to the countess of Pembroke and *An Excellent Poeme Upon the Longing of a Blessed Heart* to Lord North; in 1602 his *Soules Harmony* was dedicated to Lady Sara Hastings. However, with a receptive monarch on the throne, he dedicated his *The Soules Immortall Crowne* to James in 1605.[23] Soon after, presumably upon finding that James was less than responsive, he resumed dedicating his religious verse to non-royal figures.

Even before his accession James was having an influence on English poetry as poets anticipated his reign and worked to please him in advance. From at least 1598 it was expected that James would succeed Elizabeth, and from that time various English courtiers and poets began to court his favour. One of the best-known examples of this is Michael Drayton, who in the 1600 edition of *Englands Heroicall Epistles* and *Idea* included a poem, "To the high and mighty Prince, James, King of Scots", in which he pledges his future service to the king. Sir John Stradling later heralded Drayton as the first to salute James:

---

[21] See Margaret P. Hannay, *Philip's Phoenix: Mary Sidney, Countess of Pembroke* (Oxford: OUP, 1990), pp. 135–9.

[22] For uses of this image see Joshua Sylvester, *Divine Weeks and Works*, vol. 1, p. 204, and Joseph Hall, "Ad Leonem Anglo-Scoticum" in *The Kings Prophecie, Collected Poems*, ed. Arnold Davenport (Liverpool: Liverpool UP, 1949), p. 122.

[23] Breton also presented a manuscript version of the poem to James, presumably sometime before publication (BL MS Royal 18 A. LVII).

"Prima salutatum venit tua Musa Iacobum".[24] Once James arrived, however, Drayton did not find patronage to be forthcoming; although he was later to find a place at the court of Prince Henry.

Some English writers of the 1590s knew of James' interest in the poetry of du Bartas, and a number of passages from James' translations are included in Robert Allott's anthology *Englands Parnassus* (1600).[25] Any English poet not aware of James' admiration for du Bartas would have become so by a few sentences in the king's *Basilikon Doron*,[26] where he advises that the French poet's works are "all most worthie to bee read by any Prince, or other good Christian".[27] In addition, in a preface to *Essayes of a Prentise* entitled "To the favorable Reader", James expressed the hope that others would follow him in translating du Bartas:

> some quick sprited man of this yle, borne under the same, or as happie a Planet, as *Du Bartas* was, might by the reading of it [James' "Uranie"], bee moved to translate it well, and best, where I have bothe evill, and worst broyled it.[28]

Both Thomas Winter and Joshua Sylvester published sections from du Bartas before James' accession, but prepared fuller translations for presentation to the new king.[29] Thomas Winter quotes the section from *Basilikon Doron* dealing with du Bartas in the dedicatory epistle to Prince Henry preceding his translation of du Bartas' *Third Dayes Creation* (1604). Winter goes on to cite James' own translation of du Bartas, and his "delighting to beautifie his books and speeches with such pithie sayings, as do abound in this incomparable Poet".[30] All this gives Winter hope:

> The consideration hereof makes me presume, that this Translation which here I offer to your Princely view, shall not want gracious acceptance. Whereof I do the rather assure my selfe, remembring your gracefull embracing of my former Essay of this verie nature, coming but accidentally unto your hands.[31]

Ironically, his "former Essay", a translation of du Bartas' *Second Day*, had been dedicated to Sir Walter Ralegh, imprisoned in 1603 for his suspected involvement in plots against James.

[24] "Ad *Mich. Drayton*, poetam eximium", *Epigrammatum Libri Quatuor* (1607), p. 100.
[25] Prescott, *French Poets and the English Renaissance*, pp. 177–8, 183.
[26] Although *Basilikon Doron* was first published in Edinburgh in 1599, most Englishmen would have first read it in the London edition of 1603.
[27] *Political Works*, ed. Charles Howard McIlwain (New York: Russell & Russell, 1965), p. 50.
[28] *Essayes of a Prentise*, sig. C3v.
[29] A list of translators of du Bartas into English, including those that survive in manuscript, is found in Prescott, *French Poets*, pp. 179–80. Sir Philip Sidney was rumoured to have completed a translation, and William Lisle published selections from *La Seconde Sepmaine* in the late 1590s. In addition, there were a number of translations of du Bartas' work into Latin published in England (Prescott, pp. 179–80).
[30] sig. A2v.
[31] sig. A2v.

Joshua Sylvester presented his initial translations from du Bartas' *Les Sepmaines* to non-royal figures such as the earl of Essex; however, with the accession of James he found a new "cheefe Partaker". Sylvester asks,

> To whom should sacred Arte, and learned Piety
>   In highest notes of Heavnly Musike sing
> The Royal Deedes of the redoubted Deity,
>   But to a learned and Religious *King*?[32]

Sylvester desires the patronage of the king: at the same time he does not want to be perceived as a typical court flatterer. He expresses the hope that the court of James will be one where a court poet can be a prophetic adviser to the king, rather than a mere sycophant. He believes that James' court will be free of vice since,

> The secret vertue of [James'] sacred beames,
> Attracts th'attentive service of all such
> Whose-mindes did ever vertues Loadstone touch.[33]

In spite of this virtue, there is still the possibility that a poet will be made "drunke with folly" by the favour of the court. Sylvester ends the passage by praying, "Let me, true Honour, not the false, delight;/And play the Preacher, not the Parasite."[34] After Sylvester's death John Vicars was to eulogize him as a court-poet who had nevertheless filled the role of the prophet who castigated the nation for its sins:

> No *Temporizer*, yet, the *Court* frequenting:
> Scorning to *sooth*, or *smooth* this Ages crimes:
> At *War* with *Vice*, in all thy holy *Rymes*:
> Thine *Israels*-Sins (with *Jeremie*) lamenting.[35]

According to Vicars at least, Sylvester had secured a position at court without writing the sort of flattering verse normally associated with that role, and religious poetry seemed an appropriate means to achieve such a delicate position at court.[36]

In the words of Sylvester, a king like James could be both the "most Royal pattern and Patron of Learning and Religion",[37] but it was not always easy to

---

[32] "Corona Dedicatoria Melpomene", *Divine Weeks and Works*, vol. 2, p. 889.

[33] *Divine Weeks and Works*, vol. 1, p. 204.

[34] *Divine Weeks and Works*, vol. 1, p. 205. Du Bartas presents a similar tension between court and country life in the original.

[35] "Sacrum Memoriae Ornatissimi Pientissmique ipsius Amici, Magistri *Josuae Sylvester*" in *Divine Weeks and Works*, vol. 2, p. 926. This poem first appeared in the 1621 edition.

[36] Sylvester's 1605 edition of *Les Sepmaines* went as far as the second day of the second week; thus, it did not include the third and fourth day of that week in which du Bartas had praised James. Sylvester alludes to this in "Corona Dedicatoria Erato".

[37] *Divine Weeks and Works*, vol. 2, p. 894.

please both a God-like patron and a fellow-poet. As a royal pattern a king
could influence his subjects by inspiring imitation of his activities; as a patron
he would attract the sort of gifts of art and scholarship which would be
directed toward a king in order to appeal to his tastes. That the potential royal
patron was himself a poet led to certain tensions, and this was especially the
case when the poet was translating the same work. Sylvester could not very
well present a translation of du Bartas to James without recognizing the king's
own endeavours in that area. Thus, he begins his dedicatory sequence to
James with a French sonnet that immediately recognizes James' translation:
"Voy (Sire) ton Saluste habillé en *Anglois*".[38] Rather than following this tack,
which would leave little room to justify his own work, Sylvester turns to their
common admiration for du Bartas. He describes the French poet as "Your
Mynion Bartas",[39] a wording that exaggerates the actual position of du Bartas
in relation to James, but underlines the suitability of Sylvester's poetic gift. In
another poem in the "Corona Dedicatoria", Sylvester requests that James
accept the work for the sake of the original poet, rather than for this particular
translation:

> I know your Highnes knowes him Prince of Singars:
> And his rare Workes woorthie your Royall Fingars
> (Though heere his luster too too much obscure-I).
> For his sake therefore, and your self's Benignitie,
> Accept my Zeale, and pardon mine Indignitie.[40]

Such strategies were used often by translators in their dedications: in this way
they could plead on behalf of their work, yet maintain a suitable humility.[41]
When the king himself was a fellow translator, it was an especially wise
rhetorical gesture.

Joseph Hall's praising of the king's poetic skill in his poem *The Kings
Prophecie* also manifests the tensions inherent in a situation where the king
was both fellow-poet and potential patron. First, Hall celebrates the fact that
the hopes he expressed in an earlier poem have now been fulfilled, and how
he has "solemne vow'd that mine eternall song/Should sound thy name
unto the future seed". Then he connects this poetry with James' own poetic
fame:

> So may thy worth my lowly Muse upraise,
> So may mine hie-up-raised thoughts aspire
> That not thy *Bartas* selfe, whose sacred layes
> The yeelding world doth with thy selfe admire,

[38] vol. 2, p. 885.
[39] vol. 2, p. 888.
[40] *Divine Weeks and Works of Guillaume de Saluste Sieur du Bartas*, ed. Susan Snyder, 2 vols
(Oxford: Clarendon Press, 1979), vol. 2, p. 889.
[41] Such a strategy was especially common with biblical paraphrases in the period.

Shall passe my song, which nought can reare so hye,
Save the sweete influence of thy gracious eye.[42]

As the phrase "thy *Bartas* selfe" brings the identity of the French poet and the king very close together, we are left with an ambiguous passage: is Hall suggesting that James' patronage will make his poetry greater than the original or greater than James' own translation? In either case James is being encouraged to function primarily as a patron.

IV

William Leighton was another among those minor courtiers who perceived in the coming of James to the throne an opportunity to better their own positions. Leighton served Queen Elizabeth in some capacity, or at least so he claimed. His work of 1603, *Vertue Triumphant*, describes him as a gentleman-pensioner, but as this work was published in July of that year it is quite possible that Leighton achieved that position under James.[43] The work, as would be expected, is dedicated to the king himself, and presents a worthwhile picture of what a poet-courtier might hope for from a monarch. The epistle dedicatory is governed by the image of the monarch as fountain, and the poet-courtier as the plant which flourishes through the fountain's nurturing. Leighton writes that the "drops of your Princely favour" have brought a desire "to bring forth the fruit of my most humble zeal and faithfull service".[44] The king or court as nourishing fountain was commonplace in the language of patronage relations,[45] but Leighton is extending the imagery to complete the circle of patron-client-patron, showing that it is not just a one-way relationship. The patron, in this case the king, will receive something in the exchange: namely, the fruit that is the poem. But in what way does this poem benefit King James? Unlike some poems written by clients to their patrons, its primary function is not to immortalize the patron directly, but to celebrate and encourage the cultivations of those virtues which the king embodies. *Vertue Triumphant* concerns the four cardinal (classical) virtues, and if it is of any present value to the king, it is as an image of those virtues which lead to a happy kingdom when practised by the king. "In this, as in a Crystall thou shalt see,/What best befitteth Rule and Emperie."[46]

Leighton does not claim that the current work will be of immediate value to the king: however, if the work, like the poet, is properly nourished, it will later bring forth more worthwhile fruit. "Kirnels being set at first, in time beare

---

[42] *Collected Poems*, p. 113.

[43] The work was entered in the Stationers' Register on 4 July.

[44] *Vertue Triumphant, or a Lively Description of the Foure Vertues Cardinall* (London, 1603) (sig. ¶r).

[45] See Peck, *Court Patronage and Corruption*, p. 1.

[46] sig. A3v.

fruit; but being ungraft, never come to perfection: So, may it please your Highnesse, from this tender plant of mine, there can appeare nothing woorthie either keeping or gathering; but being grafted in the least favour of your Maiesties protection, it may hereafter bring forth matter of more approbation, content and consequence."[47] The work manages to be simultaneously the fulfillment of his duty to the king for past favour, and the invocation for more favour in the future. Of course, in the cycle of favour and fruit, the poet will claim publicly that the fruit will never sufficiently recompense the favour shown. However, if the cycle is broken by lack of favour, the poetry of praise may very well be replaced by that of complaint. At the end of *Vertue Triumphant* Leighton again apologizes for "a designe so venturous and much bolde" but hopes that "where vertue rules the minde,/ Attempts of dutie gracious pardon finde".[48] He concludes with the hope that no king with a "gust of hardest censure" will venture "to doome the wracked of turmoiled barke,/That in her failing made a King her marke". Leighton was rewarded, or at least his bark was not buffeted for his indiscretion, by being knighted, among at least 300 others on 23 July 1603.

V

Previous to James' accession to the throne, John Davies of Hereford seems to have been favoured by the Herberts and Robert Sidney; he possibly worked in the Sidney family as a scribe or writing instructor. He had dedicated *Mirum in Modum* (1602), a work of philosophical verse, to Sir Robert Sidney, William Herbert, earl of Pembroke, and Edward Herbert of Montgomery. He followed the next year with the similar poem, *Microcosmos*, dedicated to King James; while it is possible that some of the work was written before James' accession, certain parts are directed specifically to the new king, and the prefatory material shows that it was published in response to the accession. Appended to the work are a number of extra dedicatory poems to various noble figures; from the titles with which these are addressed we can determine that the work went to press between 21 July and 27 July 1603.[49] Thus, the publication was likely meant to coincide with the coronation on 25 July, St. James' day. Both the commendatory poems, and Davies' own dedication and preface, increased hopes for favour and support of such work.[50] Both Davies' own comments in *Microcosmos* proper, and its commendatory poems, repeatedly

---

[47] sig. ¶2r.

[48] sig. H1v.

[49] Wriothesley is addressed as earl of Southampton, a title which he received on 21 July, but Lord Mountjoy is not addressed with the title of earl of Devonshire, which he gained on 27 July.

[50] Prefixed to the work were commendatory poems in Latin and English by John Sanford, Robert Burhill, Nicholas Deeble, John James, T. R.[?], Douglas Castilion, Charles Fitzjeffrey, Nathanael Tomkins, Richard Davies and Edward Lapworth.

declare the connection between the poem and James' coming to the throne.[51] Nicholas Deeble describes Davies' poem as "Togither borne with *England's endlesse mirth*", and suggests that up until this time there was not an appropriate audience for such literature:

> Wast from disdaine to powre th'ambrosian dew
> (Dropping like Nectar from a sacred quill)
> Into the common Lavour, vulgar *view*;
> That Heaven deferd thy birth these howres untill?[52]

In spite of any favour he may have received from Sidney and Herbert, Davies himself attributes the sorry state of poetry to the lack of support from great men:

> What *Guift* to *Greatnesse* can lesse welcome be
> Then *Poems*, though by *Homer* pend perchaunce?
> It *lookes* on them as if it could not see,
> Or from them, as from *Snakes* away wil flee.[53]

Davies hopes that with a learned and religious monarch on the throne, such poetry as his will no longer be ignored.

Davies presents James' accession as a sort of judgement day for English poets: only the righteous ones will be allowed into his kingdom, where they will continue to write virtuous poetry.

> And who hath held their *Pens* from blott of *blame*
> And ever kept their *Muse* immaculate,
> Their conscience now takes comfort in the same,
> As if some *God* were come, (that *Vice* doth hate)
> With *Grace* their virtue to remunerate:
> As when the *Kinge* of *Kings* shall come at last
> To give all *Men* their *meede*, in righteous rate,
> The *good* alone rejoyce in their *lives* past:
> So perfect *Poets* now must comfort tast.[54]

---

[51] The majority of those writing commendatory poems to *Microcosmos* have some sort of connection with Magdalen College, Oxford. Among them, Sandford, Lapworth, and Castilion had also written commendatory poems to Thomas Winter's first translation from du Bartas, *The Second Day of the First Weeke* (1603). Some of these poets also appear in *Academiae Oxoniensis*. Davies himself had also contributed a commendatory poem to *The Second Day of the First Weeke*.

[52] vol. 1, p. 9.

[53] *Complete Works*, vol. 1, p. 49. This passage is from a section in the middle of *Microcosmos* where Davies breaks to digress on the proper role and behaviour of kings, or as he calls it, the importance of "Policy". While it is possible that the rest of *Microcosmos* could have been written before 1603, this passage clearly refers to the new reign.

[54] vol. 1, pp. 13–14.

In response to this judgement, poets write pure lines "T'expresse their *Soules'* praise-worthy avarice/To draw their *King* to read their *Subject* twice".[55] Only with poetry of a serious and pious nature could such phrases as "praise-worthy avarice" be used. In Davies' view, to desire the favour of the king can be no more wrong than to desire the favour of God. In a poem appended to *Microcosmos*, Nicholas Deeble says that Davies challenged other poets to write similar works to appeal to the king, but they failed to take up his challenge:

> for when
> (T'approve his Excellence) he challeng'd *All*
> Or *English* bred, or forraine Nationall
> To strive for *glorie*, and a golden *Price*
> (Which *one* or *both* might every sort entise)
> Unanswer'd, hee Monarchiz'd alone . . .[56]

Ironically, Davies himself did not win any prize or favour: his convoluted metaphysical verse would not have fulfilled James' desire for poetry of plain virtue, but the greater reason is that Davies, like many others, overestimated James' interest in poetry at this stage in his life. Later works of Davies were not directed to James, but he continued with dedications to such notable courtiers as the earl of Montgomery and Sir James Hay.

The outpouring of verse following James' accession was temporarily held back by the plague that struck London in the summer of 1603.[57] The plague caused the near-evacuation of London throughout the summer, and even when the printers were at work, it was not easy to get books licensed.[58] The plague also sharply reduced personal access to the king for those who hoped to resort to manuscript presentation. The Venetian secretary reports: "All those who have not urgent business are sent away from Court, nor may anyone enter the palace without a ticket, signed after an examination proving that the person has not come from an infected district."[59] Joshua Sylvester had hoped to publish his translation of *Les Sepmaines* with an appropriate dedication to James, but was forced merely to present a segment of the work in manuscript:

[55] vol. 1, p. 14.
[56] vol. 1, p. 104. Such writing of poetry within the framework of contest or competition judged by a king needs further attention. James had promoted something of this sort in his Scottish court during the 1580s.
[57] *Microcosmos* was printed at Oxford.
[58] In *Doctor Andros his Prosopopeia answered* (1605) Henoch Clapham claims he would have had his *Epistle Discoursing upon the Present Pestilence* (1603) licensed, but the bishop and his chaplains had fled the city because of the plague, "nor (as was said) might any book be receaved of them then to be perused, for feare the plague were convayd in it" (sig. B3r). His explanation is substantiated by the number of entries in the Stationers' Register from late summer 1603 that grant approval for printing, but include the provision that the book first be licensed.
[59] 28 Sept., Scaramelli to Doge and Senate, *CSPV* 10/136, p. 98.

> Beeing inforced (through the grievous visitacion of Gods heavie hand, upon
> your Highnes poore Cittie of London) thus long (& yet longer like) to defer the
> Impression of my slender Labours (long since meant unto your Matie) I
> thought it more then tyme, by some other meane, to tender my humble
> Homage to Your Highnes.[60]

Clearly, Sylvester had not merely written a work and was now casting about
for a suitable dedicatee. He felt it was essential to show to James that he was
willing to serve the new king with his poetry. As with Davies' *Microcosmos*, it
is quite possible that Sylvester presented his manuscript to James at the time
of his coronation in late July. The volume that Sylvester had hoped to publish
to greet King James was finally brought out early in 1605.[61] It is likely that
other poets' aspirations were also frustrated by the ravages of the plague that
summer.

While Davies' *Microcosmos* is primarily a work of religious or philosophical verse, he nevertheless shows a concern for more secular affairs,
and takes the bold step of advising the new king on public matters. He
exhorts the king to be merciful and just, but severe with those who plot
against him. The king should keep the nobility divided to restrict their
power. Most surprisingly, Davies asserts that in spite of Solomon's warning
in Proverbs 17 about a king's lying lips, "*Kings* sometimes must *faine* and
temporise/For their estate and *common-wealthe's* welfare."[62] Thus, religious
verse like *Microcosmos* could provide the opportunity to preach to the king
as well. In some instances the religious nature of Davies' poem and his
political concerns come together. In his dedicatory poem to the king,
Davies writes, "Then peacefull be thy Raigne (deare *Lord*) alone/To build
the *Temple* of true *Union*". This passage relies upon the common
association of James with King Solomon who, because he was a king of
peace, was allowed by God to build the Temple. David, his father, had
been forbidden to do so because of the blood he had spilt. The "temple"
that Davies anticipates James will build is neither just a set of religious
reforms, nor the inner temple of the human heart; rather the temple will
be the union of Scotland and England both politically and ecclesiastically.
This was a major goal of James' at the beginning of his English reign, and
was reflected in numerous poems greeting his accession.[63] The proclamation for union of England and Scotland was made shortly after James'
arrival in London, on 18 May, at Greenwich.[64] Earlier, there had been talk

---

[60] MS Royal 17 a xli, fol. 265 (5), quoted in *Divine Weeks and Works*, ed. Snyder, vol. 1, p. 19.

[61] Snyder suggests that the delay of Sylvester's *Les Sepmaines* after the plague had abated may
have been due to the death of the printer Peter Short who held the copyright on the work, and
questions as to inheritance (vol. 1, pp. 19–20).

[62] p. 48.

[63] The proclamation for union was made shortly after James' arrival in London, on 18 May, at
Greenwich (*CSPD*, 1603–10, p. 9).

[64] *CSPD*, 1603–10, p. 9. See Bruce Galloway, *The Union of England and Scotland, 1603–1608*.

that James desired to call himself not the king of England and Scotland, but the king of Great Britain.[65] The proposed union was not merely a political move, but a religious one, because of its apocalyptic connotations: many of the godly hoped that James, as king of Britain, would overthrow the Antichrist, that is the papacy, as they understood it.[66]

VI

Both Davies and Sylvester had merely intensified their efforts in religious verse in response to James' accession. In the case of John Harington, however, there was an explicit turning to religious verse in an effort to please the new king. Harington had a well-established place in both the literary and court world of the early 1590s. His well-known translation of Ariosto's *Orlando Furioso* had been commissioned by his godmother Queen Elizabeth. His *Epigrams*, not yet published but widely circulated in manuscript, had gained him a reputation as a court wit, a reputation furthered by his partly satiric *The Metamorphosis of Ajax* (1596). The offence that this work caused, along with a close association with the unpredictable earl of Essex, plunged Harington into disfavour with the queen during the last few years of her reign.[67] Because of these problems Harington looked forward to the coming of a new monarch. Already at Christmas 1602, he presented to James a New Year's gift consisting of his epigrams in manuscript and a lantern engraved with the words of the thief on the cross, "Lord, remember me when thow comest into thie kingdom."[68] Also included with this gift were verses entitled, "The Farewell to his Muse", where Harington recognizes that the new reign will bring with it a new type of poetry: "Now to more serious thoughts my soule aspyers,/This age, this minde, a Muse awsteare requiers".[69] Curtis Perry sees these lines as signalling the oft-noted shift to a plain style that came with James' accession. However, I would suggest that Harington is also pointing toward a new subject matter, and that his works in the years that follow are a fulfillment of these new requirements. Harington commits himself to responding to the king's tastes:

> List he to write or study sacred writte;
> To heere, reade, learn, my breeding made me fitt.

---

[65] *CSPV*, 17 April 1603, p. 5. See Bruce Galloway, *The Union of England and Scotland, 1603–1608* (Edinburgh: John Donald, 1986). Many poets at the time made reference to this reuniting of "Britain"; the term, however, was somewhat contentious: later Anthony Weldon in his vitriolic *Court and Character of James I* (1650) mocked the term as a Scottish barbarism. See Wormald, "James VI and I: Two Kings or One?", p. 206.

[66] Williamson, "Scotland, Antichrist and the Invention of Great Britain", pp. 44–6.

[67] J. E. Neale, *Queen Elizabeth I* (New York: Doubleday, 1957), pp. 379 and 385.

[68] An engraving of the lantern is found in a manuscript of his epigrams held at the Folger Library (MS V.a.249).

[69] "The Farewel to his Muse", *Nugae Antiquae*, ed. T. Park (London, 1804), p. 333.

What he commaunds, I'le act without excuse,
That's full resolvd: farewell, sweet wanton Muse![70]

Earlier in the same poem Harington had clearly recognized that the "sweet wanton muse" of such works as his *Orlando Furioso* and the very epigrams he presented to the king were not well suited for the coming court of King James.

A brief few weeks after James "came into his Kingdom", Harington wrote to Lord Thomas Howarde: "a new Kynge will have new soldiers, and god knowethe what men they will be".[71] While Harington held such hopes, his fortunes in the years 1603 to 1605 reached a nadir, not because of his poetry, but because of the problems of his kinsmen, the Markhams, who pulled Harington down with them in their financial collapse. In addition, one kinsman, Griffin Markham, was implicated in the Bye Plot to place Arabella Stuart on the throne. After these problems were cleared up, Harington began writing works with an eye toward gaining a position, either as an instructor to the young Prince Henry or as chancellor of Ireland. In the years 1603 to 1608 he wrote *A View of the State of Ireland*, a verse translation of Book 6 of the *Aeneid*, and *A Supplie or Addicion to the Catalogue of Bishops to the yeare 1608*. Of these, only the last was published.

However, the primary poetic activity of Harington in this period was his versification of the Psalms. We cannot be certain when he began work on these; however, that he presented his sister, Lucy, countess of Bedford, with a copy of three of Sidney's Psalms, numbers 51, 104, and 137, in 1600 would suggest that he had not yet composed his own.[72] He presented a manuscript of all the Psalms to James in about 1601.[73] A letter survives in which he asks for James' approval and support:

> That your Majestie will be pleased to referr the examynacion of this woorke of the Psalms drawing so nere to an end to some of your learned chaplains now resyding abowt London, and the resolucion of all doubtfull places to my Lord Bishop of Elie. And whereas I fynde Master Aton your Majesties servant very judicious in this kynde and by whose advyce I must ingenuously acknowledge I have receaved some furtherance in this worck, yt may please your Majestie to joyne him also as well as for the review of the same as for the ordring of the convenyent publishing of yt to your Majesties best lykinge.[74]

---

[70] *Nugae Antiquae*, p. 334.

[71] Letter to Lord Thomas Howarde [later earl of Suffolk], *Nugae Antiquae*, p. 337.

[72] The manuscript is in the Library of the Inner Temple, Petyt MS 538, vol. 43, f. 303b. The letter accompanying them is reprinted in John Harington, *Letters and Epigrams*, ed. N. E. McClure (Philadelphia: U of Pennsylvania P, 1930), p. 87. Also included in the presentation manuscript are some of Harington's own "shallowe meditations" [his epigrams].

[73] Three complete manuscript versions of Harington's Psalms survive; see Peter Beal, *Index of English Literary Manuscripts*, 5 vols (London: Mansell, 1980–), vol. 1, pt. 2, p. 128.

[74] *Letters and Epigrams*, ed. McClure, pp. 143–4. While McClure assigns a tentative date of 1612 to this letter, Peter Beal suggests that the manuscript was presented to James "in or after 1609" (*Index of Literary Manuscripts*, vol. 1, pt. 2, p. 122). The earlier date would situate the

Another of Harington's letters asks for patronage and help in publishing his work. It is addressed to "your Grace", presumably the archbishop of Canterbury.[75] In this letter Harington expresses the desire that these psalms be published "to gods honor and the kings". Only with religious verse could the twin goals of pleasing God, the heavenly patron, and James, his earthly counterpart, so conveniently coincide. In the same letter Harington recounts how "I have rais'd my selfe a mighty enmitie by offering my service in this kynd." We cannot tell whether this "enmitie" was that of the king or of other rival poets, but clearly turning to religious verse did not lead to the success and favour that Harington had hoped for. Harington may have offended James, who still hoped to eventually complete and publish his own version of the Psalms for use in the church, a topic that will be considered more fully in Chapter 7. At one point, Harington himself wrote that a poet needed to keep in mind that James was "not willinge a subjecte should be wiser than his Prince, nor even appeare so".[76] The "mighty enmitie" raised by Harington's Psalms prevented them from ever reaching print.

VII

With religious verse dedicated to a king, a mingling of monarchial and religious language was inevitable, especially when James himself referred to kings as "little Gods".[77] Flattery could be achieved through dedications and in allusions to the connections between God and the king. Joseph Hall presented religious verse as a suitable replacement for direct flattery:

> I would the flatterie of a Prince were treason; in effect it is so: (for the flatterer is a kinde murtherer.) I would it were so in punishment. If I were to speake before my sovereigne King and maister, I would praise God for him, not praise him to himself.[78]

By doing as Hall suggests a poet could conceivably please the king, while at the same time maintain that his poetry was of a lofty and noble purpose. As discussed above, John Harington turned the words of the thief on the cross to

Psalms as bids for favour in the court setting, rather than in "those final quieter years of his life spent at Kelston with his wife and family", as Karl E. Schmutzler suggests ("Harington's Metrical Paraphrases of the Seven Penitential Psalms: Three Manuscript Versions", *PBSA* 53 (1959): 240).

[75] Letter 61, *Letters and Epigrams*, pp. 142–3.

[76] *Letters and Epigrams*, pp. 109–11.

[77] Such a mingling of language was more common at the English court than it had been at the Scottish. Wormald notes that in 1603 the tone of addressing the king was significantly heightened: such phrases as "our soverane lord" were replaced by such as "his sacred majesty", a shift undoubtedly pleasing to James. (Wormald, "James VI and I: Two Kings or One?", p. 204.)

[78] *A Holy Panegyric* (1613), sigs E6r–E6v; *Works*, ed. Philip Wynter (Oxford, 1863), vol. 5, p. 91.

his own purposes when he requested of James in 1602, "Lord, remember me when thow comest into thie kingdom." Davies of Hereford also borrowed the language of the New Testament when he called upon James to "dwell in our *harts*".[79] At the same time poets became more inclined to apply language of royal patronage to God. A prime example of this intermingling is found in the dedicatory epistle to *The Soules Immortall Crowne* (1605), where Nicholas Breton places the poem and his service at James' feet,

> beseeching the vertue of all grace, and grace of all vertue, so to blesse you with his infinite blessings, that as vertue under heaven putteth her praise under your Patronage, so the Patrone of all vertue will so Royallize your praise in the Heavens, that to your gratious Crowne on earth, you may receive a Crowne of Eternall glory.[80]

It is a convoluted but clever rhetorical move: Breton is presenting James as one ordained to patronize the praising of virtue, for which he will be rewarded by God, "the Patrone of all vertue". In this way, the subject matter of religious verse allowed poets to raise the language of flattery to a much higher level.

Some poets at least recognized the dilemma in directing a divine work to an earthly figure. If God were the "Patron of all vertue" surely such works ought to have Him as their only dedicatee. In his *Sacro-Sanctum Novum Testamentum* (1604), John Bridges, bishop of Oxford, asks if Luke sought any other patron than the Holy Spirit in writing his Gospel and Acts. He must answer in the negative, yet Luke did direct his work to Theophilus: "Praestantem seligit unum,/Nobilitate virum, cui dictat, dedicat, offert".[81] Bridges then equates James with Theophilus, "Esque THEOPHILUS inter Reges temporis huius"; in this way Bridges' dedication to the king is justified, and James is flattered by the title "Lover of God".[82]

Like Breton, Davies of Hereford suggests the king may be God-like in his patronage:

> In common policy, great *Lords* should give,
> That so, they may (though great) much more receave:
> The more like *God*, the more they do relive . . .

However, within this same passage, Davies suggests that poets also have extra-human powers:

---

[79] *Microcosmos*, p. 11. Cf. John 14:17, II Timothy 1:14, and I John 4:12.

[80] "To . . . James", *Works in Verse and Prose*, ed. A. B. Grosart, 2 vols (London, 1879), p. 4.

[81] sig. A6r [he chose one distinguished man, a noble man to whom he speaks, dedicates and offers].

[82] sig. A6v [and you are the "lover of God" among the kings of our time]. Breton also presented a manuscript of his verse translation of the Old Testament to James (BL MS Royal 20 D.xiv–xix).

And, the more *Writers* they aloft doe heave,
The more *renowne* they to their *Race* doe leave:
For, with a *droppe* of *ynke* their *Penns* have pow'r
Life to restore (being lost) or *life* bereave,
Who can devour *Time* that doth *all* devoure,
And goe beyond *Tyme*, in lesse than an *how'r*.[83]

The power to give and take away life, usually associated with the heavenly ruler, and by extension the earthly ruler, is here claimed by the poet. James, the "God-like" royal patron appealed to earlier, is rendered a passive subject. Further, Davies seems to suggest that "the great" may need poets to touch up tarnished reality:

For, though no *praise* for *penning* it thou gaine,
Yet *praise* thou gett'st, if thou that *Pen* sustaine,
That can eternize thee in *Deathe's* despight,
And through it *selfe* thy grossest *humors* straine,
So make them pure (at least most pure in sight)
Which to *Posterity* may be a *light*.[84]

Basically, Davies is asserting that poets do not necessarily tell the truth, but since they have the power to establish the reputations of great men for ages to come, it behooves the great to treat them well. James is not explicitly named here, but as he is the dedicatee of the poem, surely the passage points to him. Davies seems to be offering to maintain the image of the virtuous king so precious to James, but at the same time suggesting that James' actual virtue may be somewhat lacking. Davies is either exhibiting an honest naivety about the decorum of praise, or intentionally subverting his own praise of the king out of distaste for the usual role of the court poet. We do not find such ambiguity in the other religious poetry directed to James in the period.

VIII

Clearly, James' accession led English poets to believe that religious and philosophical verse would hold an important place in the cultural life of his reign. Were their expectations actually met, that is, was there significant royal patronage of those poets who directed their works toward the king? Generally, these poets received less help than they had hoped for, but that seems to have been true of poets at all times. On the one hand, John Bridges enjoyed continued clerical preferment, Joshua Sylvester received a pension

---

[83] *Complete Works*, vol. 1, p. 49. Cf. also the footnote to this passage: "Good and ill renowme are immortal and prevaile even over the remembrance of Tyme, which Poets have powre to give."

[84] *Complete Works*, vol. 1, p. 49.

from Prince Henry from 1608 until the prince's death in 1612,[85] and William Leighton was knighted by James in July 1603, shortly after the publication of *Virtue Triumphant.* This was more substantial royal favour than most poets of the period ever experienced. On the other hand, both Nicholas Breton and John Davies of Hereford received no discernible favour, and returned to directing their poems to non-royal figures. In spite of high hopes, James did not maintain the interest in poetry that he had shown in Scotland: he published no poetry while king of England, and no English equivalent to the "Castalian Band" was established. Malcolm Smuts has suggested that James failed to shape culture as was often done by continental monarchs.[86] James' failure to support and direct the groundswell of religious verse inspired by his accession would seem to illustrate Smuts' thesis. However, it is also a reflection of James' changing interests. As far as poetry went, religious and philosophical verse may have been of most interest to James, but poetry as a cultural field was not particularly important to James during his English reign. In describing James' English court in 1613, Hugo Grotius writes,

> Venio ex Anglia; literarum ibi tenuis est merces. Theologi regnant: Legulei rem faciunt: unus ferme Casaubonus habet fortunam satis faventem, sed, ut ipse judicat, minus certam. Ne huic quidem locus in Anglica fuisset ut literatori; induere Theologum debuit.[87]

By about 1610 straight theology without poetic embellishment was perceived as the best way to attract the king's attention and favour. Some poets continued to direct works of religious verse to James, but those of later years generally lacked the optimism that lavish patronage would be forthcoming, and the naivety that their versifying on God, the church, and the soul would fulfill James' taste for theological complexity.

---

[85] *Divine Weeks and Works*, ed. Snyder, vol. 1, p. 21.
[86] "The Political Failure of Stuart Cultural Patronage", pp. 168–9.
[87] Letter to Joanni Meursio, 16 June 1613, *Epistolae* (Amsterdam, 1687), p. 751. [I have come from England; there the rewards of literature are few. Theologians reign, lawyers flourish, one Casaubon [Isaac Casaubon] nearly has enough supporting fortune, but he judges that it is less than fixed. Indeed his place in England was not as a literary figure, he had to appear as a theologian.]

Chapter 3

PROPHETS AND THE KING

IN his prose work *The Wonderfull Yeare*, Thomas Dekker celebrates 1603 as a year noteworthy both for the peaceful accession of a new king in the spring, and the devastating plague of that summer. The outpouring of praise and hope at James' accession has been traced in the previous chapter, but as a time of national crisis this year also elicited a much different kind of poetry. As an "annus mirabilis" it provided an opportunity for outspoken assessment of the state of England, an assessment which sometimes established itself in reference to Israel's prophets. By far the majority of works heralding the new reign were panegyric, with any instruction to the king disguised as praise; however, a few writers did adopt the more radical position of prophet. This chapter will examine two writers who in 1603 adopted a moderately prophetic stance in their writings to the king, and then compare these with the developing prophetic mode of George Wither, and the general tendency to more outspoken prophecies that emerged in the period 1619–25. However, before these individual figures can be turned to, we must consider the tradition of prophecy, as understood by Protestantism generally, and English Protestantism particularly.

James' English subjects recognized that while their new monarch had a high view of his own authority, he also saw a role for Protestant prophetic utterances and interpretation of biblical books.[1] James saw himself as a sort of prophet king, and analogies to the "royal prophet" David were common. This idea that a king might be a prophet figure himself was adopted by a number of writers of the period. Bishop John Howson, for example, defended

---

[1] The "prophetic" mode in English renaissance verse has received considerable recent attention, often with particular focus on Spenser and Milton; among the most important studies are Joseph Anthony Wittreich, *Milton and the Line of Vision* (Madison: U of Wisconsin P, 1978); Kenneth Borris, *Spenser's Poetics of Prophecy in the Faerie Queen V* (Victoria: English Literary Studies, 1991). David Norbrook, *Poetry and Politics in the English Renaissance* (London: Routledge and Kegan Paul, 1984), ranges further afield than most scholars in tracing the prophetic stance adopted by more minor poets of the sixteenth and early seventeenth centuries. He uses the term "prophet" to describe those writers who worked from a militant Protestant position in opposition to the court. However, Norbrook spends little time considering the biblical Prophets themselves, and shows few instances where early modern writers actually invoked these figures specifically.

such ceremonies as coronation on the grounds that they were what had made Saul and David prophets.[2] Many anticipated that James would be a godly king, possibly even a Protestant emperor, and prophesied along these lines, frequently drawing upon the Book of Revelation. James himself produced a paraphrase and a commentary on this book and like many Protestants, identified the Antichrist with the pope.[3] To the extent that the biblical prophetic works supported a monarch-centred extension of the true church, James was happy to promote the study of such works, and the development of new prophetic utterances. As late as 1611 he was still debating with the French Calvinist theologian Pierre du Moulin the details of prophetic interpretations of Revelation, and du Moulin was citing James as an authority on the matter.[4]

In James, royal and prophetic authority came together. This then was the conundrum that developed in the early years of his reign: the king recognized the significance of prophetic utterance, but would not recognize any earthly authority above his own, to which he must humbly submit, as did Kings Hezekiah and David. Further complicating matters was the question of whether prophetic utterance would take its seat in the royal court or in the gathered community of the godly, a body ultimately threatening to the court and king. This difficulty was one manifestation of a larger issue faced by Protestant nations in the sixteenth and seventeenth centuries: did the Reformation give the power of shaping religious life and culture to the laity, clergy, or to the king?

Many poets and preachers of the sixteenth and early seventeenth centuries did not see their prophetic role as conflicting with veneration of the king. Instead, their prophetic gifts were used to show the future glory of the king. In spite of the anti-monarchial passages in the Old Testament prophets, kingship in Christendom developed in such a way that monarchy and the church were closely related, especially in the state-churches of the Reformation. Frequently, the Old Testament prophets prophesied "against" Israel or Judah or their royal courts, but this was never their only role: Jeremiah also praised the virtuous king Josiah.[5] Similarly, those writers of the early seventeenth

---

[2] *A Sermon Preached at St. Maries in Oxford* (1603). This was preached on the anniversary of Queen Elizabeth's Accession Day, 17 November 1602.

[3] *Workes*, p. 78; this commentary, *Ane fruitfull meditatioun*, had been written and published already in 1588, but was republished in England in 1603 and again in the *Workes* of 1616. This last maintained the strong language against the pope, even though by that time James was moving away from apocalyptic speculation based on Revelation. His preface to *A Meditation upon the Lord's Prayer*, included in the 1616 *Workes*, suggests that in his old age he is moving away from the "bickerings" of controversy.

[4] Pierre du Moulin, *The Accomplishment of Prophecies* (1611), sig. A4r. Throughout Chapter 10 of this work du Moulin quotes the king repeatedly.

[5] After the death of Josiah, the last of the kings of Judah, Jeremiah sang a lament: "Jeremiah also uttered a lament for Josiah; and all the singing men and singing women have spoken of Josiah in their laments to this day. They made these an ordinance in Israel; behold, they are written

century who turned to biblical models experienced a frequent tension between being a court poet and an oppositional prophet. They vacillated between hopes for their monarch as the godly king chosen by God to overthrow the pope, and a despair at that same king's failure to fulfill his role. Along with this they move from the poetry of flattery to that of indignant criticism, caught between the two roles of the court poet and the prophetic outsider.

References in the books of Samuel and Kings indicate that once the monarchy was established, "court prophets" became a common feature, and these figures seem largely to have affirmed the king's position. At the same time, individual figures continued to prophesy against the king, often in resistance to the court prophets. In the Bible, "court prophets" are usually presented as dishonest temporizers, who prophesy that which will please the monarch or nation.[6] Most noteworthy is the story of Micaiah, whose prophecy of Ahab's death was an important one for those writers set on being foreboding prophets (I Kings 22). In this story Jehoshophat, king of Judah, collaborates with Ahab, king of Israel, against the Syrians. The court prophets (about 400 of them) predict success, but Jehoshophat asks if there is no other prophet. Ahab acknowledges that there is the prophet Micaiah, but "I hate him, for he never prophesies good concerning me, but evil" (I Kings 22:8). At Jehoshophat's insistence Micaiah is brought in: he accuses the other prophets of speaking with a lying spirit and enticing the king to a losing battle. After Micaiah's imprisonment, Ahab dies in battle. A prophet who insisted on speaking truth could, like Micaiah, expect persecution, not favour. The prophet Hanani told Asa, king of Judah, that he had done wrong in relying on an alliance with the king of Syria rather than divine aid: "Then Asa was angry with the seer, and put him in the stocks, in prison, for he was in a rage with him because of this" (II Chron. 16:7–10). For seventeenth-century writers, persecution might be read as a sign that they, like Micaiah and Hanani, were the true prophets of God.

In comparison with other parts of the Bible, the Prophets received little attention in England from the Reformation until 1640. Commentaries and sermons on the Prophets, beyond those on the messianic sections of Isaiah, were few in comparison to those on the Books of Moses and the Wisdom Literature. However, the broader world of continental Protestantism shows how the Prophets and their relevance for contemporary writers were generally understood. Calvin sees the biblical Prophets as interpreters of the law, and remembrancers to the kings and nation of God's law and covenant with Israel. King Hezekiah provides a model of how a king ought to respond to a prophet:

in the Laments" (II Chron. 35:25). This illustrates well that a biblical poet could combine dire prophecy with praise of a king, that is, if the king followed the Lord.

[6] See Micah 2:6–11.

Hezekiah, not only treated the holy man with reverence, but modestly submitted to his doctrine like one of the common people, and, what is still more, endured patiently severe reproof when it was found necessary.[7]

Such a model puts the prophet over the king, and Calvin adopts a similar stance in advising King Edward VI of England:

And here I expressly call upon you, most excellent King, or rather, God himself addresses you by the mouth of his servant Isaiah, charging you to proceed, to the utmost of your ability and power, in carrying forward the restoration of the Church, which has been so successfully begun in your kingdom.

The voices of the prophet, that of Calvin, and that of God Himself, are aligned in this passage, and the implication is that they stand in relationship to the king in similar ways. Thus, Calvin recognizes an ongoing role for prophet figures:

Hence we may learn in what manner the doctrine of the word should be handled, and that we ought to imitate the Prophets, who conveyed the doctrine of the Law in such a manner as to draw from it advices, reproofs, threatenings and consolations, which they applied to the present condition of the people. For although we do not daily receive revelation of what we are to utter as a prediction, yet it is of high importance to us to compare the behaviour of the men of our own age with the behaviour of that ancient people; and from their histories and examples we ought to make known the judgments of God.[8]

John Bale's *Images of Both Churches*, drawing on Bullinger, established an English Protestant historiography, which was further promulgated by Foxe.[9] John Knox considered himself a prophet of God, and devoted considerable time to defending this position.[10] In 1560 he was involved in a long debate with the Catholic Ninian Winzet concerning his prophetic authority. However, by no means did all Calvinists agree with the application of biblical prophecy to current events.

In England the "exercise of prophesying" developed among the godly Protestants of the southeast in the 1570s. This involved gatherings of clergy and laymen outside the worship service, where a number of sermons would be presented on a biblical text. Elizabeth recognized these gatherings as a threat to the established church, and Archbishop Grindal was suspended for

---

[7] *Commentary on the Book of the Prophet Isaiah*, trans. William Pringle (Edinburgh, 1850), p. xx.

[8] p. xxx.

[9] Borris, p. 27.

[10] J. Ridley, *John Knox* (Oxford: OUP, 1968), pp. 409, 503–4. See also Rodney L. Petersen, "Bullinger's Prophets of the "*Restitutio*'", *Biblical Hermeneutics in Historical Perspective*, eds Mark S. Burrows and Paul Rorem (Grand Rapids: William B. Eerdmans, 1991), pp. 245–60.

his support of them. As Patrick Collinson notes, these gatherings did have the potential to be "exploited for polemical and even subversive purposes".[11] The prohibition against these prophesyings was lifted in 1604.[12]

Late in the sixteenth century there seems to have been a cautious reassessment of the role of prophecy. Lambert Daneau, a highly respected French scholar,[13] provides an outline of a Calvinist understanding of "prophets" in the late sixteenth century. He suggests that the term "prophet"

> comprehendeth all those the which being moved with the spirit of God, either ordinarily or extraordinarily, either in prose or in verse doe set forth, tell, and declare the will of God, and the same either already knowen & written: or as yet hidden & unknown.[14]

For Daneau the distinguishing characteristic is that the utterance expresses the will of God by a moving of the spirit: the form of the utterance is irrelevant. Daneau rejects outright those who claim to foretell future events, a sort of prophecy that he believes ended with the Revelation of John. He also denies the application of Old Testament prophecy to current situations, but his description of acceptable prophesying would seem to include the uttering of new prophetic statements about the times.[15] Daneau hoped to defend the "exercise of prophesying", which he claimed found its roots in the New Testament church rather than the Old Testament prophets, while at the same time distinguishing it from prophetic foretelling, of which there seems to have been a rash in the 1580s and early 1590s.[16] Daneau may have been reacting against such Protestants as Giacopo Brocardo who achieved notoriety in the 1580s for his reinterpretations of biblical prophecy.[17] Also prominent at this time was one Paul Grebner, whose works caused widespread controversy in the 1580s and 1590s.[18]

Pierre du Moulin, writing during James' reign, defends his application of

---

[11] *Archbishop Grindal*, p. 234.

[12] McCullough, *Sermons at Court*, pp. 126–7.

[13] Daneau (freq. spelt Danaeus) was born in Aurelia, France in 1530; he was with the Calvinists in Geneva from about 1560 on, and later took a position at the University of Leiden. He died in 1596. (Thomas Fuller, *Abel Redivivus* [1651], p. 408.)

[14] *A Fruitfull Commentary upon the Twelve Small Prophets*, trans. by John Stockwood (1594), p. 2.

[15] p. 29.

[16] p. 16.

[17] At least one of his works was published in English: *The revelation of S. Jhon reveled, writen in Latine and Englished by J. Sanford* (1582).

[18] Grebner's works were latched on to by the Fifth Monarchists in the 1650s, see *A Brief Description of the Future History of Europe* (1650); *The Prophecie of P. G. Concerning these times* (1649); *Grebner his Prophecy concerning Charles, son of Charles* (1651); *A Paraphrase on P. Grebnerus's prophecie, in Vaticinium votivum* (1649); *Europe's Wonder: or, the Turks Overthrow Contained in a Prophecie written by that famous Divine Paul Grebner* (The Hague: John Browne, 1661).

the biblical Prophets to current events by suggesting that he is merely recognizing the fulfillment of prophecies: "the reader shall do well to consider, that it is one thing to *prophecy*, another thing to *speak of the fulfilling of prophecies*: the one is done by revelation, the other by experience".[19] As such he is not claiming any special position or authority, but merely pointing out the similarities between the biblical prophecies and current events. Such perusal of the prophets then is not mere curiosity, du Moulin asserts, and, in fact, an ignoring of them would be a rejection of God's grace.[20]

Some English preachers of James' time made efforts to temper the Protestant assertion of the supremacy of the prophet figure and the significance of modern-day prophecy. Joseph Hall, a moderate churchman, provides an instructive example of how such tempering might be manifest. His *Contemplations* were extremely popular in the period, and his description of the biblical institution of monarchy, and the relationship between king and prophet, stands in striking contrast to that of Calvin quoted above. His description of the instituting of monarchy in Israel presents it as a positive thing, and a result of the failure of the prophets/judges tradition: "The wickedness of his [Samuel's] Sonnes gave the occasion of a change: Perhaps Israel had never thought of a King, if Samuels Sonnes had not beene unlike their Father."[21] In his account of Nathan and David, the king's willingness to heed his prophet's admonition is praised, but in terms far less challenging of the ultimate authority of monarchy than in Calvin's preface to Isaiah: "Had not Nathan beene used to the possession of Davids eare, this complaint had beene suspected. It well beseemes a King to take information by a Prophet. Whiles wise Nathan was querulously discoursing, of the cruell rich man that had forceably taken away the only Lambe of his poore Neighbour, how willingly doth David listen to the Storie, and how sharply (even above Law) doth he censure the fact?"[22] The phrase "take information" is far more indirect, and places the king in the active role. Hall skips right over the post-Davidic history of Israel in his *Contemplations*, and makes no mention of the later writing prophets.

In James' reign there was also some resistance to the common Protestant analogy between prophet and preacher.[23] James himself became satiric in his attack in *The Trew Law of Free Monarchies* on those preachers who went beyond even the prophets' role in Israel:

---

[19] *The Accomplishment of Prophecies*, sig. A3v.
[20] sig. A6v.
[21] *Works* (1624), p. 1052.
[22] p. 1142.
[23] For an outspoken dismissal of the idea of modern-day prophets shortly after James' death, see Stephen Denison, *The White Wolf* (1627), a sermon preached at Paul's Cross, and particularly concerned with refuting the prophetic claims of John Hetherington.

And I think no man will doubt but Samuel, David, and Elijah had as great power to persuade the people, if they had liked to have employed their credit, to uproars and rebellions against these wicked kings as any of our seditious preachers in these days of whatsoever religion, either in this country or in France, had that busied themselves most to stir up rebellion under cloak of religion. This far the only love of verity, I protest, without hatred at their persons, ha[s] moved me to be somewhat satiric.[24]

John Donne carefully distinguishes between the two roles: "The Prophets would chide the King openly, and threaten the Kings publiquely, and proclaime the fault of the Kings in the eares of the people confidently, authoritatively."[25] Donne goes on to rebuke those preachers who assume they then have license to do the same.[26] In spite of such careful qualifying of the prophetic role, preachers in James' reign still took fair liberty in commenting on the current situation,[27] to the point that James published his *Directions to Preachers* in 1622, which limited the topics upon which clergy could preach. There was a continuing popular perception that preachers had special license: according to Drummond, Ben Jonson at one point expressed the desire to be a preacher for one day, so that he might "have favour to make one sermon to the king. He careth not what th[e]r[e]after should befall him; for he would not flatter, though he saw death."[28]

In spite of the cautious limits espoused by Hall and Donne, there were writers in the period, such as Thorne, Clapham and Wither, who maintained a Calvinist understanding of the modern-day prophet's role. However, in doing so they did not necessarily position themselves against the court. Later, when prophetic poetry flourished during the civil war and interregnum, foretelling and opposition to the court often went together. However, it is a mistake to assume that such was necessarily the case in the earlier years of the century. Many poets of the sixteenth and early seventeenth centuries did not see their prophetic role as conflicting with veneration of the king. Instead, their prophetic gifts were used to show the future glory of the king. In the same way that Jeremiah might praise the virtuous king Josiah, English prophetic poets were more than strictly oppositional in relation to the court. David Norbrook recognizes this in the case of Spenser;[29] however, I

---

[24] *Basilikon Doron*, eds Fischlin and Fortier, p. 64.
[25] John Donne, *Sermons*, eds George R. Potter and Evelyn M. Simpson, 10 vols (Berkeley: U of California P, 1953–62), vol. 2, p. 303.
[26] See Jeanne Shami, "The Absolutist Politics of Quotation", *John Donne's Religious Imagination*, eds Raymond-Jean Frontain and Frances M. Malpezzi (Conway, Ark.: UCAP, 1995), p. 387.
[27] See McCullough, *Sermons at Court*, pp. 35–9 and 47–8 on the willingness of court preachers to use the pulpit as a forum for the discussion of *arcana imperii*.
[28] *Conversations with Drummond of Hawthornden*, in *The Oxford Authors: Ben Jonson*, ed. Ian Donaldson (Oxford: OUP, 1985), p. 602.
[29] *Poetry and Politics in the English Renaissance*, pp. 59–90, 109–56.

will argue that even in more "radical" poets such as Henoch Clapham, George Wither and Andrew Melville there was a constant tension between being a court poet and being an oppositional prophet. As previously mentioned, these poets vacillated between the hope that James might be the godly king chosen by God to overthrow the pope, and despair at the failure of James to fulfill his role. What they hoped for above all was a godly court where the prophet and his words would be welcome. In chastising the errors of the king and nation, such poets as Wither and Clapham were self-consciously following in the tradition of such prophets as Jeremiah, Elijah, and Micaiah, yet they expected that with a godly king like James their admonitions would be graciously accepted and suitably rewarded. At the same time, the expectations were so high as to lead to inevitable disappointment: disgruntled poets turned their prophetic mode in the direction of criticism of the court and at times even James himself, or they began to look to Prince Henry, or later Elector Frederick of the Palatine, as the Constantinian "godly prince". With James' death, Wither would look to Charles to pick up the mantle never rightly worn by his father.

II

Among the works that greeted James in 1603 was William Thorne's *Εσοπτρον Βασιλικον*: or *A Kenning-Glasse for a Christian King*, a work of instruction for the new king. Thorne (1568?–1630) was regius professor of Hebrew at Oxford and dean of Chichester. The work is a manual of instruction to the king, but Thorne takes pains to note that he is not directly advising, that for the king there is no earthly instructor or model: according to Thorne, he is to imitate Christ or God directly. From Thorne's book, James will perceive what it means to be Christ-like.

In the dedicatory epistle Thorne presents himself as a latter-day Amos, who was forced to leave the royal chapel at Bethel and prophesy from Judah. Thorne writes, "As a Priest in the way of conscience I chose to do this, as knowing Amaziah of old, what he said unto Amos; O, thou the Seer, go, flee thou away into the land of Judah, and there eate thy bread, and Prophesie there. But Prophesie no more at Beth-il. For it is the Kings Chappell, and the Kings Court".[30] That he has been removed in "the way of conscience" suggests that Thorne objected to some aspect of worship at the Chapel Royal; elsewhere in *Amos*, the prophet attacks the idolatry of the altar at Bethel.[31] In his commentary on the twelve minor prophets Lambert Daneau comments quite extensively on this passage. He clearly sees Amaziah as a deceitful figure opposed to the true prophet of God. He also sees the chapel at Bethel as ungodly:

[30] sig. A3v.
[31] See especially Amos 3:14, and 5:5ff; cf. also I Kings 13.

The Holines is described in these wordes (*It is the Kings chappell*) the which wordes doe sound thus much, as if Amazias should say: This place is unto us all a most holy temple, ordayned by the commandement of the King, like as unto you is your Temple at Jerusalem most holy. It is therefore unlawfull for thee to speake anything against the worship and holiness of this temple. For thou mayest not here bee suffered, as namely being one that is blasphemous against our gods, and iniurious unto this place the which is so holy. After such like maner Jeroboam the first would have maintained the false and counterfeit holines of his altar in the selfesame citie Beth-el against the Prophet of God, but he was punished for his labor. For when hee stretched out his arme to have had the Prophet stayed, *his hand which hee put forth against him, dryed up, and hee could not pull it in againe to him*, I King 13, ver. 4.[32]

In the passage from I Kings, the prophet is not named, but clearly Daneau equates him with Amos. This would have increased the perception of Amos as anti-court prophet, and particularly as one who prophesied against the religious practices of the court. The prophet in I Kings 13 goes on to forecast that a King Josiah will come who will sacrifice the high priests on their own altar. The implications of Thorne's use of the analogy are clear: the king's chapel, like the altar at Bethel, is not acceptable to God. The use of the altar in the English church, and particularly in the Chapel Royal, was a focus in these years for the godly's objections, as will be demonstrated in the next chapter on the epigrams of Andrew Melville.

Because Thorne is writing from Oxford, he can indeed be compared to Amos: he writes from outside the king's court.[33] However, how far does the analogy extend? Amos had been banished because he prophesied against King Jeroboam, saying that the king would die by the sword and Israel would go into exile because of his death (Amos 7:11). Could an allusion to Amos's banishment avoid bringing with it the substance of his prophecy? If Thorne is a latter-day Amos, does that make James a latter-day Jeroboam? Perhaps, it would be more accurate to suggest that Thorne's work presents the king as a potential Jeroboam, and that $E\sigma o\pi\tau\rho o\nu\ B\alpha\sigma\iota\lambda\iota\kappa o\nu$ is a book of warning for the king, encouraging him to imitate Christ, in order to avoid that end. For the godly in 1603, the question was whether James would prove to be a Jereboam or instead a Josiah, the king of Judah who had reformed public worship, and to whose reign Amos looked forward.

The last sentence of the passage quoted above weaves together echoes and allusions from two other biblical episodes, Solomon's coronation (I Kings 1:32–40), and King Nebuchadnezzar's dream and his insistence that the Chaldeans interpret his dream (Daniel 2:4). He hopes "our great Oxford

---

[32] p. 305.

[33] As an outsider and rustic Amos would have represented a model for those prophetic poets like Wither who stressed their untutored country ways. Augustine presented Amos "as a model of "untutored eloquence" (*De Doctrina Christiana* 4:7). On the significance of Amos for early Protestants, see J. Ridley, *John Knox*, p. 409.

Hosanna to adde my Aramites [A4r] crie to, *Malco legnotemin cheiie*, God save my Lord King James for ever". The quotation is from Daniel 2:4 where the Chaldeans address King Nebuchadnezzar, but in this story they are in turn castigated by the king for their inability to recall his dream. Thorne is again depicting himself as an outsider, but in this case one who stands apart from even his colleagues at Oxford. That Thorne borrows his exclamation of praise from the story of Nebuchadnezzar also places James in a negative extended analogy. King Nebuchadnezzar was best remembered in the early modern period for his madness and eating "grass like an ox", as Daniel prophesied (Daniel 4:32–3).

Within the work itself Thorne adopts a mildly prophetic stance, by instructing James quite directly. He justifies this approach by pointing out the king's influence on the nation, and hence his responsibility: "Aswell for that a King is to compute unto God for each Christian soule in his whole Commonweale: as that the whole Common-weale is naturallie conformed unto the customes of her King".[34] The king's imitation of Christ is more important than the common man's: the king comes to stand as an intermediary between God and his country. Thorne tells James: "He [Christ] is an everlasting example for thee: Imitate him, and thy subjects will imitate thee. He is a most Exemplar states-booke for thee: Read him, [A3r] and thy Subjects will read thee." In the passage that follows Thorne touches on the sensitive and controversial matter of royally granted monopolies: "thou must, as A just STEWARD, divide aequallie; to thy selfe thine owne, to the Common weale her owne, to the Church her owne, impartiallie, without acceptation of persons: thou must scourge out all Monopoly-mongers, and such like monsters out of thy common-weale: as Christ did".[35] In this passage he criticizes those who place great men above Christ or take themselves as their own examples: "some other Anthropolatra there are (as the Emperour in his Code recordes of Nestorius) that commit Idolatry with men, that make mirrours of men: some of themselves, and some of others".[36] Thorne continues his instruction of James by warning him against those who proposed to treat him like a God: "thou must reject thy many flatterers, that will say; Thou art a God; and respect thy fewe friends, that will tell thee; Thou art a man. I have said; Yee are Gods, but yee shall dye like men" [A3v]. Thorne is quoting Psalm 82:6–7: "I say, 'You are gods, sons of the Most High, all of you; nevertheless, you shall die like men, and fall like any prince.'" The first half of the passage, which lends a quasi-divine status to the monarchy, was frequently quoted by panegyrists of James, but Thorne completes the quotation, and in doing so takes on the prophetic role of warning.

[34] sig. A2v.
[35] sig. A3r.
[36] sig. D1r.

48

In the same summer, Henoch Clapham presented a number of works that both praised James and criticized official policy, and he provides an example of a writer who oscillated between a prophetic and courtly stance in relation to King James in the early years of his reign. Clapham cannot easily be given a theological label; while many have considered him to be a Brownist, theologically he could better be described as a radical Puritan, as he never officially separated from the Church of England.[37] Clapham was ordained by Bishop William Wickham about 1591, but outside the regular ordination service. Just what he was ordained to is unclear: he describes himself "as a Sheepheard at randome to helpe where I could".[38] Through the 1590s much of his time seems to have been spent in Holland, and during this time he published a series of poetic and theological works. His most successful work was *A Briefe of the Bible*, a synopsis of the Bible in verse, published at Edinburgh in 1596, and revised for publication at London in 1603.[39] In the 1603 dedicatory epistle to Prince Henry, Clapham claims that the first edition had been approved by King James while in Scotland. *A Briefe of the Bible* is the sort of uncontroversial work of theological instruction that James would have found attractive. However, in other works written in the first years of James' reign, Clapham did not hesitate to criticize official policy, especially policy enacted for the plague of 1603. Thus, in the summer of 1603, we have Clapham celebrating the coming together of Scotland and England under one godly king, and at the same time blasting the official policy of quarantining those infected by the plague. Such a balancing act Clapham found difficult to sustain.

In *An Epistle Discoursing upon the Present Pestilence* Clapham presents the plague of 1603 as God's judgement rather than a merely physical illness, and argues that churchmen and magistrates have a duty to remain in the city at such a time. His belief in the moral basis of the plague led him to much contact with those who were ill, as he did not fear contagion. Throughout the work he invokes the examples of biblical kings and their response to national crises, and he ultimately extends this to connect himself with the biblical Prophets. In his concluding paragraph he writes, "Let Nehemiah and Daniel, Magistrate and Minister, confesse their sinnes & the sinnes of their people, and let all the people subscribe, saing, Amen." In this way, as a minister resisting the orders of both the civil magistrates and his own church leaders in regards to quarantine, Clapham aligns himself with the prophet Daniel.

An Epistle was to be Clapham's most controversial work, and it led to his imprisonment on 14 November 1603. From prison he wrote two defenses of his epistle, directed especially against Lancelot Andrewes, who had been

---

[37] Champlin Burrage, *The Early English Dissenters in the Light of Recent Research, 1550–1641* (Cambridge: CUP, 1912), pp. 194–5.
[38] *Doctor Andros his Prosopopeia answered*, sig. B2r.
[39] There were further editions of this work in 1608 and 1639.

appointed to investigate Clapham's writings and activities. Overall, his defenses of the work greatly diminish his prophetic stance: he engages in tightly argued discussions of specific passages of his epistle and Andrewes' response. Argumentation of this sort simply seems unprophetic. As he himself puts it, "I sometimes speak to Scholers schoole-wise (for now the simplicitie of the Prophets and Apostles is but meanly esteemed of so many, into such wicked times we be falne)."[40] The latter work includes "An Epistle To such as be distracted in mynd in respect of present styrres in the Church" in which he explains how he can remain in the Church of England without agreeing with all that goes on there. *Doctor Andros* ends with the words "God save King James" in large block letters (p. 83). Clearly, Clapham wanted to distinguish between attacking official policy and attacking the king himself; he still saw himself as a potential court poet and preacher, and from about 1605 his relations with the crown and church improved markedly.[41]

Of the three writers I am considering closely, George Wither took his prophetic claims furthest, and, especially in the 1640s through 1660s, was a wildly outspoken prophet figure. The prophetic element in his later poetry has been ably traced by Allen Pritchard;[42] I wish to consider more closely the relation between his earlier satires and panegyrics and *Britain's Remembrancer* (1628), his first prophetic work. Wither differs from Thorne and Clapham in that he was not ordained, and thus could not claim to prophesy as part of that calling; instead his prophetic stance was part of a very full poetic career. The prophetic mode could integrate the critical capacity of satire with what poets hoped would be a poetry worthy of respect at court, a respect based on its divine nature.[43] He is claiming to speak for God, but in his own person.

Two ideas are prominent throughout George Wither's early verse: first, he sees poetry as his calling, rather than a mere pastime or secondary interest; secondly, he expects that through this poetry he will achieve fame and a public role in the service of his nation and king. Wither's high view of poetry derives most directly from the writings of Spenser, Sidney, and du Bartas. In Spenser he found the Virgilian movement from pastoral to heroic epic, in Sidney and du Bartas his vision of the high calling of the poet.[44] In *Abuses Stript and Whipt*, he praises poetry as the highest calling: "For, of all sorts of men here's my beliefe, / The Poet is most worthy, and the chiefe".[45] He also presents the

---

[40] *Doctor Andros*, p. 3.

[41] At the time Clapham wrote this work, Andrewes was dean of Westminster.

[42] "George Wither: the Poet as Prophet", *SP* 59 (1962): 211–30.

[43] The coming together of the prophet and satirist figures has been partially traced by Raymond-Jean Frontain and Jan Wojcik in the introduction to their book *Poetic Prophecy in Western Literature* (London and Toronto: Associated UP, 1984), p. 24; they cite John Skelton, Thomas Drant and Wither as early examples of this, but find it most markedly in Dryden. On the satiric nature of the biblical Prophets themselves, see Thomas Jemielity, *Satire and the Hebrew Prophets* (Louisville: Westminster/John Knox Press, 1992).

[44] In addition to Spenser and Sidney, he praises the poetry of Daniel, Drayton and Sylvester.

[45] *Juvenilia* (1626), sig. S8r. For all references to Wither's *Prince Henries Obsequies, Abuses Stript*

idea of a "sacred Fury" that carries the poet above his usual self, and hence gives his writing further authority.[46] Wither's career began with a flurry, as he produced five works in the space of just over three years. *Prince Henries Obsequies* (1612) and *Epithalamia* (1613) are poems of praise for members of the royal family; *Abuses Stript and Whipt* (1613), *A Satyre* (1614) and *Shepheards Hunting* (1615) are all satiric works meant to correct the vices of England and warn the king against corruption. Wither considered all five of these works to be youthful, somewhat rough and rustic, and preparatory to more important poetry. Gestures to earlier or later works are typical of Wither: his poems are never isolated, but parts of an interconnected career. They announce works to come, or hark back to the success or controversy of earlier ones. Most often in the early works, even when in the role of the satirist, he is pointing forward to future poetry of importance. The early suggestions are that this "greater matter" will be of a martial nature, celebrating a future British or Protestant triumph.

For those familiar with Wither's later support of the Parliamentary cause, his persistent pursuit of royal patronage in the first twenty-five years of his poetic career may come as a surprise. Many scholars have mistakenly viewed his attacks on various courtiers in his early works as a deep-seated opposition to the king and court. In describing the early Wither as "oppositional", Christopher Hill ignores the poet's repeated petitions for royal patronage.[47] David Norbrook, in an otherwise excellent discussion of Wither and his circle, recognizes the poet's appeals for royal patronage, but dismisses them as empty gestures.[48] However, these "empty gestures" eventually led to Wither's receiving a potentially lucrative patent on his *Hymns and Songs of the Church* in 1623. Although he frequently disagreed with the policies of the king, his response was to try to show the king the wickedness of some courtiers, and persuade him to pursue a different course. For Wither, James was still potentially the godly king.

and *Whipt*, *Epithalamia*, *A Satyre: Dedicated to His Most Excellent Majestie*, *The Shepheards Hunting*, and *Fidelia*, I have cited the 2-volume Spenser Society Reprint of Wither's *Juvenilia* (1626) (Spenser Soc., 1871; rpt. New York: Burt Franklin, 1967). Due to the confusing double pagination of this reprint, I have chosen to cite by signature: these correspond to those in the original 1626 publication.

[46] p. 41. Pritchard, "George Wither: the Poet as Prophet", p. 214, notes that this idea stems ultimately from Plato's *Ion*.

[47] "George Wither and John Milton", *Collected Essays of Christopher Hill, vol. 1: Writing and Revolution in Seventeenth-Century England* (Amherst: U of Massachusetts P, 1985), pp. 133–50.

[48] Norbrook, *Poetry and Politics in the English Renaissance*, pp. 207–11. See David Cressy, "Foucault, Stone, Shakespeare, and Social History", *ELR* 21 (1991): 121–33, on the tendency of new historicists to ignore revisionist historians and base their discussions of literature on an "historical analysis which may have peaked in the early 1970s". Norbrook, at least, recognizes the arguments of the revisionists, but asserts that there were exceptional writers who questioned the traditional hierarchies (p. 11). My argument is that the Wither of the 1610s and 1620s is not among these: he merely wanted his faction, and the ideas it represented, to enjoy the king's favour.

What Wither disdained were the workings of the traditional patronage networks at court; he sings "the old harsh notes" of satire because he is not able to afford the more costly cultivation of favour which involves addressing various court functionaries to have his appeal read by the potential patron:

> I cannot bear't to runne my selfe in debt,
> To hire the *Groome*, to bid the *Page* entreat,
> Some *favour Follower* to vouchsafe his Word
> To get me a cold comfort from his *Lord*.[49]

He believed that his own high poetic calling allowed him to address the king directly, rather than seeking indirect patronage and access through courtiers who were liable to subvert his endeavours. If Wither's intended audience was primarily the king, why then did he bother to publish his poems rather than present them in manuscript form directly to the king? In Wither's case, publication created a public controversy that the king could not ignore. He argues that the "Sharpe sauce" of *Abuses* actually makes it more worthy of the king's notice, "Than those that in *Court-language* filed smooth,/Strive unbeleeved *Trophies* for to raise thee".[50] Clearly, Wither is not rejecting the poetry of courtly patronage, but merely changing the style of it. His will not merely flatter, but also advise.

Throughout James' reign, with the exception of his biblical versifications that will be discussed below in Chapter 8, Wither maintained this stance of the lofty satirist. He did not proclaim himself a prophet in the biblical sense, yet at times his outspoken and direct stance are reminiscent of that model. However, after James' death Wither went one step further. With his first work of Charles' reign, *Britain's Remembrancer* (1628), Wither adopts a stance as national prophet, which, while consistent with his earlier satire, presents a much higher claim. This lengthy work interprets the plague of 1625 as a warning to England of its sinful ways. Wither begins the poem with a long verse dedication to the king which seems to indicate that Charles was meant to receive a copy of the work before it was publicly distributed.[51] In effect, Wither desires to be a virtuous court prophet, for he claims "My *Lines* are

---

[49] *A Satyre* in *Juvenilia*, sig. Dd2r. There is a similar passage in the introduction to the first edition of *Fidelia* (1615), where he disdains to be beholden "to some under-Officer" (A4v), and that only "to part with three moyties to get one". On the importance of courtiers serving as brokers between patrons and clients see Peck, *Court Patronage and Corruption in Early Stuart England*; on the role of such brokers in literary patronage see my "'The Fruit of Favour': The Dedicatory Sonnets to Henry Lok's *Ecclesiastes*", *ELH* 60 (1993): 1–15.

[50] Epigram 2, "Another to his Maiestie", *Juvenilia*, sig. Y8r.

[51] *Britains Remembrancer*, sig. A2r–A12v. A shorter manuscript copy of the work from 1625, meant for presentation to Charles, survives (Pepysian MS 1999, Magdalene College, Cambridge). This was edited by J. Milton French as *The History of the Pestilence* (Cambridge, Mass.: Harvard UP, 1932). According to the dedicatory poem to the king accompanying the 1628 edition, the licensers refused to allow the first edition to be printed (sig. A6r).

loyall, though they bold appeare."[52] He is convinced that the personal piety of Charles will lead him to accept the wisdom of *Britains Remembrancer,* and help him to save England from the perils which the poem depicts. As with his earlier satires, he knows that some courtiers will try to misrepresent *Britains Remembrancer* to the king: for that reason the king himself can be his only patron.[53] He clearly disdained the influence of Buckingham, at whose death he composed a mock epitaph, but as with James fifteen years earlier, he was fulsome in his praise of the king himself.

There is a continuity between Wither's earlier works and *Britains Remembrancer,* but in the latter work we find a greater recklessness, and a willingness to invoke a special status related to the will of God. Wither now sees himself as God's chosen messenger, but he still desires to be the elect of earthly King Charles as well. Particularly in his dedication to the king, Wither makes repeated direct comparisons of himself to the biblical Prophets in general, and specifically to Jeremiah and Jonah. He also describes the vision in which he, like Isaiah and Ezekial, is commissioned by God to the role of prophet:

> Thy god hatht toucht thy *Tongue,* and tipt thy Pen;
> And, therefore, feare not thou the face of men,
> Lest he destroy thee. For, this day to stand
> 'Gainst *Princes,* Priests, and People of this *Land,*
> Thou art appointed.[54]

Here he recognizes his task to include standing against princes, but this does not keep him from adopting a humble attitude toward Charles elsewhere in the work. As with his later prophetic works, Wither presents contemporary troubles as God's warning to Britain, yet he has little confidence that the people and king will heed either the plague itself, or Wither, its "remembrancer".

As Wither's first prophetic work, *Britains Remembrancer* exhibits traits which were to be found throughout the later prophetic works: an emphasis on personal sin leading to national ruin, a conviction that his words would not be heeded, disregard for poetic structure, and the claiming of direct inspiration from God. However, these aspects are not discontinuous with his earlier satiric and panegyric works. We find still the references to the muses and patronage, the scathing, if indirect, depictions of individual courtiers, the loosing of his satiric dogs, which he had used in *Abuses Stript and Whipt,* and the humble attitude before the king. *Britains Remembrancer* is a striking work, then, for its melding of the two traditions, and the resulting lofty satire. *Britains Remembrancer* goes on for nearly 300 pages divided into eight cantos; it begins in epic fashion with a conference between God and the

---

[52] *Britains Remembrancer,* sig. A8v.
[53] sig. A2v.
[54] sig. O1r.

allegorical figures of Justice and Clemency, but after the first few cantos Wither's Muse "at random flyes", as he himself describes it. Generally, the work reveals a moderate religious position, cautious between the extremes of papism and iconoclastic Puritanism.

What had changed with the beginning of Charles' reign to explain Wither's shift in approach? Biographical information is scanty, but it may have been the personal circumstances or disappointments of Wither himself. Despite royal support, his *Hymns and Songs of the Church* had been blocked by the actions of the Stationers' Company; like many others he viewed the influential Buckingham with great animosity.[55] Or were these prophetic tendencies held in abeyance while James lived, as Wither felt that they would be more welcomed by Charles? However, a broader explanation, not centred on Wither himself, might be necessary; *Britains Remembrancer* was only part of a wider increase in the use of the prophetic stance in the 1620s. The last year of the previous decade had seen a widely noted spate of "odde fellowes that watching the Kings going abrode have brought him messages and admonitions from God".[56] In early 1619 a controversial work entitled *Balaam's Ass*[57] was "let fall in the gallery at Whitehall, bearing a subscription to the king"; the authorship was eventually traced to one Williams, a Roman Catholic[58] who was hanged, drawn and quartered for his utterances; during the execution he claimed that "he had inward warrant, and a particular illumination to understand certain hard passages of Daniell and the Revelation".[59] His prophecy also held that "this lord chief justice should usher the king to his grave, . . . and that Whitehall should be desolate, and be covered with grass, that so there might be store of feeding for his ass, and all this before the 7th of September, 1621".[60] Also in May of 1619, a former secretary of Lord Willoughby, named Weekes, approached James in the park at Theobalds, and commanded him to stop as he had "a message to deliver from God". He reportedly told James, in words heavily indebted to the biblical Prophets: "thou hast perverted justice and not relieved the oppressed. Therefore, unless thou repent, God hath sent the kingdom from thee and thy posterity after

---

[55] It is possible that *Britains Remembrancer* was not published until 1628 because it could not be safely disseminated while Buckingham was alive.

[56] Chamberlain to Carleton, 8 May 1619, *Chamberlain Letters*, vol. 2, p. 233.

[57] A work of this title survives in BL MS Lansdowne 213, fol. 59ff; this work is a prophetic warning to the king, but was clearly written in March of 1617, and the encouragement of persecution of recusants (fol. 70r) makes it unlikely that it is Williams' work. Overall, this *Balaam's Ass* is encouraging the king to fully enforce his proclamation ordering all to leave London who had no proper business there. The story of Balaam and his ass (Numbers 22:1–35) was frequently cited in the period; use of the story would allow the writer to speak with a less self-aggrandizing way than with a parallel to Isaiah or any other human prophet.

[58] Lorkin to Puckering, 16 March 1618/19, *Court and Times of James I*, ed. Thomas Birch (1848), vol. 2, pp. 146–7.

[59] Chamberlain to Carleton, 8 May 1619, *Chamberlain Letters*, vol. 2, p. 234.

[60] Lorkin to Puckering, 5 May 1619, *Court and Times of James I*, vol. 2, p. 158.

thee."[61] The prophetic utterances of Williams and Weekes coincided with a serious illness of the king in the spring of 1619. Through the 1620s Puritan preachers began turning increasingly to the biblical Prophets for sermon texts. In reference to the plague and other such disasters they frequently drew upon Ezekiel 5:14–17, and its depiction of them as God's arrows sent to warn the nation.

Wither's *Britains Remembrancer* was part of a flurry of prophetic utterances in 1625 that seem to have been provoked by the combined crises of a royal death and a summer plague. That summer saw the beginning of Lady Eleanor Davies' long career of vehement prophetic utterance. Davies' application of the book of Daniel to contemporary events, *A Warning to the Dragon and All His Angels*, was delivered to George Abbot, archbishop of Canterbury, in August, 1625, and printed in the same year (pp. xii and 1).[62] Like Wither she dedicated the work to King Charles.[63] Also appearing at that time were T. Brewer's *The Weeping Lady: Or, London like Ninivie in Sack-Cloth* (1625) and R. Harris' *Hezekiah's Recovery* (1626).

Clearly, the actual or feared death of the monarch brought forth prophetic utterance that was not likely or possible at other times. The passing of a monarch was a national crisis that elicited a radical response, and hopes on the part of a wide variety of figures of new directions for the nation. When, as in 1603 and 1625, this coincided with a summer plague, prophetic possibilities seemed all the greater. The year 1625, however, did not merely repeat the prophetic moment of 1603; those prophetic works of the latter year were both more outspoken and daring in their invocation of biblical precedent, as well as more widespread. This would seem to indicate a broader shift in the political and religious situation, one that was to reach its fruition during the civil wars and interregnum when prophetic utterances and works became commonplace.

Thorne was a preacher, Wither a poet, and Clapham a preacher and poet, but for them the distinction between prose and poetry seems insignificant. The content or message they provided was more important than the style in which it was delivered, and they would not have recognized the Prophets as being stylistically different from the rest of scripture. What mattered for these writers was that the biblical Prophets provided a model that allowed them to write on national issues with a tone of religious authority. For a career poet like Wither, the biblical Prophets provided an alternative to the classical figure of the laureate poet, or the modern figure of the satirist; for Calvinist preachers like Thorne and Clapham, the model of the Prophets extended their authority, and resituated their position relative to the king. In imitation of the

---

[61] Lorkin to Puckering, 4 May 1619, *Court and Times of James I*, vol. 2, p. 157.

[62] Esther Cope, ed., *Eleanor Davies: Prophetic Tracts* (Oxford: OUP, 1993), pp. xii and l.

[63] See Christine Berg and Philippa Berry, "'Spiritual Whoredom': An Essay on Female Prophets in the Seventeenth Century", *Literature and Power in the Seventeenth Century*, eds Francis Barker *et al.* (Colchester: U of Essex, 1981), pp. 45–7.

Prophets, writers such as Thorne, Clapham and Wither could continue to praise where appropriate, but also criticize and direct the king in following the ways of God. They might also at times lament the general state of the nation, or rebuke it for its sins. A very limited number of writers in the early Stuart period made use of the prophet model, and those who did seem to have tended toward the Puritan or godly part of the Church of England.[64] We must note, however, that none of those considered here rejected the court world completely – for them the monarch could still be the means by which God's will was fulfilled. These prophetic voices emerged in times of national crisis, times in which anxiety about the state of the nation would be at a high level, and the technical controls over printing loosened. Prophecy at the time might be an extension of the preaching or the poetic mode, but in neither case was it strictly oppositional; in the early Stuart period, at least, writers found a model for a more nuanced stance in the biblical Prophets themselves.

[64] This chapter has dealt largely with written works. The biblical Prophets were first of all oral figures; in this respect they may have been imitated by early Stuart "prophets" as well, who might be far more oppositional with the limited and known audience of a sermon or exercise of prophesying than they could be in published work. Even preachers reproaching the king in sermons at which he was present might be more free, for at least they were not making his faults known to the nation.

Chapter 4

KING JAMES, ANDREW MELVILLE AND THE NEO-LATIN RELIGIOUS EPIGRAM

ANDREW Melville, the Scottish scholar, preacher, and poet, is most often remembered for his confrontation with King James at the Falkland General Assembly of 1596, at which time he plucked James by the sleeve, and referred to him as "God's sillie vassal". While this is typical of the tension between the king and the *de facto* leader of the Scottish Presbyterians from the 1580s on, their relationship went through a series of stages, with frequent periods of ambivalence on the part of both men. At times, Melville was quite prepared poetically to praise James as at least a potential godly prince. He produced a great range of literary works, many of which had some relation to King James: these ranged from celebrations of Queen Anne's coronation and the birth of Prince Henry, to satiric epigrams on the English church. As a writer whose major works are in Latin he is less accessible than many better known, yet less significant, contemporaries. Although he devoted most of his life to theological scholarship and church government, his fame as a poet was widespread, and his poems, however short, circulated widely and provoked great controversy. Unlike many ecclesiastics his poetic production did not slow down later in life: he continued to write until his death in 1622 at the age of seventy-seven. An examination of Melville's writings and activities will illustrate the interconnectedness of English and Scottish ecclesiastical and theological controversies, the significance of Latin poetry in these conflicts, and the tendency for new controversies to resurrect the arguments and texts of earlier, and at times, significantly different conflicts. A study of Melville's epigrams will also shed light on the shifts in the perception of James' role in religious matters as his reign went on.

As Melville's epigrams will be the focus of this chapter, some explanation of the broader context of the genre is necessary. The epigram in general was the most fashionable poetic form of James' reign, John Owen's secular epigrams being the best known of these.[1] In describing the neo-Latin epigrams of

---

[1] Among English epigrams we find fewer of religious controversy; Sir John Harington has a few on church matters, but the only one of controversy I noted was Book 4, no. 63, "Against Pius quintus, that excommunicated Queene Elizabeth". In his index, *English Religious Poetry*

England in the seventeenth century Leicester Bradner identifies two broad types: the satirical and the sacred. By the sacred, however, Bradner means those based on biblical passages or sacred days.[2] Melville's epigrams are probably best understood within a third category, that of the humanist neo-Latin epigrams of the sixteenth century, which often included serious ecclesiastical satire. Taking their cues from *Disticha Catonis*, rather than from Martial, they served as a vehicle for serious admonitory comment; however, a satiric element was not completely absent, especially in such collections of epigrams as *Pasquillorum tomi duo* (1544), and John Parkhurst's *Ludicra sive epigrammata juvenilia* (1577), which commented directly on church matters.[3] These epigrams brought together the traditions of satire and scholarly "flyting",[4] and were often used by Protestants for pointed attacks on the Church of Rome. However, the continuation of this tradition in the seventeenth century has received very little attention from scholars.[5] These epigrams took a prominent role in the literature of religious controversy, serving as a medium that crossed linguistic and national boundaries, and one whose brevity encouraged widespread manuscript circulation and response. For British Protestants the writing of neo-Latin verse could serve to strengthen those international bonds which so many hoped would result in a strong Protestant League.[6] However, the neo-Latin epigram was also the vehicle for conflicts among Protestants, especially those related to church government and liturgy.

Theodore Beza was the most prominent of these Protestant epigrammatists, and likely served as a model for Melville. His epigrams enjoyed a wide circulation throughout Europe, and while his Roman attackers focussed on the amorous epigrams of his youth, Protestants frequently reprinted his epigrams of religious controversy. These continued to be used in inter-church polemic well after Beza's death in 1605.[7] According to Prescott, the quoting of Beza's epigrams "was part of a larger vogue for epigrams and indeed for any

Printed 1477–1640, Roman Dubinski lists over 600 religious epigrams (Waterloo, Ont.: North Waterloo Academic Press, 1996), but most of these are of the sacred rather than satiric variety.

[2] Bradner, *Musae Anglicanae* (New York: MLA, 1940; Rpt. New York: Kraus, 1966), p. 78.

[3] Mary Thomas Crane, "*Intret Cato*: Authority and the Epigram in Sixteenth-Century England", *Renaissance Genres: Essays on Theory, History, and Interpretation*, ed. Barbara Kiefer Lewalski (Cambridge, Mass.: Harvard UP, 1986), pp. 158–86.

[4] On the continuing significance of flyting in scholarly debate of the Renaissance, see Walter Ong, *The Presence of the Word* (Minneapolis: U of Minnesota P, 1981), pp. 207–22.

[5] The most thorough study of English neo-Latin writing, J. W. Binns' *Intellectual Culture in Elizabethan and Jacobean England* (Leeds: Francis Cairns, 1990), leaves epigrams, and in particular religious epigrams, largely undiscussed. As a primarily Scottish phenomenon they seem to have fallen outside the bounds of his study; however, it should be noted that while Scots were the primary authors of these, many were written while those Scots were living in England, and, in the case of Melville, elicited a significant English response.

[6] Binns, p. 109, points out the frequency with which such Scottish poets as Buchanan, Adamson, Leech and Johnston were printed on the continent.

[7] Anne Lake Prescott, "English Writers and Beza's Latin Epigrams", *Studies in the Renaissance* 21 (1974): 83–117.

useful fragments of sententious or striking poetry which, to gain variety, add authority, or suggest a consensus, could be inserted into a larger discourse".[8] Because of their brevity, epigrams were easily copied, if not memorized and spread orally. Thus, widespread circulation occurred, even though publication was rare. While many of these epigrams were composed for a particular situation or controversy, they frequently developed an afterlife, as they were resurrected for later similar controversies.

Like Beza, Melville turned to the epigram as a vehicle for ecclesiastical polemic, especially in his later years when he was excluded from direct influence on the churches of Scotland and England. Considering his significance as a major Scottish churchman and writer, Melville as poet has been relatively neglected; the early nineteenth-century biography by Thomas M'Crie is still the standard work, and M'Crie's disdain for Melville's poetic activities is reflected in the relatively short shrift they are given in the biography. In his own time Melville was well known as a humanist scholar and playfully ironic poet, as well as a fiery defender of the Presbyterian model of church government. His role in the reformation of the Scottish universities was as significant as his attempts at further reform in the church. Melville's early education was in Scotland at the time of the Reformation; he graduated from St. Andrews in 1564, and then spent time at Paris, Poitiers, and Geneva, where he associated with such poets and scholars as Beza, Joseph Scaliger and Francois Hotman. Melville's first major poetic work was *Carmen Mosis*, consisting of a verse paraphrase of the Song of Moses and part of Job as well as other short poems; it was published at Basle in 1573. The following year he returned to Scotland, where he undertook first the principalship of the University of Glasgow, and then that of St Mary's College at St Andrews. From that point until his removal to London in 1605, Melville was to be a major figure in the continuing reformation of both the Scottish church and the Scottish universities.

Melville's stature and influence during the 1570s and 1580s shifted as rapidly as the competing factions within Scotland. From 1574 until the late 1580s Melville proved himself willing to antagonize King James and the Scottish court on behalf of Presbyterianism and further reformation. Throughout this time Melville's standing with the court varied depending on who controlled the king. During the regency of Morton he fared well, playing a key role in drafting the *Second Book of Discipline* (1581), which attempted to rid the Scottish church of all remnants of episcopacy. With Esmé Stuart's rise to prominence in the early 1580s, Melville and the other Presbyterians found themselves in direct conflict with the court. He rose with the Ruthven Raiders, and then fell when James was rescued from them. Upon being charged with treason he fled to London in 1584.[9] With the fall of James

---

[8] Ibid., pp. 94–5.
[9] On Melville in England, see Gordon Donaldson, "Scottish Presbyterian Exiles in England, 1584–8", *Scottish Church History* (Edinburgh: Scottish Academic Press, 1985).

Stewart, earl of Arran, in 1585, and the Scottish alliance with England, he could once again return to Scotland, and participate in the continuing struggles over church government. However, by 1586 his reputation for speaking out in his sermons was such that he was permitted only to preach in Latin, thus limiting his audience to the learned.[10]

By the time of the coronation of Queen Anne on 17 May 1590, James and the Presbyterians were on unparalleled good terms, and Melville functioned at that ceremony as something of a court poet. With the Armada the Scots had been frightened by their common enemy the Roman Catholics, and, as chancellor, John Maitland of Thirlestane promoted co-operation between competing groups. The service for Anne's coronation, held at the chapel at Holyrood, was a soundly Presbyterian ceremony, complete with clarification that the coronation was a civil rather than ecclesiastical affair.[11] Originally, plans had called for the bishops to participate in the ceremony, but at some point between 4 May and 17 May, the ministers Robert Bruce, Patrick Galloway and Melville were substituted.[12] According to Spottiswood, Melville had originally objected to the Ceremony of Unction as a Jewish or papist ceremony, but relented when James threatened to get a bishop to perform it.[13] Anne was anointed by the staunch Presbyterian Robert Bruce, and after the crown was placed on her head by Bruce, John Maitland of Thirlestane, and David Lindsay,[14] Melville rose and pronounced a Latin poem based on the text, "Iustitia stabilit thronum Regis" (Proverbs 16:13). Thus, the Presbyterian clergy were filling the courtly roles usually filled by the bishops and archbishop. According to Adrian Damman's account of the ceremony, Melville "grandique ad Regem carmine fatur/Ausonio, monitisque docet prudentibus artem/Imperii".[15] A "carmine Ausonio", an Italian song, is the sort of courtly verse one would expect from a time-serving flatterer, not a preacher-prophet such as Melville, but in such poems we see again how the usual dichotomy between prophet and court poet breaks down. In the poem, entitled Στεφανισκιον, Melville praises James for his courage in braving the North Sea to bring home his bride. There are allusions to James' poetry, and most importantly a section where the connection between God, the king and the church is clearly enunciated:

> o quam sumus una
> Coniuncti qui regnamur cum Rege catena?
> Virtutis secat ille viam dux praevius? ultro

---

[10] *DNB*, p. 233.

[11] *CSP, Scotland*, vol. x, p. 299.

[12] *CSP, Scotland*, vol. x, p. 289.

[13] John Spottiswoode, *History of the Church and State of Scotland*, 4th edn (1677), pp. 381–2.

[14] Lindsay was minister of Leith in 1584, and imprisoned at the time of Black Acts.

[15] [he speaks to the king in a grand Italian song, and teaches in prudent warnings the art of empire] *Schediasmata Hadrianus Dammanis A Bisterveld Gandavensis* (Edinburgh: Robert Waldegrave, 1590).

Nos comites. Fertur preceps per devia? iam nos
Praecipites. Vernat Zephyris felicibus? & nos
Floremus. Lapsum urget hyems? nos flore caduci
Defluimus, ruimusq[ue].[16]

Figuring largely among Melville's concerns is the topic of virtuous kingship; the tone, however, is a moderate one of praise rather than didacticism. Melville does not hesitate to use language that links the king with God himself: he describes James as "viva Dei viventis imago" [the living image of God himself].

By the time of Prince Henry's baptism three years later, neither Melville nor the Presbyterian establishment enjoyed so unquestionably the light of the king's favour. In the spring of 1594 Melville was suspected of assisting the earl of Bothwell in his plots against the king, but he seems to have cleared himself by the time of the baptism on 30 August 1594. Once again Melville played a public role in the affair, composing verses entitled *Principis Scoti-Britannorum natalia*, which were printed at the king's command.[17] In this work Melville anticipates that James and Henry will one day rule over both England and Scotland. The work addressed James as "Scoto-Britanno Rege" and hoped that Henry would lead a united Britain against the various forces of the Roman Catholic world:

fulmine luridum
Trudente ad orcum ter sacratum
Pontificem, atque Italum, atque Iberum.[18]

The composition of the verses, and most particularly, James' command for them to be printed, was a great offense to Queen Elizabeth, who remained throughout her life unwilling to name a successor.[19] The work was also printed in Holland, and from there circulated widely in England; in fact Robert Bowes, the English ambassador in Scotland, came to know about it through a report from England.[20] A flurry of diplomatic activity followed the

[16] [O how are we joined as one, we who are reigned with a kingly chain? The leader of virtue going before us marks the way of virtue. Beyond we are companions. Is he borne headlong through an erroneous way? Then we are borne headlong. Does he flourish with the happy west winds? So we flourish. Does winter push him with a downward movement? We descend with the fallen flower, and are ruined.] Στεφανισκιον, ll. 98–104.
[17] The ceremony of the baptism is described by William Fowler in *A True Reportarie . . . of the Baptism of . . . Prince Henry* (Edinburgh [1594]). This work was reprinted in London in 1603. According to Allan F. Westcott, Fowler "as assistant to Sir Patrick Lesly was chief contriver of the celebration at Prince Henry's baptism" (*New Poems by James I of England*, p. xli).
[18] [with a thunderbolt pushing to ghastly death the three: sacred Pope, Italian and Spaniard.]
[19] The birth of Henry elicited a more private poetic celebration in England as well: later, in 1603, Joseph Hall reports that he had written a translation of Virgil's Eclogue 4 on the occasion, *The Kings Prophecie* (1603) in *Collected Poems*, p. 112. This was presumably left unpublished, and no manuscript copy survives.
[20] *CSP, Scotland*, vol. 11, pp. 430–1.

publication of *Principis Scoti-Britannorum Natalia.* Bowes demanded an apology, first from the printer Robert Waldegrave, and then from the king. Waldegrave excused himself on the grounds that he could not read Latin, and the king claimed not to have read the verses before granting approval. James tried to dismiss the matter, asserting that "poets and scholars would oftentimes and without good discretion publish 'conceiptes' occupying their heads and pleasing their minds, notwithstanding their actions therein little profited".[21] However, the conceit of the "British" king probably pleased him as well, and it is unlikely that one who took such interest in matters of kingship and poetry, and who recognized the influence of Melville, would have haphazardly approved a work without being aware of its contents. As with the coronation of Anne, Melville was serving in the role of court poet, one who prophesied, but whose "prophecies" betokened the success of the Stuart line, and its important place in the coming of Christ's kingdom.

After the conflict at Falkland of 1596 there was increasing tension between James and Melville, as the king excluded him from subsequent General Assemblies of the church. Westcott suggests that "when James in *Reulis and Cautelis* warns poets to avoid matters of the commonwealth, which 'are to grave materis for a Poet to mell in', he is doubtless speaking from his experiences with the verse satirists of the Kirk party in Scotland".[22] When Melville got hold of a copy of James' *Basilikon Doron,* printed only as a private edition for Prince Henry in 1599, he severely criticized the claims of royal authority the king made.[23] In July of 1602 James personally ordered that Melville not be allowed beyond the confines of his college, St Andrews;[24] it was from this situation that the poet celebrated James' accession to the English throne the following year.

Throughout Melville's years in Scotland he experienced a tension between serving a godly prince, and criticizing that prince who too often failed to measure up to Melville's understanding of godliness. Like many other Scots of the time Melville hoped that James would be a Constantinian godly prince, reigning over a renewed Christian empire.[25] Yet, at the same time, Melville was repeatedly frustrated by James' refusal to heed the church as it expressed itself in the General Assembly. Yes, Melville hoped for a godly prince, but wanted one that would also receive instruction from preachers like himself.

---

[21] *CSP, Scotland,* vol. 11, p. 431. The whole affair is similar to the dispute between England and Scotland over Book 5, Canto 9, of Spenser's *Faerie Queene* that took place two years later. At that time as well there was a diplomatic crisis based on the question of whether a monarch was responsible for a work published in her honour.

[22] *New Poems by James I of England,* ed. Allan F. Westcott (New York: Columbia UP, 1911. Rpt. New York: AMS Press, 1966), p. xlvi. James might even be punning on Melville's name at this point, a practice common in the Latin poetry addressed to him at the time.

[23] Thomas M'Crie, *Life of Andrew Melville* (Edinburgh, 1824), vol. 1, p. 488n.

[24] David Calderwood, *Historie of the Kirk of Scotland,* ed. T. Thomson (Edinburgh, 1845), p. 472.

[25] See particularly his verses on the baptism of Prince Henry, *Principis Scoti-Britannorum Natalia* (1594).

Above all Melville's opposition to episcopacy was incompatible with a king who increasingly saw such a system of church government as politically essential, if not divinely ordained.

MELVILLE AND THE KING OF ENGLAND

Melville celebrated James' accession to the English throne in three poems, which remained unpublished until 1619.[26] As with the poems on Henry's baptism, these celebrate the possibility of a Protestant empire with James as its head. The promise pointed toward in the poem at Henry's birth is now fulfilled: James is truly a "Scotangle Princeps", or "Scotobriton-hiberne Princeps".[27] The longest of these poem harks back to the defeat of the Spanish Armada, a moment when England and Scotland were united in a common purpose and militant Presbyterians were influential with James. As king of England, however, James established peace with Spain, and the Hampton Court Conference made clear that there were serious limits to his toleration of further reform, much to the disappointment of Melville and those who shared his views. Nevertheless Melville would still join in the general celebration of James' deliverance from the Gunpowder Plot, penning "Conjuratio pulverea. anno 1650 [sic] Novemb. 5".[28]

Unlike many Scottish subjects Melville did not follow his king south; however, he maintained an interest and involvement in English affairs that would plague King James and eventually lead to imprisonment in the southern kingdom. Melville seems to have recognized early that developments in the English church after 1603 were likely to affect the Church of Scotland as well: James' desire for union between the two kingdoms was not likely to exclude religious or ecclesiastical union. In England some of the godly hoped that James' accession would lead to the English church becoming more like that of Scotland. The Millenary Petition was privately presented to James in the spring of 1603: it called for an end to such "Popish" elements as the use of the sign of the cross in baptism, the surplice, and the observation of feast days; it also asked that the problems of ecclesiastical pluralities and underpaid preachers be addressed. The petition provoked a hostile response from Oxford, published in the fall of 1603 as *The Answer of the Vice-Chancellor, the Doctors with the Proctors and other Heads of Houses in the University of Oxford*; included in this work was a letter from the vice-chancellor of Cambridge supporting the Oxford position.[29] This work attacked the petition as a seditious libel against the king, and a factious blow to the English church

[26] They appeared then in *Viri Clarissimi A. M. Musae, et P. Adamsoni vita et Palindoia* (1620) (*STC* 17810), an anthology of poetry by Melville and Patrick Adamson, archbishop of St Andrews from 1576 until his death in 1592, and a frequent opponent of Melville.
[27] "Kalend. Aprilis. 1603. Ad Regem", *Viri Clarissimi*, p. 13.
[28] *Viri Clarissimi*, p. 15.
[29] *STC* 19010.

in that it controverted matters which were wholly indifferent.[30] In attacking the petitioners, the Oxford work links them with the Scottish Presbyterians, but even without such provocation Melville might have become involved. Melville defended the petitioners with *Pro Supplici Evangelicorum Ministrorum in Anglia ad Serenissimum Regem . . . sive Anti-Tami-Cami-categoria* (1604).[31] The poem is addressed to the king, and in harsh biting terms Melville mocks those features of English worship to which the petitioners had objected. In reference to the English liturgy, he asks, "sacra vox sacrata im-/ Murmuret unda/Strigis in morem?" [Does the sacred voice murmur with the sacred wave of a screech-owl at death?]. Melville uses the strategy of invoking the broader European conflict between Protestants and the Church of Rome: thus, the English Puritan John Rainolds is held up alongside Martin Bucer, Peter Martyr and Beza. However, he does this in a way that connects James to these pan-European Protestants as well: like the Petitioners themselves Melville still hopes that James might be the godly prince leading the nation, and bring the English church closer to continental Calvinism.

> solumque
> Et salum coeli aemula praecinentis
>   More modoque
> Concinunt Bezae numeris modisque
> Et polo plaudunt: referuntque leges
> Lege quas sanxit pius ardor & Rex
>   Scotobritannus.[32]

The poem was not published, however, until 1620, when it was appended to David Calderwood's account of the Perth Assembly, *Parasynagma Perthense*.[33] The controversy stirred at that time will be discussed later in this chapter.

Melville's next conflict with the Church of England came in the fall of 1606. The previous year James had been angered by the General Assembly of the Church of Scotland at Aberdeen, which had been held without his leave. As a result, in May 1606 Melville and seven other Presbyterian ministers

---

[30] This matter of "things indifferent" or "adiaphora" was to occupy much of Melville's struggles with the English church through the rest of his life.

[31] This poem survives in a number of different forms: I am quoting the version appended to Calderwood's *Parasynagma Perthense* (1620). The date 1604 is given in the 1620 publication of *Anti-Tami-Cami-Categoria* with *Parasygnagma Perthense*. As Melville's poem includes no reference to the Hampton Court Conference of January 1604, it seems most likely that it was written in late 1603 or very early 1604.

[32] [And the earth and the open sea, vying with singing heaven harmonize, and in the numbers and measures of Beza they beat: and they bring back the laws, those which holy love and the Scoto-British king consecrated by law.]

[33] No place of publication is given: the Catalogue of the Edinburgh University Library suggests St Andrews. Three years later Melville's *Anti-Tami-Cami-Categoria* appeared once again in an appendix to another of Calderwood's works on the controversy, *Altare Damascenum* (1623). An English edition of this work had appeared in 1621 without Melville's poem.

were summoned by James to appear in London.[34] Upon meeting with James, Melville and the others refused to condemn the assembly, and were subsequently compelled to hear four notable English churchmen, William Barlow, John King, Lancelot Andrewes, and John Buckeridge, preach sermons at Hampton Court, all designed to show Melville and his fellow Presbyterians the proper way.[35] The sermons stressed the significance of the English liturgy, the legitimacy and benefit of episcopacy, and the king's prerogative in ecclesiastical matters.[36] That the proposed union between England and Scotland was approaching a crisis in parliament only heightened the significance of the event. In an opening speech to parliament James had called for "one church and one king".[37] Unable to respond to this barrage by preaching or publishing, Melville turned to the satiric epigram. After the first sermon of the series, by William Barlow on the "Antiquitie and Superioritie of Bishops", Melville penned a scathing epigram, ridiculing Archbishop Bancroft, whom Barlow had held up as a prime example of the benefits of episcopacy.[38] This was just one of a number of epigrams attacking Bancroft later included in *Viri Clarissimi*, for which the period 1606–07 is the most likely time of composition.

After this series of sermons was concluded on 28 September, Melville was required to be present at the celebration of the festival of St Michael at the English Chapel Royal at Windsor. In response to what he saw there he penned the following lines:

> Cur stant clausi Anglis libri duo regia in ara,
> Lumina caeca duo, pollubra sicca duo?

[34] Spottiswoode, *History of the Church of Scotland*, ed. M. Russell (Edinburgh, 1851), vol. 3, pp. 177–82, provides a detailed description of these meetings, as does Calderwood, *Historie of the Kirk of Scotland*, ed. T. Thomson (Edinburgh, 1845), vol. 5, pp. 559–97. A central contentious issue seems to have been the treatment of the Presbyterian ministers, Charles Farum, John Munro, Robert Youngson, James Irvine, William Forbes, James Greig, Nathaniel Inglis, and John Ross, whom James had charged with treason, but whom Melville and the others insisted on praying for as "persons in trouble and distress". For a more English perspective, see Roland Usher, *The Reconstruction of the English Church* (New York: D. Appleton, 1910), vol. 2, pp. 162–6.

[35] This was only one of many instances where James set up English theologians to counter Scottish Presbyterian arguments: in 1608, George Abbot was sent to Scotland, as the chaplain to the earl of Dunbar, to address the General Assembly at Linlithgow (Paul A. Welsby, *George Abbot* [London: SPCK, 1962], pp. 30–1; John Spottiswoode, *History of the Church of Scotland* [1851], vol. 3, p. 180). Similarly, Dr Downham's sermon in defense of episcopacy was widely distributed in Scotland in the same year.

[36] All these sermons were printed in 1606 or 1607.

[37] Godfrey Davies, *The Early Stuarts, 1603–1660*, 2nd ed. (Oxford: Clarendon Press, 1959), p. 9, quotes *Commons' Journals*, pp. 314–15.

[38] Usher, *Reconstruction of the English Church*, vol. 2, p. 162. He is citing Row, *Historie of the Kirk of Scotland*, p. 236. Usher describes it as "too coarse to be reprinted". According to M'Crie, Barlow responded to Melville's epigram on Bancroft with one of his own, and directs readers to Walton's *Lives*, ed. Thomas Zouch (York, 1796), p. 353.

Num sensum cultumque Dei tenet Anglia clausum,
  Lumine caeca suo, sorde sepulta sua?
Romano an ritu dum regalem instruit aram,
  Purpuream pingit relligiosa lupam?[39]

Like Melville's *Anti-Tami-Cami-Categoria*, these few lines were to play an inordinately large role in the struggles over liturgy in the English and Scottish churches. James was shown a copy of the verses by one of his chaplains, and subsequently called Melville before the Privy Council.[40] When Melville appeared, he claimed that he had intended to show the verse to the king,[41] and turned his attack upon Archbishop Bancroft for his 1590 tract on the succession. However, no such manoeuvres could prevent his confinement, first with the dean of St Paul's, John Overall, and then Bishop Bilson of Winchester.[42] One immediate result of the imprisonment was that Melville could not take part in the General Assembly of the Church of Scotland at Linlithgow the next month, an assembly at which bishops were given an official place in the kirk.

Spottiswoode's account suggests that Melville's insolence before the council, rather than the poem itself, was the reason for his imprisonment; however, the only formal charge brought against him in April 1607 was the epigram itself. M'Crie speculates, with just reason, that the actions of the Privy Council against Melville simply furthered the awareness and effect of the epigram.[43] About the same time he further increased the English-Scottish tension by writing an epigram mockingly contrasting the English St George with the Scottish St Andrew.[44] Melville might be imprisoned, but his verses on the royal altar took on a life of their own, as in the words of Izaak Walton they were "writ and scattered".[45] They circulated widely in manuscript in subsequent years, and were frequently responded to.[46]

---

[39] The earliest published version is found in *Viri Clarissimi*, p. 24. [Why do these two closed books stand on the altar of the English king? Two blind lights, two dry wash-basins? Or does England hold back the judgement and care of God, because of her blind light, her buried filth? While she sets up a royal altar according to the Roman ritual, she fights the Roman wolf-bitch [whore] zealously [my trans.]] The first published English version seems to have been by James Melville, Andrew's nephew, and printed in *The Blacke Bastel* in 1634. It begins, "On Kingly Chappels altar stand, blinde candlestickes, clos'd bookes".

[40] John Spottiswoode, *History of the Church of Scotland*, ed. M. Russell (Edinburgh: Oliver & Boyd, 1851), vol. 3, p. 183.

[41] Usher, *Reconstruction of the English Church*, vol. 2, p. 164, notes that James was not present at this meeting of the Privy Council.

[42] A poem by James Melville, dated 5 November 1606, suggests that his uncle was already imprisoned at that time (M'Crie, *Life of Andrew Melville*, vol. 2, p. 459).

[43] M'Crie, vol. 2, p. 177.

[44] M'Crie, vol. 2, p. 172.

[45] *Life of Herbert* (1670), p. 35.

[46] Antoine Le Fevre de la Boderie, *Ambassades de M. De la Boderie*, vol. 1, p. 458, and vol. 2, p. 209, reports on the widespread conversation about them in London.

Eventually the lines would be known on the continent as well.[47] The brevity of the epigram made circulation easy, and it became a central focus in the struggles between the churches of England and Scotland, and between the godly and the conforming within the Church of England. In a later collected edition of Melville's poems the poetic battle is playfully referred to as an "Arimachum" and "Aricolam". The epigram provided an opportunity for other poets to express their loyalty to James and the English church. As Thomas Dempster notes "In eum tunc eruditi quique, cum ut arrogantis hominis audaciam castigarent, tum ut regi suo placerent, stylum strinxerunt".[48]

Some of these responses remained in manuscript only, while others were published, along with Melville's original, in later years. Joseph Hall, later bishop of Exeter, penned two epigrams in response, preserved in Bodleian MS Rawlinson poet. 246, f. 16.[49] One of these is in Latin, the other English, and both counter the specific details of Melville's attack. In the English epigram Hall mocks Melville as a latter-day Oedipus pondering "what might these riddles meane?" The final lines of the epigram direct the significance of the items on the altar against Melville: they are "to teach in forreigne guise/To have blind eyes, clos'd lips, hand voyd & free/From foule suspect of wrongfull Jelousy". Ultimately, the epigram is dismissive of Melville, suggesting he would complain regardless of what he found on the English altar. In the same manuscript, on a facing page, another anonymous response to Melville is found. Like those by Hall, this one also responds directly to the objections expressed in what it calls Melville's "divinis libellis".[50]

Melville lingered in the Tower for nearly four years, and this time was one of frustration both for him and James. While denied pen and paper at first, he later was able to continue his writing, including a defense of himself entitled *Prosopopeia Apologetica* and a versification of the Psalms.[51] However, the most celebrated writing of his that emerged from this time was another epigram, which concerned both his imprisonment for the earlier altar poem and Sir William Seymour's imprisonment in the Tower for his secret marriage to Arabella Stuart in 1610:

> Communis tecum mihi causa est carceris, Ara-
> bella tibi causa est; Araque sacra mihi.[52]

---

[47] M'Crie, vol. 2, p. 177.

[48] [Then certain learned men turned against him, so that they might restrain the audacity of this arrogant man, then so that they would please their king, they attacked his style.] *Historia Ecclesiastica* (Edinburgh: Andreas Balfour, 1829), vol. 2, p. 497.

[49] Fram Dinshaw, "Two New Epigrams by Joseph Hall", *Notes and Queries* 29 (1982): 422–3.

[50] MS Rawl. Poet. 246, fol. 15v.

[51] M'Crie, vol. 2, pp. 203–15.

[52] [The cause of your imprisonment and mine is the same: a beautiful "Ara" is the cause of yours, a sacred "Ara" (altar) the cause of mine.] This epigram circulated in a variety of forms, all with the same basic sense, but different word order; this would suggest that its prime

Melville sent these lines to Seymour, and they also circulated widely at court.[53]

Throughout these years of imprisonment Melville was disappointed in what he perceived as the abandonment of Scottish tradition by those courtiers who had accompanied James down to his southern kingdom.[54] During his trial in April 1607 he had called upon the earls of Lennox and Mar as fellow Scots to come his defense, a gesture that greatly angered the king.[55] Melville certainly had connections at the court of James: his nephew James Melville, who experienced much the same persecution as his uncle, had some hope that the earl of Dunbar would intercede on their behalf. In fact, Dunbar actively worked against the Melvilles, and there may be a connection between his death in 1610 and Melville's release the following year.

Melville's release was likely due to a number of such developments in England and on the continent. Archbishop Bancroft had also died in 1610, and this removed what seems to have been a personal antagonism between Melville and the English archbishop. Melville's imprisonment had damaged James' reputation on the continent; that a theologian and churchman so widely respected by Protestants across Europe was being held prisoner by a Protestant prince was perceived by many as scandalous. During Melville's imprisonment a number of continental Protestant universities sought his release so that he might join them in their work. Also in these years, Archbishop Spottiswoode suggested that Melville return "to teach in Glasgow, if he pleased",[56] but it is unlikely that Melville would have enjoyed much freedom if he had accepted this offer. Finally, through the intercession of a leading French Protestant, Henri, duke of Bouillon, Melville was released in 1611 to take up a position at the University of Sedan. James gave him 60 pounds as a sendoff.[57] By this time James may have felt that the battle over church government in Scotland had been won by the supporters of episcopacy; in addition, removal from England might also diminish his public profile. Finally, Melville's theological skills might actually be useful to James if he were released and safely established in France. Already in 1607 Melville had been consulted by continental theologians about the emerging theology of Arminius, and by 1611 the emerging controversy of Vorstius'

---

means of circulation was oral. For example, "Causa mihi tecum communis carceris, Ara/ Regia, bella tibi, Regia sacra, mihi" appears in MS Rawl. Poet. 246, fol. 16r. See also *Court and Times of James I*, ed. Birch, vol. 1, pp. 127 and 132.

[53] M'Crie, vol. 1, p. 262; see *Memorials of Affairs of State* (London, 1725), vol. 3, p. 201, and John Row, *Historie of the Kirk of Scotland, 1558–1637*, 2 vols (Edinburgh: Maitland Club, 1842; rpt. New York: AMS, 1973), p. 173.

[54] A letter of the earl of Salisbury from 15 April 1607 recommends adding a number of Scots to the group prosecuting Melville, "in order that their presence may give a good reputation to the sentence in Scotland" (*CSPD, 1603–10*, p. 354).

[55] M'Crie, vol. 2, p. 175.

[56] Calderwood, *Historie of the Kirk of Scotland*, vol. 7, pp. 4, 5ff, 46.

[57] *CSPD*, vol. 9, pp. 21, 23. 6 and 11 April 1611. See also M'Crie, vol. 2, pp. 262–3.

theology, which carried on that of Arminius, seems to have been a higher priority than the struggles within the English church.[58] In this fashion the theological skills of Melville might be put to a use compatible with the king's interests. The radical theology of Vorstius thus brought about a sort of peace between Melville and the king, as their shared orthodox Calvinism over-shadowed their differences over church government.[59]

It seems that silence on British affairs was a condition of Melville's release, and for a few years he observed this. However, he and his earlier works were not forgotten by the Scots and English. While Melville remained on the continent for the rest of his life, he still functioned as a significant figure in the affairs of the Church of Scotland, and as a symbolic figure, continued to raise problems for King James. With the conflict provoked by the Perth Assembly of 1617–18, Melville's name and epigrams once again came to prominence. At the Perth Assembly struggles similar to those of the Hampton Court Conference were played out again, as James tried to impose a more English style of worship in Scotland. At James' insistence the General Assembly brought forward five articles: the lawfulness of private baptism and commu-nion, confirmation by bishops, celebration of such holy days as Christmas and Easter, and kneeling at communion. Archbishop Spottiswoode began the proceedings with a negative reference to Melville, arguing that episcopacy was the original church government of the Scottish reformed church, "and had continued the same, if the death of the Regent, the Earle of Marr, had not intervened; & that a seditious fiery man Mr. Andrewe Melvine come here to disturb all good order".[60] The 1617 General Assembly passed a watered-down version of the articles, which did not satisfy James, and the assembly at Perth in August 1618 was called upon to reconsider them. An assembly stacked with laymen whom the Presbyterians claimed had no right to vote passed the articles. The controversy had only just begun: for the next four years, there was a series of proclamations ordering compliance, protests from Scottish congregations and individuals, and defenses of the articles and James' policy. In this controversy both Melville's earlier poems, and some newly composed ones, figured prominently.

The first writer to attack Melville on behalf of James and his policy was George Eglishem, physician to the king, who in 1618 published six "Prophy-lactic Epigrams" in response to Melville's 12-year-old epigram on the royal altar.[61] These were published as an appendix to Eglishem's *Duellum Poeticum*, a

[58] On James' intense opposition to the appointment of Vorstius to the University of Leiden, see F. Shriver, "Orthodoxy and Diplomacy: James I and the Vorstius Affair", *English Historical Review* 85 (1970): 449–74.
[59] The Vorstius affair created strange bed-fellows: assisting James in his own writings against Vorstius was the crypto-Catholic George Calvert. Also writing against Vorstius was George Eglishem, the poet-physician who will be discussed below.
[60] Calderwood, *True History of the Church of Scotland* (1678), p. 478.
[61] Eglishem attracted much greater attention at the end of James' reign when he claimed that

work in which the physician-poet presented a challenge to the Latin versified psalms of the king's former tutor, George Buchanan. Eglishem's versification of Buchanan, like his response to Melville, was no mere literary exercise, but a challenge to one who had denied the king's absolute authority and was much cited by the Puritans: he charges that Buchanan "impietatem in Deum, perfidiam in Principem, tyrannidem in Muses exercuisse quantumvis ab impuro puritanorum caetu laudibus ad caelos feratur".[62] Thus, Eglishem is bringing together two attacks against infamous Scottish opponents of James. Eglishem's epigrams confront Melville's objections to the specific items on the altar, noting their symbolism and holy mystery. He warns, "Lumina non oculo, sed concipe mente, profanis/Claude Libros, lachrymis Pollubra sicca reple".[63] Eglishem emphasizes the sacramental and symbolic appropriateness of the altar. In the final epigram, his response becomes *ad hominem*, concluding, "Sordidus est, tumido caecus amore sui" [He is sordid, blind with his own swollen love].[64] The details of Melville's epigram were still germane; in his 1617 trip to Edinburgh, James had redecorated the royal chapel at Holyrood; the Presbyterian John Row's description of the altar dwells on the same details addressed in Melville's epigram: "a glorious altar sett up, with two closed Bibles, two unlighted candles, and two basins without water sett thereon".[65] In a similar vein the next year, Thomas Wilson brought out a collection of the late Archbishop Patrick Adamson's poetry, with which he included a preface attacking Melville.[66] As the archbishop of St Andrew's, Adamson had been a staunch supporter of episcopacy in Scotland and a long-time foe of Melville.

Also appearing in this context was the largest published collection of Melville's verse, *Viri Clarissimi A. Melvini Musae, et P. Adamsoni vita et Palindoia*, a counterblast put together by a supporter of Melville. While it included epigrams attacking Melville, the bulk of the collection was made up of Melville's own epigrams. These epigrams ranged from Melville's celebratory panegyrics written at James' accession to the English throne, to his notorious lines on the royal altar. The main goal of the collection seems to have been to counter Wilson's attack in the preface to *De Sacro Pastoris*

---

both James and the marquis of Hamilton had been poisoned by the doctors appointed by the duke of Buckingham (*Prodromus Vindictae* [1626]). Hamilton had been a lifelong patron to Eglishem.

[62] [had exercised impiety toward God, bad faith toward the Prince, and despotism toward the Muses, however much he is borne to the heavens with praises from the impure assembly of Puritans.] *Duellum Poeticum* (1618) sig. A2v.

[63] [Do not grasp the candle with your eye, but with your mind, do not close the books with profane words, fill up the dry basin with tears.]

[64] The version that Eglishem quotes is somewhat different from that most commonly circulated; its final two lines are, "Romano ritu Regalem dum instruit aram,/Romanam pingit relligiosa lupam".

[65] David Mathew, *James I* (London: Eyre & Spottiswoode, 1967), p. 258, quoting Row, *Historie of the Kirk of Scotland*, vol. 1, p. 113.

[66] Patrick Adamson, *De Sacro Pastoris Munere* [ed. Thomas Wilson] (1619), sig. G2v–G5v.

Munere. Included in *Viri Clarissimi* are poems by John Gordon and John Barclay responding to the epigram on the royal altar.[67] Like that of Eglishem, these epigrams respond to the details of Melville's poem. Gordon suggests that the lights of the English altar are dim, and the books closed, because the English have closed themselves to the leadership of the pope.[68] In his epigram Barclay defends the ornamentation of the English church, and suggests that Melville desires God to be worshipped in "haram/Porcorum stabulum".[69] Barclay had achieved a position at James' court in 1605, prominently serving as a learned assistant to James in his theological disputes, and it seems likely that Barclay's responses were written shortly after Melville's own epigram; however, his flight to Rome in 1615, and the suspicion that he had a hand in the vicious satire against James, *Corona Regia*, the following year, would render his defense of the English church an irony worth attacking. The editor of this volume pointedly refers to him as "Barclaius pontificius" in the one poem's heading. Such defenders could only bring the Church of England into disrepute. Included are five more in response by Melville.

The years following the Perth Assembly also saw the composition of new poems in response to Melville. Thomas Atkinson, a student at St John's College, responded to Melville in a satire entitled "Melvinus Delirans".[70] This poem was dedicated to Laud sometime between December 1616 and June 1621, the time when Laud was both dean of Gloucester and president of St John's College. However, the most notable response to Melville in these years was that of George Herbert in a series of Latin epigrams entitled *Musae Responsoriae*, dedicated to King James.[71] In the years following the Perth Assembly, Herbert held a number of Cambridge appointments: lecturer of rhetoric in 1618, deputy orator in 1619 and orator from 1620, and Herbert may have perceived his satiric rebuttal of Melville as consistent with his official duties. After all, *Anti-Tami-Cami-Categoria* had been an attack on Cambridge as well as the liturgy of the church. In this series of epigrams Herbert is responding most directly to *Anti-Tami-Cami-Categoria*, but also

---

[67] M'Crie speculates that those ascribed to Barclay and Gordon might be Melville himself, and represent a "poetical *just* or mock encounter" (vol. 2, p. 157n), but provides no evidence to support this.

[68] *Viri Clarissimi*, p. 24. The identity of this John Gordon is not clear. John Gordon, dean of Salisbury, had been Melville's "keeper" at one point during his imprisonment, and was known for his writings in support of the king and the English church. However, it seems likely that Melville or the editor would have given him that title, rather than simply referring to him as "Johannis Gordonii Scoti". In addition, the author of this poem is clearly Roman Catholic. However, I would suggest that Melville would not be displeased if readers mistook this for the thoughts of the dean of Salisbury.

[69] *Viri Clarissimi*, p. 25.

[70] BL MS Harl. 3496.2. See Thomas Fuller, *Church History* (1655), vol. 10, p. 70.

[71] A fuller discussion of Herbert's work is given in my article, "The Contexts of George Herbert's *Musae Responsoriae*", *George Herbert Journal* 2 (1992): 42–54. A translation of *Musae Responsoriae* is found in *The Latin Poetry of George Herbert: A Bilingual Edition*, eds Mark McCloskey and Paul R. Murphy (Athens: Ohio UP, 1965), pp. 8–11.

includes some reference to the epigram on the royal altar. He simultaneously celebrates the moderate orderliness of English worship and ridicules the zeal and obstinacy of the Scots. He also celebrates James as the leader of the forces against the Puritans: "Cum tu contundis *Catharos,* vultuque librisque".[72]

While the Perth Assembly sat, Melville composed a new collection of aphorisms published anonymously as *De Adiaphoris. Scoti TOU TUXONTOS aphorismi* ([Amsterdam, AEgidius Thorp], 1622), and he may have also had a hand in *Scoti TOU TUXONTOS Paraclesis contra Danielis Tileni Silesii Paraenesin* (London, 1622), a work that responded to Daniel Tilenus' defense of the Perth Articles.[73] Thus, right until his death in 1622 Melville continued in his established role as theologian and epigrammatist. Melville's career as a poet represents an inversion of the usual: rather than turning from satire and invective in his younger days to panegyric and loftier genres in his later days, he went the other way, as his circumstances separated him from the usual positions of power and influence a scholar of his status would normally have enjoyed.

Clearly, poets were engaging with Melville's past works in an attempt to court the king's favour; but how significant were these "epigram wars" in the public affairs of the time, and to what extent did James heed the exchanges? Epigrams, or "libels", are much reported on in the newsletters of the times, and there seem to be particular years where the "buzz" created by them is most noticeable. In the early 1620s the furor over English foreign policy and the Spanish match generated a wealth of manuscript-circulated epigrams. Among those circulating were some believed to be by King James himself.[74] In a time when printed books and sermons were being carefully monitored and suppressed, epigrams provided a means of surreptitious comment, one that could be easily circulated, and where authorship could remain hidden.[75]

The career of Andrew Melville, both in its clerical and poetic facets, was closely tied to James and his vision of the church. Ultimately, Melville's desires for the Church of Scotland and Protestantism in general were defeated by the policy of James. The "godly prince" had led, or misled, the church in other directions. In his final years Melville became a byword for an intransigent Presbyterian, a figure who could be attacked as a gesture of support for King James' ecclesiastical policy. The use of the satiric religious epigram in this internecine fashion reflected the fracturing of the Protestant unity which had been the chief dream of both Melville and James in the last decades of the sixteenth century.

---

[72] "When you subdue the Puritans through your countenance and books" [my trans.], Epigram 1.

[73] M'Crie believes that the work was by Melville's friend James Sempill (vol. 2, p. 319). The British Library Catalogue ascribes it to David Calderwood.

[74] See *The Chamberlain Letters,* 25 January 1622/23, *Court and Times,* 18 January 1622/23 and 14 February 1622/23.

[75] I am now engaged on a study of epigram circulation in the period.

Chapter 5

FROM CONSTANTINIAN EMPEROR TO *REX PACIFICUS*: THE EVOLVING ICONOGRAPHY OF JAMES I

THE iconography of James I drew on a substantial number of previous models – biblical, imperial and British. William Germano, in an unpublished dissertation on dedications to King James, notes that "As early as 1604, James had been hailed as any number of biblical kings, as a Caesar (particularly Constantine and Titus), a Noah, someone vaguely related to Apollo or Apollo himself, Atlas, and even Homer."[1] Classical and biblical prototypes would often be brought together in describing James: Robert Burton describes him as "a wise, learned, religious king, another Numa, a second Augustus, a true Josiah".[2]

As I suggested in the preface, many recent scholars have concentrated on the classical iconography used to celebrate James' reign, especially at his accession.[3] Correspondingly, the large body of biblical references applied to the king has been relatively neglected. Ultimately, there was perceived to be a closer correspondence between James and a biblical *king* than between him and a pagan *emperor*. Widely overlooked as well has been the important model that later Christian emperors such as Constantine provided for the iconography of the time. The emphasis on classical models may be a reflection of scholars' attention to drama and the masque:[4] considerations of the iconography of James must move beyond the limited visual worlds of the theatre, architecture and art, to consider a wide variety of prose and poetry. This chapter then will provide an overview of the biblical kings to whom James was frequently compared, and then turn to a consideration of how the iconography of James as a Constantinian prince was gradually displaced by his image as a Solomon-like "Rex Pacificus".

Increasing the complexity of any study of biblical iconography are the contemporary differences over what the parallelism signified. For some it

[1] William P. Germano, "The Literary Icon of James I", Ph.D., Indiana University, 1981, p. 68.
[2] Burton, *Anatomy of Melancholy*, fasc. of 1621 (Amsterdam: Theatrum Orbis Terrarum, 1971), p. 52.
[3] See for example *James I and the Politics of Literature*.
[4] Collinson, *Birthpangs of Protestant England*, p. 113.

might be merely a comparison of praise, for others a means of advising. For some it functioned in the same way that classical parallels did, consistent with the classical tradition of a history of constant return: "To see ourselves again, we need not look for Plato's year; every man is not only himself; there have been many Diogenes, and as many Timons, though but few of that name; men are lived over again; the world is now as it was in ages past."[5] Such a view would be in conflict with a chiliastic [or teleological] Christian conviction that all history is leading to eventual fulfilment.[6]

However, for many Protestants an analogy to a biblical figure might have a greater, typological significance as well. They might see the parallel as a divinely ordained one: God had chosen this figure to be the fulfilment of Solomon or David, or a latter-day Constantine leading God's church. This more profound correspondence is sometimes described as "neo-typology", and in it the types of the Old Testament found their fulfilment not only in the person of Christ, but also in individual believers of the New Covenant. A medieval reader of the Psalms looked for elements that prefigured Christ; a Reformation reading would see in them a pattern for the spiritual struggles of every believer in Christ.[7] Thus, biblical figures in the poetry of Donne and Herbert are more often working typologically than tropologically. It is not that Donne has chosen Jacob, nor that Walton, in his *Lives* of these men, simply finds their circumstances similar to their biblical forebears; but that they see God working in their lives in similar ways, and the two men responding in like fashion. Such neo-typology could also be applied to monarchs; it was not only that James had similar qualities to Solomon, but that God might be perceived as using James as he had used Solomon, to bring peace, or to further devout worship. Kings, however, were in a unique position, for in their office, rather than their person, they might embody their Old Testament predecessor. A king in the Christian era might also be a "formae perfectior", not just another Solomon, but a better, because Christian, Solomon.

In discussing the use of classical parallels, Annabel Patterson notes that they were most often oblique and indeterminate, and their indeterminacy led them to be read in different ways at different times.[8] The same was true of biblical analogies, including typological comparisons. Certain biblical parallels were so common that the very mention of the biblical figure would compel readers to search for a contemporary, in the assumption that a parallel must be intended. At the same time, few historical figures were without blemish: King

---

[5] Sir Thomas Browne, *Religio Medici*, in *Religio Medici and Other Works*, ed. L. C. Martin (Oxford: Clarendon Press, 1964), Book 1, Sect. 6.

[6] See William Lamont, *Godly Rule: Politics and Religion, 1603–60* (London: Macmillan, 1969).

[7] Lewalski, "Typology and Poetry: A Consideration of Herbert, Vaughan and Marvell", *Illustrious Evidence: Approaches to English Literature of the Early Seventeenth Century* (Berkeley: U of California P, 1975), p. 48.

[8] *Censorship and Interpretation*, p. 57.

David had sinned with Bathsheba and in the death of Uriah, Constantine had murdered his own son. Solomon, for all his wisdom and the building of the Temple, had been attracted to magic, and had fallen into pagan worship at the end of his life. Most writers who invoked the biblical king as a prototype for James overlooked these things, but in a biblically literate society, they might come to a reader's mind unbidden, and in non-analogical discussions they might arise in a way that commented upon the present. Thus, in discussing the possibility of backsliding in his conversation with Archbishop Bancroft, Tobie Matthew pointed out that King Solomon "grew to be such a kind of not only monster but devil, that at the instance of his Pagan concubines he fell flat from the service and worship of Almighty God".[9] By considering John Harington's description of the masque performed for King Christian's visit in the summer of 1606, William Tate demonstrates how the positive Solomonic iconography could be given a satiric twist.[10] John Chamberlain's description of James' funeral sermon also highlights the negative possibilities of any analogy: "The Lord Keper hath shewed a greate deale of witt and learning in comparing King James to King Salomon in all his actions saving his vices."[11] Biblical parallels could also be used for the purpose of direct critique or satire; thus, during the 1610 parliament James was compared to King Joram,[12] and Absalom and Achitophel were frequently invoked as symbols of court corruption.

The Bible provided iconographers of James' reign with a host of kings as possible models or comparisons: David, Solomon, Joash, Josiah, Hezekiah were all frequently invoked. James himself recognized the significance of these biblical kings for monarchs such as himself, counselling his son that "for there [in Kings and Chronicles] will ye see yourself as in a mirror, in the Catalogue either of the good or the evil kings".[13]

As the greatest of biblical kings, David was the most frequent model invoked in the early modern period. Thus, it is not surprising that Andrew Willet celebrated James through extended comparison to David in a 1604 sermon.[14] What is striking then is how seldom, relatively, James is compared to David. The parallel was usually drawn in reference to his composition of the Psalms, which James as poet-king was known to be translating.[15] Very few pushed the analogy to David, the shepherd-warrior, to suggest that James would lead them into battle. Linking the comparison to David with other

---

[9] *A True Historical Relation of the Conversion of Tobie Matthew* (London, 1904), p. 82.

[10] "King James I and the Queen of Sheba", *ELR* 26 (1996): 563–76.

[11] *Chamberlain Letters*, 21 May 1625, vol. 2, p. 619.

[12] David Harris Willson, *King James VI and I* (London: Jonathan Cape, 1956), p. 267. There were actually two biblical kings named Joram or Jehoram, the one a son of Ahaziah, and king of Israel, the other a son of Jehoshaphat, and king of Judah. Neither was a positive figure.

[13] *Basilikon Doron*, eds Fischlin and Fortier, p. 106.

[14] Graham Parry, *The Golden Age Restor'd* (Manchester: Manchester UP, 1981), p. 231.

[15] This aspect of James' career will be considered below in Chapter 8.

biblical kings such as Josiah and Solomon – as a number of poets and speakers did on James' return trip to Scotland – was a common practice.[16] In other comparisons to David, peaceful elements of that biblical king might be highlighted: James would tame the pope with his harp, as David had tamed Saul.[17]

Josiah had become king of Judah at the age of eight, when his father Amon was slain by his own servants (II Kings 21:23–22:1.), a situation thus with particular relevance for James. Josiah was noted for his praiseworthy religious reforms, including the repair of the Temple and the stamping out of pagan worship (II Kings 22–3 and 33–4). As such, he provided a model for those Protestants encouraging James to enact harsher measures against recusants. John Taylor noted that both James and Josiah were taken away "by unlook'd for death".[18]

"Joash" or "Jehoash" was the name of two separate biblical kings, one the son of Ahaziah and the eighth king of Judah, and the other son and successor of Jehoahaz and the twelfth king of Israel. The former, like Josiah, was a boy king, coming to the throne at the age of six, and a restorer of the Temple. He was a favoured figure in the iconography surrounding James. However, as the killer of the prophet Zechariah, and a victim of assassination, such an analogy brought with it certain difficulties. Hezekiah was another opposer of idolatry, which English Protestants usually associated with the Roman church. John Speed's *History* describes James' reception of the Millenary Petition in this way: "[he] resolved now by his Princely judgement, as another Hezekiah to breake the Brazen-Serpent, if Idolatry were thereunto committed, and like a second Josiah, to read the law of the Lord him selfe: whereupon by Proclamation hee commanded an assembly of selected Divines".[19] The analogy with Hezekiah became especially pertinent in James' later years, after the recovery from his 1619 illness.[20] Thus, in his sermon at James' death Daniel Price recalls an earlier illness at Royston, when "Our Royall Hezekias recovered miraculously to Gods glory, the good of the Church and State, and great comfort of all his good Subjects."[21] What is missing in Price's statement is that Hezekiah's recovery was also a personal one, giving him more time for repentance.

Of all biblical kings, however, Solomon provided the most significant

---

[16] John Adamson, Τα των μουσων εισωδια: *the Muses Welcome* (1618) p. 41.

[17] Williamson, *Scottish National Consciousness*, p. 104.

[18] "A Living Sadnes in Duty Consecrated to the Immortall Memory of our Late Deceased all-beloved Soveraigne Lord, the Peerelesse Paragon of Princes, James . . .", in *Works* (1630), p. 323.

[19] John Speed, *History of Great Britain* (1611), p. 163.

[20] On the figure of Hezekiah and his life as a model for illness leading to repentance, see Kate Frost, *Holy Delight: Typology, Numerology, and Autobiography in Donne's Devotions Upon Emergent Occasions* (Princeton: Princeton UP, 1990), pp. 28–35.

[21] Daniel Price, *A Heartie Prayer* (1625), p. 32.

prototype for those intent upon celebrating James' reign. A figure of wisdom, learning, and peace, a restorer of the Temple and a writer of poetic theology, Solomon was an ideal fit for the king. Comparisons of James to Solomon were manifold, and the intention of this chapter is not to trace them all, but simply to give a summary of the main features by which the two kings were held to be alike, before turning to the special affinity between James and Solomon in terms of peacemaking.[22]

Already as a 14-year-old king of Scotland in 1579, James had been celebrated in a pageant that invoked the Judgement of Solomon (I Kings 3:13–28).[23] As king of both Scotland and England, James reminded some of his subjects of Solomon's reign over both the northern and southern kingdoms of Israel. Such iconography was particularly widespread in the years immediately following 1603, as James pushed for a union of the kingdoms. John Thornborough, bishop of Bristol at the time, used the Judgment of Solomon to argue for the Union (I Kings 3:16–28). Solomon's reign was also generally perceived as a time of wealth and plenty; Henry Farley borrows biblical language to describe James' reign:

> Yet for his wealth, his wisedome, strength and all,
> A second Salomon you may Him call;
> His Land the Israel that flowes with milke,
> And honey sweet, corne, cattell, cloth, and silke,
> Gold from all parts, spice, oyle, and wine,
> Treasures from East and West, Pearls rich and fine . . .[24]

Bacon dedicated *The Advancement of Learning* to James and invoked the figure of wise Solomon, claiming that "there hath not been since Christ's time any king or temporal monarch, which hath been so learned in all literature and erudition, divine and human".[25] For Bacon, Solomon was also a natural philosopher, and thus James as a new Solomon should promote the study of the same.[26] In addressing parliament in 1621, James opens by quoting Solomon: " 'In multiloquio non deest peccatum' ", said the wisest king."[27]

Solomon was generally credited with authoring the Wisdom books of the

---

[22] On Joseph Hall's comparisons of James to Solomon, see Frank Livinston Huntley, *Essays in Persuasion* (Chicago: U of Chicago P, 1981), pp. 49–56.

[23] Roy Strong, *Britannia Triumphans: Inigo Jones, Rubens and Whitehall Palace* (London: Thames and Hudson, 1980), p. 20. Strong goes on to demonstrate the significance of the Judgment of Solomon during James' attempt at union of Scotland and England in the early years of his English reign.

[24] *The Complaint of Paules to all Christian Soules* (1616), p. 29.

[25] *The Advancement of Learning and The New Atlantis*, ed. Arthur Johnston (Oxford: Clarendon Press, 1974), p. 4. On Bacon's use of Solomonic iconography, see William Tate, "King James I and the Queen of Sheba", pp. 576–85.

[26] William Tate, p. 577.

[27] *CSPV, 1619–21*, p. 582. James is quoting Proverbs 10:19.

Bible: Proverbs, Ecclesiastes and the Song of Solomon. As a king who appeared in print before his people (more than he ever appeared in the flesh) a comparison of the royal author James to his biblical predecessor Solomon was natural for his subjects. He was frequently presented as a monarch who ruled with the pen as much as the sword; John King, bishop of London, celebrated James as a king who would combine authority with eloquent persuasion: "the colours of life and grace are in his lips, where *sceptrum* & *plectrum*, authoritie and eloquence will kiss each other".[28] Some writers made a more direct comparison to Solomon; Henry Farley describes James in this way:

> For Proverbs to his sonne he ded declare,
> Then next a preachers part he did not spare,
> The third his song of songs most sure shall be,
> That shall set forth His Kingly love to me [St. Paul's].[29]

In the right margin next to this passage are listed "1. Basilicon doron. 2. His Apology for the Oath of Allegiance. 3. Canticum Canticorum".[30]

David had not been allowed by God to build the Temple because he was a man of war, and so that duty fell to his Solomon in his reign of peace.[31] This aspect could be approached both in symbolic or literal terms; as a promoter of faith and patron of the church, James was a latter-day Solomon who built up the spiritual Temple, but he also actively promoted physical restoration of church buildings. These had been relatively neglected in the reign of Elizabeth, and while James was not as active as his son in church restoration, his attempts were noted by contemporaries. John Taylor celebrates James' success in this area:

> Besides for Churches, it most plaine appeares,
> That more hath bin repair'd in twenty yeeres,
> (In honour of our God and Saviours name)
> Then in an hundred yeeres before he came.[32]

Late in his reign James also took on a more literal temple-building role in his campaign to repair St Paul's Cathedral, which had remained in a badly

---

[28] John King, *A Sermon at Paules Crosse on behalf of Paules Church* (1620), p. 53.

[29] *The Complaint of Paules*, p. 28.

[30] The third reference presents something of a mystery; Farley is pointing toward some future work; the most likely would be James' versification of the Psalms, which will be discussed in Chapter 8 below, but the marginal reference "Canticum Canticorum" belies this; is it possible that James was considering a verse paraphrase of that work as well? Or has Farley received misinformation?

[31] See I Chronicles 28:1–6.

[32] "A Living Sadnes in Duty Consecrated to the Immortall Memory of our Late Deceased all-beloved Soveraigne Lord, the Peerelesse Paragon of Princes, James . . .", in *Works* (1630), p. 325.

damaged state since the fire of 1561. On 26 March 1620, James led a procession to Paul's Cross, where a special ceremony was held, inaugurating the campaign of repair.[33] John King's sermon announced the project of restoration, noting that this was the first occasion upon which James had attended a Paul's Cross sermon.[34] The major obstacle to the repair was a shortage of funds, and little seems to have been done until Charles' reign. King associates the Temple with St Paul's, but never invokes the figure of Solomon; however, he does connect the ruined "Temple" with the body of James, whom many had feared the year before was nearing death.

And how were James/Solomon's English subjects to respond to their biblical sovereign? A favourite device was to present them as taking the role of the queen of Sheba, admiring the wisdom and glory of the king:

> Graunt that his dayes may be like Salomon,
> A mirrur unto all the world beside,
> That those which heare his fame farre of to ring,
> Like Sabaes Queene, may all admire our King.[35]

James himself had introduced this conceit in *Basilikon Doron*, where he encouraged Prince Henry to cultivate a decorous court, in order "that when strangers shall visit your court, they may with the Queen of Sheba, admire your wisdom in the glory of your house and comely order among your servants".[36] As the iconography of James as Solomon developed, all people, both his own subjects and foreigners, might be construed as playing the role of the admiring queen of Sheba.[37] The image was adopted widely in sermons, treatises and even masques in subsequent years.[38] One further example will suffice; in his dedication to *Pseudo-Martyr* (1610) John Donne borrows her words to praise James: "Happie are thy men, and happie are those thy Servants, which stand before thee alwayes, and heare thy wisedome".[39]

CONSTANTINE AND REX PACIFICUS

The most significant aspect of Solomonic iconography applied to James was as a peacemaking king. However, this must be viewed in relation to a competing model of James as a latter-day Constantine. The emperor

---

[33] William MacDonald Sinclair, *Memorials of St. Paul's Cathedral* (Philadelphia: Jacobs, n.d.), pp. 180–2.
[34] *A Sermon at Paules Crosse* [p. 57].
[35] Samuel Rowlands, *Ave Caesar*, 1603, qtd. by Willson, *King James VI and I*, p. 169.
[36] *Basilikon Doron*, eds Fischlin and Fortier, p. 137.
[37] Tate, pp. 561–85.
[38] Robert Wakeman, *Salomons Exaltation: A Sermon Preached Before the King's Majestie at Nonesuch, Apr. 30, 1605*, takes as its text 2 Chronicles 9:8, the words of the queen of Sheba to Solomon.
[39] Curtis Perry, *The Making of Jacobean Culture*, p. 40, quoting *Pseudo-Martyr*, sig. A3–A3v.

Constantine was the most significant non-biblical ruler for those developing a Christian iconography for King James. As a Christian "king" and Roman emperor, Constantine embodies both the Christian and Classical traditions. In discussing the iconography of James, both Goldberg and Parry largely ignore the connections between imperial imagery and the apocalyptic associations based on the analogy to Constantine. For Goldberg, a reference to Constantine is only one more classical, imperial reference. Where Parry does discuss religious culture and the comparisons of James to Constantine, he overlooks the contentious nature of such an analogy – that to praise James as a Constantine was to direct or encourage a particular foreign and religious policy. It is true that the notion of a godly prince ruling over Britain was less important for his English subjects than for his Scottish ones; however, in 1603 his new English subjects were quick to take on the language and imagery of Britain.[40] In addition, Parry does not ultimately take this celebration of James seriously, and does not conceive that the composers themselves did either: he treats it as mere flattery divorced from actual expectations.[41]

In the European context the idea of the "godly prince" went back to the figure of the Emperor Constantine, who had converted the empire to Christianity. That Constantine was the son of a British mother certainly heightened the significance of his model, even if some sceptics were to maintain that his mother, Helena, was a barmaid, and never married to Constantius.[42] His example was attractive to those who hoped for Britain to once again play a leading role in Christendom. Among the Marian exiles of the 1550s the idea of an elect British nation – England and Scotland ruled together by one monarch, who would lead the Protestant powers against the papacy – had great appeal. It was nearly always linked with the idea of a Constantine-like leader. In Scotland the idea of a new "godly prince" in the mould of Constantine was introduced by Knox, and developed by later Reformers. In England it became widely known through Foxe's *Actes and Monuments*.[43] The new emperor or prince they expected would struggle against and overcome the Antichrist (understood most often as the papacy, but sometimes as the Turkish empire), and rebuild a Christian empire. As late as his Scottish trip of 1617 such vehemence might find expression; a speech by John Stewart of Perth calls him a "second Constantine to support Sions second daughter; the Lyon comming out of the forrest, to deplume the Eagle; to darken the Starr in the Crescents bosome, and to strype the strumpet of Rome stark naked".[44]

---

[40] See, for example, Davies of Hereford's *Microcosmos*.

[41] Germano suggests that the assumption that praise of Elizabeth was serious, while that of James was not, has been a recurring and wrong-headed feature of much scholarship (*The Literary Icon of James I*, p. 5).

[42] Winifred Joy Mulligan, "The British Constantine and English Historical Myth", *JMRS* 8 (1978): 257–79.

[43] *Actes and Monuments* (1570), vol. 1, pp. 290–1.

[44] Included in John Adamson, Τα των μουσων εισωδια: the Muses Welcome (1618) p. 138.

In Constantine, Roman might and authority came together with leadership of the church. Constantine was held up as a model by a wide range of writers and preachers, not just the more militant Calvinists. Thus, Patrick Adamson, about 1584 used the figure of Constantine to defend episcopacy, calling on James, to be, like Constantine, "a bishop of bishops".[45] Some Calvinists began to have doubts about the notion of a Constantinian godly prince as the sixteenth century went on; the Scottish biblical commentator (and inventor of logarithms) John Napier had promoted the idea of the godly prince in his early writings, but by the 1580s was rejecting the Constantinian model and the idea of an elect nation.[46] Thomas Brightman, in his *Revelation of the Revelation,* also rejected Foxe's Constantinian model.[47] As James' personal and political tendencies developed, the inappropriateness of the Constantinian model became clear. Williamson suggests that in the 1590s James tended to focus on the model of David rather than Constantine as a safer model for the imperial vision.[48] As the image of a Solomon-like peacemaker came to the forefront, the Constantinian model needed to be downplayed. However, it is not just that one image replaced the other, rather there was a tension between those who wished to see James as a Constantinian emperor, leading Protestant Europe, and those who saw him as a peacemaker. It must be stressed that at various times in his career, James accepted or endorsed both images.

During his English reign the idea of James as Constantinian ruler continued to find occasional, if more muted expression. Joseph Hall's sermon on the tenth anniversary of James' accession provides an extended consideration of the Constantinian model by a moderate churchman in the middle of James' reign.[49] Hall takes as his text I Samuel 12:24–5, which is Samuel's farewell warning to Israel: "Only fear the Lord, and serve him in truth with all your heart: for consider how great things he hath done for you. But if ye shall still do wickedly, ye shall be consumed, both ye and your king." Hall parallels himself with Eusebius and Sozomen, the early biographers of Constantine, who celebrated the tenth anniversary of Constantine's rule as a special occasion.[50] Midway through the sermon he begins an extended comparison of England to Israel; they are nations similar for the many blessings they have received. This leads naturally into a comparison of James with biblical kings: he is the king "whom the Lord hath chosen".[51]

Hall compares James' mercy to that of various emperors: Anastasius,

---

45 Arthur Williamson, *Scottish National Consciousness*, p. 44.
46 Ibid., p. 21.
47 Ibid., p. 32.
48 Ibid., p. 41.
49 *A Holy Panegyrick* (1613).
50 Ibid., sig. B2r.
51 Ibid., p. 60.

Vespasian, Mauricius, and Theodosius.[52] His leadership among the present-day kings of Christendom is suggested by Hall: "all Christian Princes rejoice to follow him as their worthy leader, in all the battels of God; and all Christian churches in their prayers and acclamations, stile him, in a double right, *Defender of the Faith*, more by desert, then inheritance".[53] What Hall meant was that the Protestant princes and churches looked to James as their natural leader, and these hopes had been encouraged by the marriage of his daughter Elizabeth to the Elector Frederick of the Palatine the previous month. The extended comparison to Constantine takes up the latter part of the sermon. Hall begins by noting the two leaders' commitment to the dissemination of scripture: "Constantine caused fiftie Volumes of the Scriptures to be fayre written out in parchment, for the use of the Church, King James hath caused the bookes of Scriptures to bee accurately translated, and published by thousands."[54] Secondly, as controversialists working against heresy, Constantine and James share a role; Constantine had published edicts against the Novatians, the Valentinians and Marcionites, James had famously written against both the pope and Vorstius. They had both taken legal steps against heretics as well, James suppressing meetings of "Papists and Schismatickes". Both worked closely with their bishops and encouraged their children to continue in their ways. Finally, James was like Constantine as a builder of churches; the emperor had built churches in Jerusalem and Nicomedia and James was like him, not in the physical construction of churches, but in his founding of that "one Colledge, which shall help to build and confirme the whole Church of God, upon earth".[55] Hall is referring to Chelsea College, which was to have been a centre for Protestant theology, and while much talked about in these years never became fully functioning. This reference gives to James a limited Constantinian role: he will lead in Europe, but through the pen and controversy rather than by the sword. Graham Parry presents Hall's sermon as "affirm[ing] the establishment line"[56] but this raises the question of whether there was a static "establishment line": James' religious policy shifted in response to domestic and foreign developments, and by 1613 Hall may have perceived that the "establishment line" of theological dispute with the papacy, particularly over the Oath of Allegiance, was ebbing. His sermon then is a call to maintain a Constantinian position, a view that he would continue to express ten years later in his sermons *The Best Bargaine* (1623) and *The True Peacemaker* (1624) which will be discussed below in reference to James as Solomonic peacemaker.[57]

[52] Ibid., p. 67.
[53] Ibid., p. 70.
[54] Ibid., p. 81.
[55] Ibid., p. 83.
[56] *Golden Age Restor'd*, p. 235.
[57] On Hall's use of the rhetoric of the *Via Media* to further a militantly Protestant agenda, see Peter Lake, "The Moderate and Irenic Case for Religious War, Joseph Hall's *Via Media* in

Richard Crakanthorpe, a renowned scholar, produced a massive work against papal claims in 1621, entitled *The Defence of Constantine*. For Crakanthorpe the central issue was the relationship between imperial and religious power: was the Donation of Constantine genuine? Crakanthorpe sets out to deny the "Popes temporall Monarchy, which utterly subverts the Imperial Dignity and Rights both of Constantine and all other Princes".[58] The work's dedication to James provides another extended comparison of the two leaders. Crakanthorpe includes many of the attributes suggested by Hall, but with considerably more detail. Constantine is not just a ruler who works closely with his bishops, but who sat "Bishop of them all". However, he also points out the differences: that Constantine, like David, conquered with the sword, but "your majesty like Salomon, a King of Peace".[59] In this way the tension between Constantine and Solomon is established, and in comparing Constantine and James as writers of treatises, Crakanthorpe once again slides into the Solomon analogy: in response to James' writings readers break "into those patheticall admirations of the Queene of Sheba".[60]

Constantine provided a model for church leadership in which the lay ruler held sway over the ecclesiastical structure.[61] As an emperor of the East, Constantine provided an alternative to the domination of Rome, in matters both political and religious. It could be invoked both by those seeking to uphold the English church hierarchy with the king firmly at the top, and those more militant Protestants seeking a godly prince as divinely appointed leader. For those in the late 1610s encouraging James to call a church council open to all but supporters of the papacy's secular claims, Constantine, who had overseen such councils as that of Nicea, was an important precedent. However, by 1621 the image of Constantine had clearly given way to that of Solomon, the *rex pacificus*, in the dominant iconography surrounding James.

JAMES AND THE ICONOGRAPHY OF PEACE

An early portrait of James, reproduced as the frontispiece to Theodore Beza's *Icones* (1580), shows the young Scottish king holding a sword in one hand and an olive branch in the other; beneath is the motto, "In utrumque paratus".[62] While such a portrait represented the stance of peaceful war-readiness that many militant Protestants hoped James would adopt, the

Context", *Political Cultural and Cultural Politics in Early Modern England*, eds Susan D. Amussen and Mark A. Kishlansky (Manchester: Manchester UP, 1995), pp. 55–83.

[58] sig. A2r.

[59] sig. A4v.

[60] sig. A5r.

[61] Constantine had been used by Henry VIII to bolster his position against the papacy; see Mulligan, "The British Constantine and English Historical Myth", pp. 269–70.

[62] Bingham, *The Making of a King*, p. 93.

reality became that James highly favoured the role of peacemaking over war-making, and in time the iconography surrounding James would come to dwell much more closely on his peace-loving and peacemaking attributes than his military capabilities. This peacemaking was most often framed in biblical terms, with supreme emphasis on Solomon as a biblical prototype of James. In the area of peacemaking, particularly in the years 1618–24, the analogy took on a particular importance, for it provided a positive model for a frequently criticized stance.[63] As restlessness over James' anti-military stance grew in the second half of his English reign, supporters of the king developed a response that would emphasize the worthiness of this approach. William Germano has argued that the iconography surrounding James was far more static than that of Elizabeth;[64] that is certainly the case, but it is also true that through his reign the significance of various iconographies changed, as did the concrete implications. This is very much the case with the iconography of peace and peacemaking. "Peacemaker" was a much less contentious term early in James' reign: relief at initial domestic peace was only slowly eroded by dissatisfaction in some quarters at James' foreign policy.

A celebration of kingly peacemaking faced a number of inherent difficulties in the period. First, there was not a strong tradition of Christian pacifism; the most noted adherents of such an ideology were the Anabaptists of the sixteenth century, whose radicalism hardly could appeal to James or the majority of his subjects. Maurice Lee also notes the difficulties of peace-making within the European situation of the early seventeenth century: James was the only leader with an ideological commitment to peace.[65] The biblical tradition established the king as the bearer of God's sword: a king who disdained that role, or upheld it only in its civic rather than foreign sphere, might seem to be denying part of his God-given mandate. On a more practical level, military success was a highly visible and effective means to popularity and support – in the seventeenth or the twentieth century. In addition, while supporters of James might celebrate his peace*making*, thus giving him an active role, that same stance might appear more passive to other subjects, particularly ones not privy to the larger vision of James' foreign policy, who could not see the ends, only the means.

While James' role as Solomon-like peacemaker has been occasionally noted, most scholars have refused to take it seriously, dismissing it instead as mere weakness or vain folly on the king's part. Their tone is ultimately borrowed, I would argue, from the militant Protestants of James' own time, who wished him to take a more active part in European conflicts, particularly

---

[63] The iconography and language of the virgin queen in reference to the last years of Elizabeth have been much discussed, but not the imagery established to validate the reality of James' last years.

[64] *The Literary Icon of James I*, p. 47.

[65] Maurice Lee, Jr., *Great Britain's Solomon: James VI and I in his Three Kingdoms* (Urbana and Chicago: U of Illinois P, 1990), p. 267.

by leading a Protestant league to save the political fortunes of his son-in-law Frederick, Elector Palatine.[66] I counter that James' pacifism emerged from deep-seated ideological convictions, and was received as such by many of his subjects. In addition, the diplomatic accomplishments of James are often underemphasized.[67] Through his 22-year reign in England, he avoided completely both internal and external armed conflict, something which cannot be said of other sixteenth- and seventeenth-century English monarchs. Even such a virulent anti-Stuart propagandist as Anthony Weldon conceded that "he lived in peace, dyed in peace, and left all his kingdomes in a peaceable condition, with his own motto: *Beati pacifici*".[68] It was an age of peace, and especially with the questioning of the "high road to revolution" by revisionist Stuart historians, the accomplishments of James in this area can now be more fully appreciated.[69]

Especially in the later years of his reign, the phrase "Beati Pacifici", blessed are the peacemakers, from the Sermon on the Mount (Matt. 5:9) came to be frequently applied to James, and readily accepted by him as a personal motto.[70] It appeared over his portrait in the 1616 *Workes*, and was emblazoned on one of the standards displayed at his funeral.[71] Frequently, James was given the similar epithet "Rex Pacificus" or "Jacobus Pacificus"; he himself comments on this in his *Meditation upon the Lords Prayer*. "I know not by what fortune, the dicton of PACIFICUS was added to my title, at my comming in England; that of the Lyon, expressing true fortitude, having beene my dicton before: but I am not ashamed of this addition; for King Salomon was a figure of CHRIST in that, that he was a King of peace."[72] Such language and iconography was broad enough to satisfy a range of conflicting stances: few would disagree that peace was a desirable and blessed state, but a wide range of options was available for how that peace might be "made". As

---

[66] An extreme example of this is found in Willson, *King James VI and I*, pp. 399–424.

[67] I am in general agreement with Fincham and Lake, "The Ecclesiastical Policy of King James I", and their argument that James' ecclesiastical policy proved successful until the crisis brought on by Frederick's acceptance of the Bohemian crown. For a recent very positive view of James' diplomacy and peacemaking, see Patterson, *King James VI and I and the Reunion of Christendom*, pp. 293–338.

[68] Weldon, *Character of King James* in *Secret History of the Court*, vol. 2, p. 12, quoted in Robert Ashton, *James I by his Contemporaries* (London: Hutchinson, 1969), p. 12.

[69] On the changing reputation of James, see Lee, *Great Britain's Solomon*, pp. xi–xv.

[70] In his epigrams John Owen includes one entitled "Beati {Muni/Paci} fici": "Iacobus laceras Britonum res munit et unit;/Munificus Rex est noster et Unificus" (Liber Quintus, no. 24), *Ioannis Audoeni Epigrammatum*, 2 vols, ed. John R. C. Martyn (Leiden: E. J. Brill, 1978), vol. 2, p. 46.

[71] Lansdowne MS 885, fol. 117. Anthony Weldon was to use it ironically in a frontispiece to *Court and Character of King James* (1650).

[72] *Workes*, 1616, fasc. edn (New York: George Olms Verlag, 1971), p. 590. John King in 1606 described him as "our Solomon or *Pacificus*" (qtd. Fincham and Lake, "The Ecclesiastical Policy of King James I", p. 169); Arthur Johnston entitled his obsequy on James *In Obitum Jacobi Pacifici*; and John Milton referred to him as "Pacificus" in "In quintem Novembris".

John Stradling points out, "Peace may be understood more waies then one,/ The word is full of ambiguitie."[73] In *The True Peace-maker* (1624) Joseph Hall comments that "Iustice comprises all vertue, as Peace all blessings".[74] For James and his subjects "peace" could take a variety of forms; there could be peace within the church, either on a national or universal level; there could be political peace, between different factions within the nation, or between the nations of Christendom,[75] and there could be peace between individuals, which found particular expression in James' acts and proclamations against duelling. Robert Aylett distinguishes among "Eternall, inward, and externall peace",[76] and Thomas Adams described some of these varieties in the dedication to his 1622 sermon "Eironopolis: the City of Peace":

> There is *pax fundamenti*, the peace of doctrine; and *pax ordinis*, the peace of discipline. The heretic would pull down the first pillar, the schismatic the other. The former would break our peace with Christ; the latter with ourselves and the church: both these are almost desperate. But there is a third, *pax politica*, a civil peace; and the common disturbers of this are such contentious spirits, that either unprovoked, out of mischievous intentions, or being provoked, out of malicious revenge, set all in uproar, make a mutiny in manners, an ataxy in the course of life.[77]

Such a variety of meanings offered James' subjects a vision or public discourse that could be continuously reworked. Thus, a subject could choose one of these "peaces" as the focus of celebration, and ignore the others, or suggest that peace was the proper policy in one facet, but not in another. While all might agree on the virtue of peace within a kingdom and within Christendom, a more vexing question was whether there could there be peace between Christendom and the Islamic world. After all, the only militaristic work that James penned was "Lepanto" which celebrated the defeat of a Moslem foe by united Christendom.

From youth, James was apprehensive of violence and warfare: legend had it that he could not stand the sight of an unsheathed sword; while some were to blame this on the traumatic death of his mother's Italian secretary David Rizzio who was murdered while James was *in utero*, he was certainly directly exposed to enough violence as a child to explain his abhorrence of the sword. Through his Scottish years James frequently found himself at the mercy of the physical power of various Scottish factions, held as a near-captive by them. Robert Pricket, soldier and later preacher, greeted James' English accession with two books, *A Souldiers Wish* and *A Souldiers Resolution*, in which he presents himself, as soldier, in service to James, and hopes for a militant

---

[73] *Beati Pacifici* (1623), p. 1.
[74] sig. B1v.
[75] On James' ecumenism, see Fincham and Lake, pp. 182–6; and W. B. Patterson, *King James VI and I and the Reunion of Christendom*.
[76] Aylett, *Peace and her Foure Garders* (1622), p. 3.
[77] *Works*, ed. Joseph Angus, 3 vols (1861–2), vol. 2, p. 310.

approach to the papacy on James' part. However, James would have little
need, and less use, for military men in his reign; it was said by Weldon that Sir
Robert Mansell was the only military man the king could abide.[78] Within the
first two years of his English reign he established a peace with the traditional
enemy Spain, and throughout his reign aspired not only to keep England at
peace, but to serve as a peace-broker among the nations of Christendom. He
consistently attempted to achieve peace, not through the sword, but through
alliances, including the matrimonial ones of his children, and through the pen.

James' English reign had begun in a strikingly peaceful way; as the
impossibility of a direct heir to Elizabeth became clear in the 1580s and
1590s, English fears at the consequences of her eventual death increased.
Memories of the struggles of the 1550s surfaced. Thus, it was with considerable relief and even surprise that England greeted James' peaceful accession.
In his chronicle, *The Wonderfull Yeare*, Thomas Dekker celebrates this
peaceful transition in the face of the expectation of anarchy:

> The losse of a Queene, was paid with the double interest of a King and Queene.
> The Cedar of her government which stood alone and bare no fruit, is changed
> now to an Olive, upon whose spreading branches grow both Kings and
> Queenes. Oh it were able to fill a hundred paire of writing tables with notes,
> but to see the parts plaid in the compasse of one houre on the stage of this new-
> found world! Upon Thursday it was treason to cry God save king James king of
> England, and uppon Friday hye treason not to cry so. In the morning no voice
> hearde but murmures and lamentation, at noone nothing but shouts of gladnes
> & triumphe.[79]

Memories of this moment continued to influence perceptions of his reign:
looking back from 1622 Thomas Adams asked, "When he was first
proclaimed, what heard we but peace?"[80]

James' reign of peace began with the hope that with his accession to the
English throne, the long-standing tension between England and Scotland
would come to end, and James signalled this with the disarming of the
garrisons at Berwick and Carlisle.[81] In 1604 he achieved a treaty between the
English and Spanish, ending a conflict that had been going on, in at least a
cold fashion, since the early 1580s. Peace also made good economic sense, and
had been greatly supported by Cecil in the early part of the English reign for
that reason.[82] King James continued his success in fostering European peace
with his intervention in the Cleves-Julich succession (1609–10). He achieved
this through diplomatic negotiation and the threat of military intervention.

[78] qtd. by Ashton, *James I by his Contemporaries*, p. 13.
[79] *Non-dramatic Works* (1863), pp. 96–7.
[80] *Works*, vol. 2, p. 326.
[81] Spottiswoode, *The History of the Church of Scotland* (1851), vol. 3, p. 156.
[82] Maurice Lee, Jr., *James I and Henri IV* (Urbana, Chicago and London: U of Illinois P, 1970), pp. 18–19.

Maurice Lee, however, argues that only "The murder of Henri IV saved the peace-loving James from an entirely unlooked-for and unwelcome involvement in a major war."[83] His confidence increased, James took a similar role in the war between Sweden and Denmark in 1613, and his success there, according to Lee, "led him, in the opening phases of the German crisis, repeatedly to overestimate what mediation could accomplish".[84]

In spite of such success, vocal resentment of James' non-military approach began to be heard, by 1612 if not earlier. Some Englishmen began to long for the more militant days of Queen Elizabeth: the greatest living hero from that time, Sir Walter Ralegh, was still imprisoned in the Tower, and his *History of the World* (1614) presented King Ninias of Assyria in an effeminate manner against which James took offense.[85] The navy was in a woeful state of unreadiness,[86] a situation lamented in William Browne's *Britannia's Pastorals, The Second Booke* (1616).[87] Their own times seemed weak and effeminate to these men. Some of the dissatisfied turned their attention to Prince Henry, and for a few brief years his court and future reign held out the promise of coming military glory, but these hopes were dashed by his death in 1612.[88]

In ecclesiastical matters, James was engaged in a continental war, but one of the pen, not the sword. A poem from the time prays, "God keep our King and them from Rome's black pen",[89] and the controversy over the Oath of Allegiance was frequently described in militaristic terms. James consistently resisted both English and foreign Protestants who desired an escalation of the conflict; in 1611 the notable French Protestant du Plessis dedicated a work advocating this to James, but he responded by saying that the time was not right to exchange the pen for the sword.[90] However, even theologians were not convinced that such an approach could be effective. Some who participated in James' war of the pen remained sceptical about its chance of success: Lancelot Andrewes, writing in 1613, suggested that the "Revising of the Council of Trent is a matter of great importance, but God and Christian Princes must take up this matter by other means than the pen."[91]

The religious wars of the pen in which James took part so eagerly were like their conventional military counterparts in that they involved an ever-shifting web of allegiances. James would at times be simultaneously engaged in contesting the limits of spiritual and temporal powers with the pope and his

[83] Ibid., p. 167.
[84] Lee, *Great Britain's Solomon*, p. 264.
[85] Germano, *The Literary Icon of James I*, p. 173.
[86] See Samuel Rowson Gardiner, *History of England, 1603–1642*, 10 vols (1883–4), vol. 3, pp. 203–5.
[87] Song 4, line 81.
[88] See Parry, *The Golden Age Restor'd*, pp. 68–9; and Roy Strong, *Henry, Prince of Wales and England's Lost Renaissance* (London: Thames & Hudson, 1986).
[89] Qtd. by Roy Strong, *The Cult of Elizabeth* (London: Thames and Hudson, 1977), p. 183.
[90] *New Poems*, ed. Westcott, p. 61.
[91] Andrewes to Dudley Carleton, 24 Feb. 1612/13, *CSPD, 1611–18*, p. 171.

writers, the necessity of episcopacy with Scottish Presbyterians, and defending Calvinist orthodoxy on predestination against Dutch Arminians. In all these battles James enlisted supporters and soldiers of the pen. At times a Scottish Presbyterian or French Huguenot might join him in attacking the Church of Rome, or the errors of Arminianism. Similarly, the Roman Catholic Becanus proved an ally against Vorstius.[92] James' allies at any particular moment depended upon which struggle was currently of greatest concern.

The policy and iconography of peacemaking were thrown into crisis by the attempt of James' son-in-law, Frederick of the Palatine, to take the Bohemian crown in 1619. This was done at the invitation of the Protestant nobility of Bohemia, but there were serious deficiencies in his claim, and the act put James in the untenable position of either abandoning his son-in-law or supporting a claim which he did not feel was justified and was bound to lead to great conflict within Europe.[93] James was invited by the Spanish to broker a peace, but this would by necessity be one unsatisfactory to Frederick and the more strident English Protestants who supported him. Central to James' peace efforts through this period was the proposed dynastic marriage between Charles and the Spanish Infanta, a scheme which Lee describes as "the most serious tactical error [James] ever made in the conduct of his foreign policy".[94] Such discussions were ongoing through the late 1610s and early 1620s, and led to an increasing closeness between the English and Spanish courts; when this diplomacy led to the execution of the Elizabethan naval hero, Sir Walter Ralegh, a significant part of the English population was angered by this sort of peace.

Early in the Bohemian crisis, a work entitled *The Peace-maker* appeared in London bookstalls;[95] although primarily the work of Thomas Middleton, it presents James' vision of himself as a peace-bringing king.[96] While the work's

---

[92] Ralph Winwood, English agent at the Hague, notes Becanus' work with approval, and suggests that William Trumbull, ambassador at Brussels, encourage others to do the same: "If you have any good Acquaintance with any smart Jesuite who hath a quick and nimble Spirit, who would at your Instance (though you be not seen in it) bestow a few Lines agaynst the Atheisms of thys Wretch, and yf by the way he did give a gentle Remembrance upon our Grudges in Holland, who forget both God and their best Freinds, assure your self you shall do a Service well pleasing to his Majesty"; 12 December 1611, *Memorials of Affairs of State*, vol. 3, p. 311.

[93] Lee, *Great Britain's Solomon*, pp. 269–70. Lee places responsibility for the fiasco squarely at the feet of Frederick.

[94] Ibid., p. 267. Lee's comment is based on the fact that it would not have solved the European situation, particularly the dilemma of the Elector Frederick, and that James failed to consider the deep opposition to it within England. For a more sympathetic reading of James' position, one that focusses more heavily on his religious convictions, see W. B. Patterson, "King James I and the Protestant Cause in the Crisis of 1618–22", *Studies in Church History*, 18, ed. S. Mews (Oxford: B. Blackwell, 1982), pp. 319–34.

[95] The work was registered in July 1618 and appeared in London bookstalls in either late 1618 or early 1619.

[96] On the authorship of the work, see Rhodes Dunlap, "James I, Bacon, Middleton, and the

final focus is on a specific type of peacemaking – the outlawing of duelling – the general ideology reflects James' role in continental affairs as well. The work was given a special patent by the king, and on its title page appears the words, "Cum Privilegio". The preface is in the voice of the king: "To all our true-loving and Peace-embracing Subjects". While Rhodes Dunlap argues that this too was written by Middleton, his argument is based only on stylistic evidence.[97] It would be more credible to see the preface as the king's, and the rest of the work as Middleton's expressing of official royal policy. In the preface James strives to overcome the perception that peace is merely the result of inactivity or passivity. Instead, peace is presented as the result of a pursued policy; it does not simply happen, but is made. Thus, he begins by talking about the glory of "Action": "The glory of all virtues is action, the crown of all acts perfection; the perfection of all things, Peace and Union."

The religious roots of peace are also presented: "My subject hath her being in heaven, her theory in holy writ, and her practice in England, Insula Pacis, the Land of Peace under the King of Peace."[98] In a state of peace, Heaven and Earth are drawn together; James' reign fulfills a biblical or heavenly paradigm. He suggests that various refugees "all seek shelter under the shadow of thine olive branches".[99] This reference is a variation upon a deep tradition of biblical iconography, frequently applied to James' peaceful reign. Frequently mentioned in such celebrations were the blessings of peace, especially the biblical image of every man "sitting beneath his own fig tree". This image was found in a number of Old Testament books. For James' purpose it was most significantly used in reference to Solomon's reign: "For he [Solomon] he had dominion over all the region on this side the river, from Tiphsah even to Azzah, over all the kings on this side the river: and he had peace on all sides round about him. And Judah and Israel dwelt safely, every man under his vine and under his fig tree, from Dan even to Beersheba, all the days of Solomon" (I Kings 4:24–5). Micah 4:4 used the same language in reference to the end-times: "But they shall sit every man under his vine and under his fig tree; and none shall make them afraid: for the mouth of the Lord of hosts hath spoken it." Among the works that had celebrated James in terms of these passages was Richard Crackenthorpe's *A Sermon Preached at the Solemnizing of the Happie Inauguration of our Most Gracious and Religious Soveraigne KING JAMES* (1609). James himself invoked it in his opening speech to parliament in January 1621, a speech that vigorously defended his record of peace:

Making of *The Peace-Maker*", *Studies in the English Renaissance Drama*, eds Josephine W. Bennett *et al.* (New York: New York UP, 1959), pp. 82–94. Recently, William Patterson, *King James VI and I and the Reunion of Christendom*, p. 296n, has reasserted James as the primary author of the work as a whole.

[97] Dunlap, p. 92.

[98] p. 325.

[99] p. 325.

I have reigned 18 years and you have enjoyed peace and plenty under me. If this is wrong I ask pardon, as I judged it an honour to be a peacefull king. You have been able to enjoy peace under your fig trees and no one suffers want except those who have dissipated their inheritance or who will not work.[100]

That James can use the allusion without explanation demonstrates how well known it had become. After his death, John Taylor's elegy drew on the image in a longer celebration of the past peaceful reign:

> No thundring Cannons did our Peace molest.
> No churlish Drum, no Rapes, no flattring wounds;
> No Trumpets clangor to the Battell sounds,
> But every Subject here enjoy'd his owne,
> And did securely reape what they had sowne.
> Each man beneath his Fig-tree and his Vine,
> In Peace with plenty did both suppe and dine.[101]

Occasionally, the image is extended as the fig tree and vine are replaced by the olive, traditionally associated with peace.

The fig-tree and vine were not only images of peace, but also the prosperity which peace led to; James' bounty and generosity were well known, but from a negative perspective could also be seen as profligacy.[102] "Plenty" could easily be portrayed as wanton luxury, and leading to a softness in the national spirit. In the words of Arthur Wilson, "Peace begot Plenty, and Plenty begot Ease and Wantonness, and Ease and Wantonness begot Poetry, and Poetry swelled to that Bulk in his time, that it begot strange Monstrous Satyrs against the King's own Person."[103] Middleton anticipates objections to the peace being enjoyed, rehearsing the usual complaints about this soft, easy time. The figure of Peace uses the biblical story of Exodus to respond to the detractors: "Shame, murmurer, hadst thou rather with the forgetful Israelites go back to the flesh-pots of Egypt".[104]

In the main body of *The Peace-maker*, the motto "Beati Pacifici" is echoed repeatedly. Other nations (specifically, Scotland, Ireland, Spain) all exclaim, "Beati Pacifici".[105] Wise Solomon as judge plays a role here as well: "Here sits Salomon, and hither come the tribes for judgment. Oh happy moderator, blessed father, not father of thy country alone, but father of all thy neighbour

---

[100] *CSPV, 1619–21*, p. 581.
[101] "A Living Sadnes in Duty Consecrated to the Immortall Memory of our Late Deceased all-beloved Soveraigne Lord, the Peerelesse Paragon of Princes, James . . .", in *Works* (1630), p. 324.
[102] On the presentation of this aspect of James' reign, see Perry, *The Making of Jacobean Culture*, p. 115
[103] Arthur Wilson, *Life and Reign of James I*, p. 792, quoted in Robert Ashton, *James I by his Contemporaries* (London: Hutchinson, 1969), p. 18.
[104] p. 328.
[105] pp. 326–7.

countries about thee."[106] James' peace, in the vision of *The Peace-maker*, also involves the restraining of religious persecution; the king is not a maker of martyrs: "Are not the flesh-eating fires quenchd, and our faggots converted to gentler uses? Oh, but those corn-fields must never be without some tares, until the general harvest."[107] The second sentence accepts a church that is not a gathered one of the saints, but a national one that includes all; in particular Middleton seems to be advocating a peace-producing approach to recusancy. In this he is resisting those Protestants who were calling for a more strenuous enforcing of the recusancy laws. This point is important in distinguishing *The Peace-maker*'s vision from that of more radical Protestants; Middleton does not anticipate the kingdom of God on earth; for him the peaceful kingdom will be less than a perfect one. There will still be envy, schism, law, drunkenness, and pride.

The more particular agenda of the work is established in the final pages: James is a peacemaker in his efforts to suppress duelling.[108] In the process he presents arguments against duelling that had earlier been rehearsed by James himself, as well as Bacon and the earl of Northampton:[109] that reputation, which duelling is often believed to uphold, is insubstantial, that crediting the words of an opponent simply dignifies him, that death comes to all, and finally that it is a risking of one's soul.

In the years following *The Peace-maker*, James' position became increasingly controversial and in need of defense. When the Palatine was invaded by Spinola in September 1620, James had reason to intervene. While he could not support Frederick's attempt at the Bohemian crown, neither could he accept the loss of the rightful lands of his son-in-law. From this point his strategy was to call for peace and the restoration of rightful claims, but at the same time show a willingness to adopt military means if necessary. Thus, parliament, sitting from January 1621, was to vote supply for military purposes, to threaten the Hapsburg powers into a negotiated peace.[110] However, parliament took this opportunity to discuss the proposed Match and England's foreign policy in general, matters which James believed were strictly his prerogative. With these developments the rhetoric of peace took on new complexities. And as James was not publicly expressing his goals, various interpretations of his peacemaking efforts circulated. Maurice Lee describes it well: "[James] was going to call for military action – and then not supply it. He was going to dwell on the wrongs of his children – and continue

---

[106] p. 327.

[107] p. 329.

[108] pp. 337–46.

[109] See Francis Bacon, *The Charge of Sir Francis Bacon Touching Duells* (1614) Fasc. (Amsterdam: Theatrum Orbis Terrarum, 1968); and *A Publication of his Maties Edict and Severe Censure against Private Combats and Combatants* (London, 1614), a work combining the efforts of King James and the earl of Northampton.

[110] Lee, *Great Britain's Solomon*, pp. 274–8.

to negotiate with the wrongdoer."[111] We must not approach sermons or poems of these years as explaining James' peace policy to the nation. Instead they were attempts to interpret and direct James' peace. Or at least we need to distinguish between official proclamations and utterances of those close to the king, such as John Williams, the bishop of Lincoln and the lord keeper, and those of others.

Among those developing an iconography for James' position in these years was Robert Aylett in his poem *Peace and her Foure Garders* (1622). Aylett, a lawyer, had earlier been patronized by John King, bishop of London, and in the early 1620s sought the support of Williams, one of the strongest supporters of the peace policy. The moral meditation in verse seems to have been Aylett's prime genre, and these meditations were collected and shaped in a variety of ways in the early 1620s: *Thrift's Equipage* (1622) on Frugality, Providence, Diligence, Labour and Care, and Death, and *The Bride's Ornaments* (1625), five meditations on Knowledge, Zeal, Temperance, Bounty and Joy. *Peace and her Foure Garders* treats the five virtues of Peace, Chastity, Constancy, Courtesy and Gravity", and the preliminary material and the celebration of Peace serve as an indirect comment on the controversy over Frederick's attempt to take the Bohemian crown and James' unwillingness to support him. Aylett's support for the peace policy is notable throughout the preliminaries to the volume, and it is also clear that for him Peace is associated with the king and the court. In an untitled prefatory verse he associates those of the war-party with the Israelites, longing for Egypt during their forty years in the wilderness, "Some loathing Peace, wish Warre, because unknowne,/To them Peace is like Manna, common growne."[112] These lines recall the rebuke of the murmurers by Middleton. Unlike *The Peace-maker*, Aylett's work suggests that passive peace itself, simply as the absence of war, is of the kingdom of God.

> Peace types us out the Blisse of our Creation,
> Warres shew our fall from Glory to damnation . . .[113]

In addition, it immortalizes that king who is responsible for it: "Sweet Peace to Subiects doth all blessings bring, / Immortall honour to a mortall King."[114] In the dedicatory poem to Williams, Aylett continues the association of peace with James and his court:

> Thou great Peace-Keeper, whom the greatest King,
> That our great God of Peace did ever bring

---

[111] Ibid., p. 279.
[112] sig. A2r.
[113] sig. A2r.
[114] sig. A2r.

> To rule these Westerne Iles, in happy Peace,
> For Honours, Arts, and Piety's increase.[115]

While Aylett draws most heavily on the Christian tradition to celebrate the peace of James, he does also draw upon the classical in encouraging Bishop Williams to be like Maecenas, assisting James to shut up the doors of Janus' temple:

> These Precedents imboldend have my Muse,
> For Patron of the Graces, thee to chuse,
> Whom great Augustus with his Seale doth grace;
> Oh be a true Mecenas in thy place:
> Seale up for ever Ianus Temple doore,
> And let Bellona's voice be heard no more . . .[116]

There is some recognition in Aylett's work of the possibility of false peace or "feigned peace".[117] He also recognizes that external peace is secondary to the eternal peace of God and the internal peace of the believer. Near the end of the meditation on Peace, the subject becomes another means of requesting patronage, as Aylett bemoans the lack of peace he has in which to celebrate the king's peace:

> Or were she able, on a high-strain'd string,
> To sing the Honour of my Soveraigne,
> That grand Peace-maker, Britaines peaceful King,
> Who through the Christian world doth Peace maintaine:
> God grant, for peace on earth, thou heav'nly peace mayst gaine.
> But ah! how can my soule opprest with Care,
> And worldy tumults, of such Glory sing,
>   Since quiet peace her selfe removeth farre
>   From Discord, Strife, Contentions, Quarrelling?[118]

However, he concludes the meditation by reflecting on eternal peace, and ending with a prayer. Thus, while James as peacemaker plays a significant role in the meditation, his iconography does not overwhelm the standard structure that Aylett pursues throughout his works.

Because of the conflicts on the continent, England's peace could be held up as its glory or its shame. Samuel Buggs stressed the glory in his Paul's Cross sermon of July 8, 1621:

---

[115] sig. A3r.

[116] sig. A3v. Earlier, Bishop Williams, while addressing the 1621 parliament, had used the image in reference to the end of the peace: "Janus' temple is now opened that hath been shut these nineteen years." Qtd. by Conrad Russell, *Parliaments and English Politics, 1621–1629* (Oxford: Clarendon Press, 1979), pp. 125–6.

[117] pp. 5–6.

[118] p. 10.

The Christians in Polonia cry out for ayde: The Protestants in Bohemia groane under a heavie and intolerable burden: The Protestants of France send many sighs to heaven for peace or bare security. Happy Britaines, wee sit under our owne vines, and our own Fig-trees.[119]

On the other hand, the peace and prosperity of England could be held up as a judgement on her failure to support the Protestant brethren on the continent. They suffered, martyr-like, for the faith, while England indulged itself with idleness. For these men, the biblical motif of "Crying peace, peace, when there is no peace" was applicable to England.[120] Hers was not a true or positive peace, but a peace of avoidance and blindness. Another ominous biblical text was Jesus' statement that he came "not to bring peace, but a sword". In this way biblical language of peace was turned against James. An outspoken critique of the softness that peace brings can be found in *Tom Tell-Troath: or a Free Discourse Touching the Manners of the Time, Directed to His Majesty* [1622]:

> Of all the benefits that descend from heaven to earth there is none to be received with more prayse, and thankefulnes, then that of peace. But a man may have too much of his fathers blessing. And I feare we have too much cause to complaine of your Majesites unlimited peace.[121]

Many writers, however, were not content to argue simply for or against peace. For them the key matter was the interpretation of that word "peace", or what peace might make possible. A notable example of this tendency is found in John Stradling's poem *Beati Pacifici* (1623). Like *The Peace-maker*, this poem had the warrant of King James, receiving a royal patent, and claiming on its title page that it had been "Perused by his Maiesty, and printed by Authority".[122] The poem is written in rather awkward six-line verses rhyming ababcc, and Stradling readily admits his lack of poetic polish: "I have not learning, neither Poets skill,/Yet out of zeale will utter my good will."[123] Like other celebrators of James' peace, Stradling anticipates objections to his

---

[119] Maclure, *Register of Sermons Preached at Paul's Cross, 1534–1642*, rev. by P. Pauls and J. C. Boswell (Toronto: CRRS, 1989), p. 119, describes this as being preached on 8 July 1621 by Samuel Buggs, minister of Coventry, *Davids Strait* (1622).

[120] This phrase is found in a number of places in the Old Testament: Jeremiah 6:14: "They have healed also the hurt of the daughter of my people slightly, saying Peace, peace; when there is no peace." Cf. Jeremiah 8:11 and Ezek. 13:9–10. "And mine hand shall be upon the prophets that see vanity, and that divine lies; they shall not be in the assembly of my people, neither shall they be written in the writing of the house of Israel, neither shall they enter into the land of Israel; and ye shall know that I am Lord God. Because, even because they have seduced my people, saying Peace; and there was no peace; and one built up a wall, and, lo, others daubed it with untempered morter".

[121] *Harleian Miscellany*, vol. 3, ca. pp. 428–39, quoted in Ashton, *James I by his Contemporaries*, p. 220.

[122] The work was entered in the Stationers' Register on 4 June 1623.

[123] p. 17.

95

panegyric; where he has chosen the biblical model of Solomon, someone might counter with names of great war-like kings such as Nebuchadnezzar and Alexander.[124] His response is to ask "What got those great ones by their feats of warre?" and trace their violent ends.[125] When Stradling does admit that there are occasions upon which a king must use force – 'Though loth they are, yet somtimes strike they must,/To curbe injustice, or to master pride" – he is careful to cite "Basilicon Doron lib. 5" in the margin.[126] Stradling recognizes that there have been kings who combined just war with peace, and provides the example of David. However, a marginal note reminds the reader that "David forbid by God to build the Temple", and this provides an opportunity to celebrate Solomon, the maker of peace and builder of the Temple.[127]

Stradling's central concern, however, is not to celebrate peace in itself, but to encourage the nations of Christendom and the various churches to put aside their differences for the good of the common faith, and to present a united front against the Turks. Aylett by way of contrast had looked for peace with the Turks as well.[128] In presenting this argument at a time when Europe was engulfed in a war largely between Catholics and Protestants, Stradling recognizes the hostility that he might face, and responds "I looke here to be tax't by some Divine,/ As though I tended to newtrality,/ And care not on which side the Sunne doth shine."[129] He anticipates that some "precise" figure on either side will raise the example of Phineas who had zealously slain an Israelite man and Moabite woman as they engaged in intercourse; his response to this parallel is the simple, but highly contentious claim, "Here be no Moabites".[130] Stradling's position is consistent with James' own view at this time that Rome constituted a true church that erred, rather than the idolatrous seat of the Antichrist. Despite Stradling's celebration of peace, his final gesture is in the direction of war, as he invites Christians to lay their quarrels aside in order to turn against the Turk, concluding that such would be "a holy quarrell".[131] Further on, he returns to the same point:

> Once more I will be bold to speake a word
> (I hope without offence) to my dread Lord;
> Here is a cause wherein to draw your sword.[132]

These lines suggest something less than complete confidence, and a suspicion that he has moved beyond the king's stated aims for his policy of peace. A

[124] pp. 7–8.
[125] p. 9.
[126] p. 11.
[127] p. 11.
[128] p. 3.
[129] p. 17.
[130] p. 18.
[131] p. 23.
[132] p. 37.

similar note is present in lines that follow: "I thinke I doe perswade not much awry,/ Nor greatly straying from your Princely minde."[133] He then invokes military heroes of the past, the very rhetorical strategy rejected earlier in the poem: among these he cites "John of Austrich" whose victory over the Turks at Lepanto had been celebrated in James' poem.[134] After a few more pages of virulent language against the Turks, Stradling admits: "Heere zeale (I see) transports me somewhat farre", and he attempts a return to his theme of peace.[135] However, in the process he has come close to turning James once more into the Constantinian emperor. In fact, in the process of rebutting Machiavelli's complaint that Christianity makes men soft and cowardly, Stradling cites the great Christian warriors Charlemagne, Constantine and Richard the Lion-Hearted.[136] Thus, *Beati Pacifici* as a motto was malleable enough to encourage a different sort of militancy: peace can make possible a just war against the Turks, and that war itself is presented as something that will bring about "peace universall".[137]

Stradling was not the only one to suggest that peace within Christendom might be rightly used to begin a final war against the Turk.[138] In his "Memorables of King James", Laud writes in hindsight: "He was not only a preserver of peace at home, but the great peacemaker abroad; to settle Christendom against the common enemy, the Turk, which might have been a glorious work, if others had been as true to him as he was to the common good."[139]

The international situation and attendant iconography changed abruptly with the return of the unwed Charles from Spain on 5 October 1623; England responded with rejoicing at the failure of the marriage negotiations, and quickly the temper and policy of peace were replaced by a vigorous militancy. Charles and Buckingham, with the support of Secretary of State Conway and members from both Houses of Parliament, pressed toward English participation in a "common cause" against the Hapsburg powers of Europe. What they envisioned was a confederation that would go well beyond the Protestant League, and include France, Venice and Savoy. As such, the distinctly Protestant fervour so often expressed by those supportive of Frederick and Elizabeth would need to be muted. Cogswell notes that after 1623 positive commentary on peace largely disappeared, even in underground works, and concludes that "the anti-war argument was a fairly artificial one which James largely foisted on his subjects. It follows therefore that once strong royal

---

[133] p. 38.
[134] p. 38.
[135] p. 43.
[136] p. 65.
[137] p. 47.
[138] Cogswell presents this poem within the context of other attempts by Bacon to encourage a new crusade in place of internecine Christian warfare (pp. 38–41).
[139] *Works* (Oxford, 1847–60), vol. 6, p. 6.

support for this unpopular position ceased, as it did in 1624, the pacifist position would suffer a swift eclipse."[140] Cogswell points out how Thomas Lushington's sermon of Easter 1624 was out of step in its criticism of military enthusiasm, and he was forced to a retraction the following week.[141] Bishop Williams was also among the few who maintained an outspoken advocacy of peace. However, even those who supported the war effort might not completely dispose of the rhetoric of peace; some simply redefined it for the new situation: James might still be the "Peacemaker", but that peace might now be achieved through military means.

In the new situation of 1623–24, sermons extolling the blessings of peace were replaced with ones proclaiming the necessity of war. Janus' doors had been opened and militant Protestantism could once again be publicly voiced.[142] Numerous preachers noted that James' ambitions had been worthy, but that peace with Rome or Spain was impossible, and presented examples from the Old Testament which underlined Israel's separateness from the surrounding heathen nations.[143] Preachers urged that "Christ was not to send peace, but a sword."[144] Some argued the economic benefits of war, claiming that "Warre was a Blessing", a phrase which ironically reversed the long-standing motto of "Beati Pacifici".[145] At this time Charles and Buckingham were at the forefront of overseeing war preparations, and James and his iconography became secondary. A letter of the Venetian ambassador, Alvise Valaresso, from May 1624 suggests the king's isolation and his pulling back from public affairs,[146] and William Laud notes that "He was from the beginning of his sickness scarce out of an opinion that he should die; and therefore did not suffer the great affairs of Christendom to move him more than was fit, for he thought of his end."[147] Cogswell suggests (and this contrasts with those quoted above) that "Until his final illness he remained vigorous" and active in foreign affairs,[148] but it is at least clear that he and his son were working at cross purposes.[149] Whatever popular support Charles might have, James was still king, and Cogswell points out the irony that "only *Rex Pacificus* could save Europe".[150]

---

[140] p. 310.
[141] Thomas Cogswell, *The Blessed Revolution: English Politics and the Coming of War 1621–1624* (Cambridge: CUP, 1989), pp. 273–4. His source is Robert James [Thomas Lushington], *The Resurrection Rescued* (London, 1659).
[142] Cogswell, pp. 44–5.
[143] Cogswell, p. 285.
[144] Quoted in Cogswell, p. 297.
[145] Cogswell, p. 286. He is citing Thomas Scott's *The Belgick Soldier* (Dort, 1624).
[146] 17 May 1624, *CSPV, 1623–5*, pp. 309–10.
[147] *Works*, vol. 6, pp. 6–7.
[148] Cogswell, p. 315.
[149] Lee, *Great Britain's Solomon*, p. 291, notes that throughout this parliament James kept meeting with the Spanish envoys "to Buckingham's vast annoyance".
[150] Cogswell, p. 71.

While the hopes of militant Protestantism fixed upon the heir Charles, as they earlier had upon Prince Henry, some writers also reconfigured James as a military king, leading Britain or even Protestant Europe into battle. Cogswell states that "In any other year but the last one of James's 59-year life, such a prophecy would have been wildly absurd; but in 1624 it embodied the hopes that many Englishmen felt for James as well as for Charles."[151] This, however, overlooks the discussion of this role in the 1590s and early 1600s. Thus, the 1624 prophecies were more of a revival of earlier hopes than a pure expression of a new ethos.

Joseph Hall can once again be turned to as a figure of moderate Protestantism, whose sermons both before and after the return of Charles from Spain were sceptical about the possibility of peace. Hall was among the few noted by Cogswell who had been willing to question the price of peace before the failure of the Spanish match; he had done so in his 1623 sermon *The Best Bargaine.*[152] In 1624 the same position could be articulated before the king and accepted. His sermon of 19 September 1624, preached before James at Theobald, presents peace as arising out of a valiant commitment to justice.[153] The very title of the 1624 sermon, *The True Peace-Maker*, seems to be a rebuttal of earlier false models of peacemaking.[154] The sermon takes its text from Isaiah 32:17, "Opus Iustitiae pax". Justice is the means, and peace the fruit, and peace can only be achieved through a rigorous application of justice. Hall applies this to both the spiritual and civil realms. Most striking are the violent images which he uses to describe peace in its dependence upon justice: after describing various instruments of punishment – the gibbet, the stocks, etc. – he writes, "upon all these engines of Iustice [gibbet, stocks, etc.] hangs the garland of peace".[155] Hall cites a story about Louis the Pious of France that provides a biblical counterpoint to James' motto of Beati Pacifici: he notes that King Louis reversed a pardon he had given after reading Psalm 106:3 "Beati qui faciunt iustitiam in omni tempore", a passage that in its very phrasing suggests a counter-wisdom to James' motto.[156] In Hall's sermon, peace is frustrated by the sinfulness of humankind: he goes through a long list of how the victims of injustice or the upholders of justice are blamed for the breaking of peace: "Thus in family, countrey, citie, commonwealth, Church, world, the greatest part seeke a licentious peace in a disordered lawlesse-nesse."[157] According to Hall, it is the injustice of Rome that has prevented

---

[151] Cogswell, p. 298.
[152] Cogswell, p. 45. Lake, "The Moderate and Irenic Case", p. 65, stresses how Hall's critique of irenicism worked "within the parameters laid down by James' own rhetoric and concerns".
[153] Letter to Mead, 24 Sept. 1623, *Court and Times of James I*, vol. 2, p. 419.
[154] Huntley, *Essays in Persuasion*, pp. 49–56, seems to overlook that the sermon is ultimately arguing in favour of war.
[155] sig. B4r.
[156] sig. B5r.
[157] sig. C4r.

peace within Christendom, and the Protestant response cannot simply be acquiescence.[158] Like Stradling, Hall suggests that God is both "the Lord of Hosts" and "the God of Peace":

> And if any shall offer wrong to the Lords anointed in his person, in his seed, the worke of that injustice shall be war; yea Bellum Domini, the Lords war; (2 Sam.25.28); Then let him who is both the Lord of Hosts, and the God of peace, rise up mightily for his anointed, the true King of Peace; that he who hath graciously said al this while, Da pacem, Domine, Give peace in our time, O Lord; may superscribe at the last his iust Trophees, with Blessed bee the Lord which teacheth my hands to warre, and my fingers to fight.[159]

Only at the end of the sermon does Hall specifically refer to James and his iconography of peacemaking:

> Blessed be God, and his Anointed, we have long and comfortably tasted the sweetnesse of this blessing [peace]; the Lilies and Lions of our Salomon have beene iustly worded with Beati pacifici: Would we have this happinesse perpetuated to us, to posterity? Oh let Prince and people meet in the ambition to be Gens iusta, a righteous nation.[160]

The sermon thus affirms the traditional Solomonic iconography, while at the same time inviting the king to join with his people, in effect to follow their lead, in becoming a just nation, engaged in the continental conflicts that are the only guarantee of future peace. While Constantine is not specifically evoked, James' role would be a reflection of that model of Christian kingship.

While both Stradling and Hall's writings are militaristic, it is a militarism which refuses to abandon completely the rhetoric of peace. Instead, peace is redefined, or at the very least, new approaches to peace suggested. The iconography of peacemaking was too well established to be abandoned completely, and as will be discussed in the final chapter, it was as the peace-loving Solomon that James was put to rest.

Ultimately, the ideology and iconography of James' peacemaking were unsuccessful in convincing the nation and parliament that it was a laudable and feasible position. However, while James' stance may not have not been accepted by many of his subjects, his rhetoric of peacemaking was not an empty one. While he lived there was not war with Spain; at his death, his daughter wrote "Now you may be sure that all will go well in England",[161] meaning that she and Frederick might expect military support, and shortly afterwards Charles and Buckingham set the war in motion. Later in his reign, Charles was to join in the elevation of James' peacemaking activities, but as

---

[158] sig. B6v–B8v.
[159] sig. C5r.
[160] sig. C7r.
[161] Lee, *Great Britain's Solomon*, p. 291, quoting Oman, *Elizabeth of Bohemia* (1964), p. 290.

Cogswell points out, "father and son arrived at the same place by radically different routes. While James followed the maxim, 'beati pacifici', out of preference, Charles did so after 1629 out of necessity. Even in the halcyon days of peace in the 1630s, Charles's preferred image of himself was that of a martial king in full armour on horseback."[162] In that respect, the Constantinian model of Christian kingship clearly triumphed in the early Stuart period.

---

[162] Cogswell, p. 62. Throughout these pages Cogswell stresses the attraction of war for the young Charles; this contrast between father and son was especially significant during 1624, as Charles and Buckingham loudly called for war, as James continued to negotiate with Spain.

Chapter 6

KING JAMES AND THE POLITICS
OF CONVERSION

"but unmoved thou/Of force must one, and forced but one allow"
(John Donne, "Satire 3")

AROUND 1614, the Dutch painter Adriaen Pietersz. van de Venne produced a canvas entitled "Fishing for Souls", which shows a wide river, with crowds of men portrayed on either bank – well-known Protestants on the right-bank of the river, and Roman Catholics on the left. In the midst of the river are a number of boats, each attempting to haul in various swimming or drowning figures. The painting effectively conveys the vigour with which the two halves of western Christendom attempted to win converts, especially converts of political or scholarly significance.[1] The year of the painting is also significant, for while this battle for allegiance was ongoing from the Reformation, it reached a period of intensity from about 1607 to 1618. As David Mathew notes, in 1614 "there began the slow piecemeal conversion [to the Church of Rome] of small individual princes",[2] and these years were also a period of intense conversion activity within England. Prominently appearing on the right bank in the painting is King James, along with his daughter Elizabeth, and her husband, Frederick, Elector of the Palatine.[3] The painting appropriately presents King James as a figure deeply concerned with significant conversions, both within England and across Europe. Through direct personal contact, as well as through his churchmen, scholars and ambassadors, James sought to bring Roman Catholics into the Church of England, and, wherever possible, prevent the falling away of English scholars, churchmen

---

[1] Wormald, *Court, Kirk and Community*, p. 134 refers to the "belief [of the Presbyterians] inherited from Calvin and Beza in the efficacy of the conversion of a single noble".

[2] Mathew, *James I*, p. 251. Among the converts listed by Mathew are the count of Pfalz-Neuberg, Count John III of Nassau-Siegen and the prince of Nassau-Hadamar.

[3] The most thorough discussion of the painting is found in Gerhardus Knuttel, "Das Gemalde des Seelenfischfangs von Adriaen Pietersz. Van de Venne" (diss., The Hague, 1917). Laurens J. Bols, *Adriaen Pietersz. van de Venne: Painter and Draughtsman* (Doornspijk: Davaco, 1989), pp. 34–41 provides a briefer and more readily available discussion of the painting. Bols suggests that the Roman church is presented in the painting as more aggressive in its fishing, using a variety of baits and lures, and hauling its catch in with a net.

and gentlemen from their national church. James took a personal interest in the conversions, and saw them as a central part of the theological and political controversies that were raging at the time.

These conversions, while noted and explored within the context of individual lives, such as those of John Donne and Marco Antonio de Dominis, the archbishop of Spalato, generally have not been approached as a broader phenomenon. Recently, Michael C. Questier has greatly expanded our understanding of the personal dynamics of such conversions, especially through his emphasis that "conversions in religion, authentic experiences of grace, could be politicised without being entirely under the regime of politics".[4] This chapter, while not denying the significance of personal choice that Questier delineates, focusses on the public ramifications, and King James' fostering of conversions, especially of notable clergy, nobility and gentry.[5]

James' role in these conversions is best seen within the context of his broader involvement in matters of theological controversy. In the middle years of his English reign, James deliberately fostered a loose community of scholars dedicated to the task of defending Protestantism in its English form against both Roman and more radically Protestant positions. This theological culture was not developed solely, or even primarily, for domestic consumption; as a mainly Latin phenomenon it was engaging in a broader continental struggle. This was the case even when James' motivations might appear to be more domestic, arising from threats to his position as king of England and head of the Church of England. While writings of controversy might be the arms of this spiritual battle, individual human souls were the *spolia*, and these spoils would include churchmen, gentlemen and scholars, from both England and the continent. This chapter will consider both the effort and results of this program of attempted conversions, coming to focus finally on the notorious and frequently misunderstood figure of the archbishop of Spalato.

---

[4] *Conversion, Politics and Religion in England, 1580–1625* (Cambridge: CUP, 1996), p. 58. See also J. C. H. Aveling, *The Handle and the Axe: the Catholic Recusants in England from Reformation to Emancipation* (London: Blond & Briggs, 1976) on the significance of conversions to the Church of Rome.

[5] Peter Milward, *Religious Controversies of the Jacobean Age: A Survey of Printed Sources* (Lincoln: U of Nebraska P, 1978), pp. 165–71 and 187–95, provides a brief commentary and preliminary bibliography of material arising from the conversions. See also Calvin F. Senning, "Vanini and the Diplomats, 1612–1614: Religion, Politics, and Defection in the Counter-Reformation Era", *The Historical Magazine of the Protestant Episcopal Church* 54 (1985): 219–39. Michael C. Questier, "John Gee, Archbishop Abbot, and the Use of Converts from Rome in Jacobean Anti-Catholicism", *Recusant History* 21 (1993): 347–60 is primarily concerned with the reconversion of Gee in 1623, after James had ceased to play a significant role in such endeavours. The only other recent study of such a figure is Neil Davie, "Prêtre et Pasteur en Angleterre aux XVI et XVII Siècles: La Carrière de John Copley (1577–1662)", *Revue d'histoire moderne et contemporaine* 43 (1996): 403–21, which passes over the conversion of Copley from a Jesuit to a priest in the Church of England rather quickly while emphasizing the uniqueness of the event; part of the present article will be concerned with showing just how a common pattern this in fact was.

There is a danger in using the term "conversion" to describe the phenomenon of shifting ecclesiastical allegiance in the period. For us, the term denotes a dramatic inner change, a reversal of a belief system that is primarily spiritual in nature. Many seventeenth-century figures were engaging more strictly in a political decision that substituted the authority of one church or regime for another. However, this is not to reduce their decisions to merely pragmatic or political ones; both Catholic and Protestant controversialists at the time recognized that conversion might be brought about by ulterior motives, but that these motives might also ultimately lead to a true inner conversion.[6] Secondly, the term "conversion" does not do justice to the broad range of figures to which it was applied: many wavered between one allegiance and another, many slowly moved from one to the other, and still others were seeking some accommodation between the Roman Catholic and Protestant churches. Finally, to call them "convertitos" or "convertites", the popular Italian terms that came to be used in England as well, is to adopt the viewpoint of the more militant elements of Protestantism and Catholicism, the framework of understanding of the continental Calvinists and Jesuits.[7] While I will use these terms for the sake of expediency, and to acknowledge how the situation was broadly perceived, I will attempt also to demonstrate the more nuanced vision of such movements held by some in the period.

This struggle over souls found two different foci for King James. One was within England, and usually concerned high-born Englishmen or English clerics who wavered between allegiance to the Church of Rome and the Church of England. The other involved the fleeing to England of Roman Catholic clergy, particularly Venetian ones who had established anti-papal leanings because of the conflict between Venice and the pope. The period of intense conversion activity began in 1607 with the twin crises of the Oath of Allegiance and the Venetian Interdict. The failed Gunpowder Plot of November 1605 drastically altered the unofficial position of Roman Catholics in England, who up to this point in James' reign had been little bothered.[8] In response to the plot James began a process that led to the Oath of Allegiance, an oath that he argued even Roman Catholics could accept.[9] However, its institution led Pope Paul V to issue an edict forbidding

---

[6] Aveling, p. 350. To avoid making one church or the other central, I have used the term "conversion" to refer to movement of either direction, and generally avoided such terms as "apostacy".

[7] The word "convertine", one about to be converted, was also used.

[8] Elliot Rose, *Cases of Conscience* (Cambridge: CUP, 1975), p. 106.

[9] See William Patterson, *King James VI and I and the Reunion of Christendom*, pp. 75–123, and Johann Sommerville, "Absolutism and Royalism", *The Cambridge History of Political Thought, 1450–1700*, eds J. H. Burns and Mark Goldie (Cambridge: CUP, 1991), pp. 347–73; and "James I and the Divine Right of Kings: English Politics and Continental Theory", *The Mental World of the Jacobean Court*, ed. Linda Levy Peck (Cambridge: CUP, 1991), pp. 55–70.

Catholics to take the oath. This led to an extended war of the pen, nicely summarized by Thomas Fuller:

> And now, the alarm being given, "whether this oath was lawful or no", both parties of Protestants and papists drew forth their forces into the field. King James undertook the pope himself; the wearer of three, against the wearer of a triple crown (an even match,) effectually confuting his briefs. Bishop Andrews takes Bellarmine to task; Bishop Barlow pours out upon Parsons; Dr. Morton, Dr. Robert Abbot, Dr. Buckeridge, Dr. Collins, Dr. Burrel, Mr. Thomson, Dr. Peter Moulin, maintain the legality of the oath, against Suarez, Eudaemon, Becanus, Cofteteus, [Coeffeteau,] Peleterius, and others.[10]

While this controversy was at its most intense from 1608 to 1614, tracts on it were published as late as 1620.[11] The Oath of Allegiance forced many Englishmen to make publicly clear their religious position, and Michael Questier notes that there was a surge of conformity between 1612 and 1615 in response to greater enforcement of the recusancy laws.[12] Some Roman Catholics took the oath, some avoided the dilemma as long as possible, others fled to the continent.

In these same years the conflict between Venice and the Church of Rome was at its peak; tensions between the civil government of Venice and the ecclesiastical authority of Rome had been longstanding. In 1606 they reached a new height as Venice was put under an interdict by Rome, and in response Venice expelled the Jesuits. The English saw the quarrel between Venice and Rome as the counterpart to their own struggle: in both cases the civil government was challenging what they saw as the intrusion of the pope into matters of secular authority.[13] In the years following the interdict, and to a lesser degree after, Venice proved a ripe field for conversions to Protestantism, and from 1609 until the late 1610s a continual stream of *convertitos* made their way to England. On the English side of the channel, Archbishop Abbot was the prime intermediary for convertites; his letters to Dudley Carleton, ambassador at Venice and The Hague, and William Trumbull, ambassador at Brussels, are frequently concerned with the movements of English apostates on the continent and would-be convertites who might come to England.[14]

Efforts at notable conversions dwindled from about 1618 on, for a number

---

[10] Fuller, *Church History of Britain* (1868), vol. 3, p. 252.
[11] See Milward, pp. 114–19, for a fuller list.
[12] *Conversion, Politics and Religion in England*, pp. 137 and 148.
[13] See J. H. M. Salmon, "James I, the Oath of Allegiance, the Venetian Interdict, and the Reappearance of French Ultramontanism", *The Cambridge History of Political Thought, 1450–1700*, eds J. H. Burns and Mark Goldie (Cambridge: CUP, 1991), pp. 247–53. See also William Patterson, *King James VI and I and the Reunion of Christendom*, pp. 115–17.
[14] See particularly the letters in *HMC* (75) Downshire, vols 3–6. See Questier, *Conversion, Politics and Religion*, pp. 350–1, on Abbot's continuing interest in converts, both English and European.

of reasons. One seems to have been a growing cynicism about many of the Italian *converititos*; secondly, James' involvement in European affairs changed with the advancing of the Spanish match, and finally, his war of the pen became overshadowed in those years by the literal war that engulfed Europe. The period of intense conversion activity also roughly coincided with the papal rule of Paul V, known for his militant stance towards Protestantism and his strong assertion of papal authority.

While a few notable conversions proved practically useful to the pope or King James in ecclesiastical or diplomatic affairs, the symbolic importance of these figures was always paramount: their allegiance to the Church of England would validate its authority and correctness; similarly, any apostasy from it reduced its significance in the eyes of Christendom. Both sides would make extensive propagandistic use of any conversion. Frequently, the convertite would publish a pamphlet explaining his actions and the errors of the church he had left, and others would appear attacking him, both on theological and personal levels. Propaganda would even exploit a conversion that was not yet, nor might ever be, a reality. The English particularly accused the Jesuits of such distortion. Henry Wotton claims in 1609 in reference to a supposed conversion that "I dare not believe, growing every day to me (as I must confess) more and more uncertain whom I shall think white or black, through the skill of the Jesuits, who knowing that example and number have *vim aggregandi*, work upon report and, either dead or alive, blemish all alike."[15] Such "cataloguing" of converts or adherents was not merely metaphorical: appended to the Jesuit work, *A Reply made unto Mr. Anthony Wotton and Mr. John White Ministers* (1612), were "A Catalogue of the Names of some Catholike Professours", and "A Challenge to Protestants: requiring a Catalogue to be made of some Professours of their fayth, in all ages since Christ".[16]

While a living convertite could publicly pronounce or even publish his new commitment, death-bed conversions had the advantage of not being susceptible to later recantation.[17] The death of Englishmen abroad was particularly susceptible to rumours of death-bed apostasy. Frequently, rumours were spread regardless of what actually happened at death; Wotton makes reference to "their [the Jesuits] fashion of working even by false example".[18] The Venetian churchman Paolo Sarpi's death was marked by two conflicting rumours – one suggesting faithfulness to Rome at death, the other a commitment to Protestantism.[19] Similarly, the death of John King,

---

[15] Wotton to the Earl of Salisbury, 18 June 1609, *Sir Henry Wotton: Life and Letters*, ed. Logan Pearsall Smith (Oxford: Clarendon Press, 1907), vol. 1, p. 457.

[16] This work was frequently reprinted and enlarged in later years; see Milward, pp. 144–5.

[17] For a partial listing of death-bed conversions and their attendant literature, see Questier, *Conversion, Politics and Religion*, p. 192n.

[18] "To the Earl of Salisbury", 31 August 1607, *Life and Letters*, vol. 1, p. 398.

[19] David Wootton, *Paolo Sarpi: between Renaissance and Enlightenment* (Cambridge: CUP, 1983), p. 120.

bishop of London, in 1621, was followed by a book entitled *The Protestants Plea*, which suggested that King "had become a convert to Rome on his death-bed, through the agency of one Thomas Preston".[20] John Chamberlain reports on the death of the marquis of Hamilton in 1625 that "The Papists will needs have him [Hamilton] one of theirs, which neither appeared in his life, nor in his death, that we can anyway learn; but it is no new thing with them to raise such scandals and slanders."[21]

At a number of points in his life, King James took a personal role in the work of conversion. As an earnest teenaged king he endeavoured to bring his beloved cousin Esmé Stuart to the Protestant faith; and he made similar efforts with the earl of Huntly a few years later.[22] Early in his English reign, there were rumours that he had persuaded the earl of Northampton to convert; an epigram by Sir John Davies suggests that "Curio" (Northampton) had been moved only by "Basilius" (the king), not out of respect for the great Reformers.[23] Before Bartholomew Legate was burned at Smithfield for his heretical Arian views, James personally met with him and attempted to sway him from his beliefs.[24]

JAMES AND CONVERSION WITHIN ENGLAND

When James came to the English throne in 1603 there was a substantial section of the population still faithful to the Church of Rome, and another segment of "Church Papists" who, while outwardly conforming, would welcome any movement of the Church of England back toward Rome.[25] Frequently, like John Donne, these figures came from traditionally Roman Catholic families. Others had newly converted to Rome, or for many years had wavered or explored. This situation is ably described in John Donne's Satire III:

> To adore, or scorn an image, or protest,
> May all be bad; doubt wisely; in strange way
> To stand inquiring right is not to stray;
> To sleep, or run wrong is.

---

[20] Maclure, *Register of Sermons Preached at Paul's Cross, 1534–1642*, p. 118. Henry King, his son, attacked the rumour in a sermon at Paul's Cross, 25 Nov. 1625, published as *A Sermon Preached at Pauls Crosse* (*STC* 14969).

[21] Chamberlain to Carleton, 12 March 1624/5, *Chamberlain Letters*, vol. 2, pp. 504–5.

[22] Willson, *King James VI and I*, pp. 37, 99.

[23] "In Curionem", *Poems*, ed. Krueger, p. 182. There is little evidence in the years leading up to Northampton's death in 1614 that he was anything but a faithful Roman Catholic.

[24] See Fuller, *Church History* (1868), vol. x, 62ff.

[25] John Bossy, "The English Catholic Community 1603–1625", *The Reign of James VI and I*, ed. Alan G. R. Smith (New York: St Martin's Press, 1973), p. 101, estimates, on the basis of recusancy statistics, that there were 35,000 thousand Roman Catholics in 1603.

These English Catholics hoped that their position might be improved with James' accession; there were even rumours that James intended to bring the nation back to the Church of Rome. Any such hopes were dashed by the Gunpowder Plot and the official measures adopted in response to it. The required Oath of Allegiance restricted the options for many in England. It was no longer possible "To stand inquiring right", nor "To sleep". The result was a host of new "converts" to the Church of England, and a number of "Church Papists" whose conformity could not extend to taking the oath, and thus became more committed in their allegiance to the Roman church. A frequent scenario was an attempt to combine spiritual allegiance to the Church of Rome with temporal allegiance to the English monarch, with attendant suspicions on both sides. Dudley Carleton put it well when he asked "whither a new Romanist can retain his old Affections and continue a good Englishman".[26]

Most frequently in England, the struggle for converts involved the young. At a number of points steps were taken by the king or parliament to bring about Protestant education for the children of Catholic families; however, these seem to have had little effect.[27] On the other hand, young gentlemen seemed most susceptible to conversion to the Church of Rome.[28] A continual fear was that young gentlemen travelling on the continent would be converted; for this reason, among others, travellers needed to be licensed, and in most cases were required to avoid Rome. As the preacher Thomas Adams put it, "Straggling Dinahs seldom return, but ravished, home"[29] and upon leaving for a diplomatic mission in Spain, John Sanford reports that King James "bid me take heed I did not turn Jesuit".[30] Joseph Hall produced a 90-page book, *Quo Vadis?* (1617), which cited religious apostasy as the chief reason why Englishmen should avoid foreign travel, except for matters of business or state. He devotes a number of pages to a description of how continental Roman Catholics gradually seduce their English visitors.[31] Henry Wotton suggests that under Clement VIII (1592–1605), a sustained policy of "invitation and allurement of all nations and religions promiscuously" was adopted.[32] If anything, this approach became more enthusiastically pursued

[26] Carleton to Trumbull, 2 April 1611, *Memorials and Affairs of State* (1725), vol. 3, p. 270. Carleton does not identify the individual being discussed.

[27] Bossy, *The English Catholic Community, 1570–1850* (New York: OUP, 1976), pp. 161–3; it seems that such attempts were most successful when the children came under the authority of the Court of Wards; see *CSP, Ireland, 1615–25*, p. 83, June 1613, for a list of Catholic heirs to be brought to England and raised as Protestants.

[28] See Chapter Ten of John Gee's *The Foot out of the Snare* (1624).

[29] Adams, *Spiritual Navigator*, in *Works*, ed. Angus, vol. 3, p. 49.

[30] John Sanford to William Trumbull, 7 April 1611, *HMC* (75) Downshire, vol. 3, p. 56. In February 1606, Sir Edward Hoby reported the rumour that the English ambassador in Spain had been left nearly without servants because of conversions (*Court and Times of James I*, vol. 1, p. 49).

[31] *Quo Vadis?* (1617), pp. 57–62.

[32] Wotton to the Earl of Salisbury, 18 August 1605, *Life and Letters*, vol. 1, p. 332.

under Pope Paul V, 1605–21. Wotton reports in 1608 that Florence in particular is a dangerous city for young Englishmen to visit.[33] He speculates that the pope and the Jesuits are pursuing the strategy of separating "by some device their guides from our young noblemen (about whom they are busiest), and afterwards to use themselves (for aught I can yet hear) with much kindness and security, but yet with restraint (when they come to Rome) of departing thence without leave".[34] Later in 1617, William Trumbull reports that "In these Provinces [the Spanish Lowlands] now governed by the Archduke there be more of his Majesties vassalls poisoned in their relligion (and consequently in their allegeance and loyalty towards him) then in all the rest of Europe."[35]

A list of English apostates of high birth from these years would include the courtiers Francis Cottington and Sir Walter Aston, Henry Neville of Abergavenny, Sir Herbert Croft, William Cecil (Lord Roos), and Sir Tobie Matthew. An examination of the last three figures will demonstrate the range of forms such conversions could take, and how their resultant relationships with James and other English official could differ.

The conversion and flight to Rome of Sir Herbert Croft seems to have been an act of immediate desperation. Sir Herbert came of the Croft family of Croft Castle, Herefordshire, and was educated at Christ Church, Oxford. He sat in parliament from 1589 to 1614, and was knighted by James, with so many others, in that glorious spring of 1603. Thus, it was as a well-established and mature figure that he turned to Rome in 1616–17. Already in May of 1617 there were rumours he had fled to France because of financial problems.[36] John Chamberlain sums up wonderfully the English perception of many such conversions: "We heare that Sir Harbert Crofts is turned popish, which seems straunge to many, but yt is no great marvayle, for desperation hath made more monckes then him."[37] In his hasty flight Croft left behind his wife and children. His conversion took on a public role in that he published a number of works to justify his step and to convince his family to follow him: *Letters Persuasive to his Wife and Children in England to take upon them the Catholic Religion, Arguments to shew that the Rom. Church is the true Church,* and *Reply to the Answer of his Daughter M. C. (Mary Croft), which she made to a Paper of his sent to her concerning the Rom. Church* (all 1619). His son Herbert eventually followed him to the continent and joined the Roman church, but was reconverted by Thomas Morton, bishop of Durham, and after the

---

[33] Wotton to the Earl of Salisbury, 5 September 1608, *Life and Letters*, vol. 1, p. 434.

[34] Wotton to the Earl of Salisbury, 18 June 1609, *Life and Letters*, vol. 1, pp. 456–7. The most notorious incident like this involved the tutor of Lord Roos, John Mole, who remained imprisoned in Rome for thirty years after his trip there with his young master (*Chamberlain Letters*, vol. 1, p. 265n).

[35] Trumbull to Winwood, 26 September 1617, *HMC* (75) Downshire, vol. 6, p. 296.

[36] Chamberlain to Carleton, 24 May 1617, *Chamberlain Letters*, vol. 2, p. 76.

[37] Chamberlain to Carleton, 18 October 1617, *Chamberlain Letters*, vol. 2, pp. 105–6.

Restoration became bishop of Hereford. Herbert Croft the Elder seems to have retired to the monastery of St Gregory at Douai, and stayed there until his death in 1629.[38]

While the younger Herbert Croft was to become an English bishop, Sir Tobie Matthew attained fame as a Roman Catholic convert because he was the son of the archbishop of York who bore the same name. Matthew is also rare among lay converts in that he left a lengthy memoir, a rather extraordinary volume, which recounts for Dame Mary Gage the circumstances under which he became Roman Catholic, and the English attempts afterward to reconvert him. After time at Oxford and Gray's Inn, Matthew travelled to the continent in July 1604, despite the fearful opposition of his parents. Through personal observation of the Lenten season and the influence of Sir George Petre, Robert Cansfield, and the renowned Robert Parsons, he was soon led to accept the Roman church in the late winter of 1606. Wotton blames the conversion on bad influence, and not just that of Italy: "Neither do I think that before his meeting with that mountebank Bagshaw at Paris he was wholly apostamated."[39] Wotton zealously saw the potential for contagion in such conversions; in a letter of warning from a few months later, Wotton suggests that in Florence there is "a certain knot of bastard Catholics, partly banished and partly voluntary residents there, whereof Tobie Mathew is the principal; who with pleasantness of conversation, and with force of example, do much harm, and are likely to do more, considering the correspondency they hold with the English in Rome".[40] He suggests in this same letter that it might be wiser for James to allow Matthew to return home than to allow him to spend his banishment in this fashion. As an archbishop's son, Matthew had more to offer Rome than his "pleasantness of conversation": he represented a major success upon which to build. By September of that year he returned to England, and soon after Archbishop Bancroft and Thomas Morton, among others, attempted a reconversion of the imprisoned apostate; his meeting with Lancelot Andrewes is described in greatest detail in his memoirs. While some of these discussions focussed on theology, it seems that the king would have been satisfied were Matthew to take the recently introduced Oath of Allegiance.[41] This he absolutely refused to do in spite of the example of such prominent Catholics as the archpriest George Blackwell. He penned a letter to the king himself, which while expressing loyalty, stopped short of confirming the oath; however, upon the advice of Robert Cecil, earl of Salisbury, he refrained from sending it to the king.[42]

[38] Hasler, *The House of Commons, 1558–1603* (London: HMSO, 1981), p. 671.
[39] Letter to Sir Thomas Edmondes, 3 August 1607, *Life and Letters*, vol. 1, p. 395. The figure is the famous Roman priest Christopher Bagshaw.
[40] Wotton to the earl of Salisbury, 5 September 1608, *Life and Letters*, vol. 1, p. 434.
[41] Tobie Matthew, *A True Historical Relation of the Conversion of Sir Tobie Matthew* (London, 1904), p. 76.
[42] Ibid., p. 115.

Matthew returned to the continent – unconverted – in the spring of 1608, and would remain there until 1617, despite a number of attempts to return home. For his part, Matthew refrained from seeing his conversion as a renunciation of his Englishness or his allegiance to the king; he seems to have followed Bacon's earnest advice that he keep "within the bounds of loyalty to his Majesty, and natural piety towards your country".[43] Hence, in 1611 he wrote to Salisbury for permission to return home, claiming that he had not cultivated contact with foreign princes, and abstained "from using any ostentation of my conversion to Catholique relligion". Thus, he hoped to be invited back to his country "which so many in my case do injoy".[44] It was still not clear that he would take the Oath of Allegiance; in 1616 Dudley Carleton comments: "I doubt his stiffness in refusing the oath is rather more confirmed than altered with time, only his heat in disputing is qualified, which would make his being for a small space in England to dispatch his affairs less dangerous if it might be admitted." This return finally took place in 1617, after the successful intervention of Francis Bacon and George Villiers. From Matthew's correspondence with Bacon it seems that Abbot gave way before the king did, who still insisted that Matthew take the oath.[45] Chamberlain wrote to Carlton that "your frend Tobie shall remain here as yt is bruited, and be dispensed withall for taking the oath of allegeance, which were yt not in him I shold thincke yt might prove a case of strange consequence".[46]

Even with Matthew's return to England, suspicions of his dangerous effect on others remained. He was reported to have "perverted [Lady Exeter] to become a Romane Catholique, which I shold be sory shold prove true, or that yt shold be blased too far".[47] His failure to take the oath, and his being, as Thomas Lorkin put it, "a dangerous man for our collapsed ladies", eventually led to his banishment once again in late 1618.[48] However, from this time Matthew's situation in relation to the king was eased, as the potential of the Spanish match made his connections in that country valuable to the king. His case demonstrates well the way in which changing circumstances affected the politics of conversion. His Catholicism remained untempered through the early 1620s, but now his position seems to have been more accepted. He seems to have been intimate with Buckingham's mother and wife, whose conversions will be discussed later in this chapter. Matthew's diplomatic work eventually led to his knighting in October 1623, and in the next year he was appointed to the unsuccessful Royal Academy. He continued in a variety of roles under Charles.

Among those believed to have been influenced by Matthew was William

---

[43] *Letters and Life of Francis Bacon*, ed. James Spedding (London, 1861–74), vol. 4, p. 10.
[44] 13 April 1611, SP 14/63/fols. 44–5.
[45] *Letters and Life of Francis Bacon*, vol. 6, p. 215.
[46] Chamberlain to Carleton, 20 December 1617, *Chamberlain Letters*, vol. 2, p. 123.
[47] Chamberlain to Carleton, 10 January 1618, *Chamberlain Letters*, vol. 2, p. 128.
[48] Lorkin to Puckering, 18 December 1618, *Court and Times of James I*, vol. 2, p. 114.

Cecil, the young Lord Roos, great-grandson of the first Lord Burleigh. Carleton reports from Venice in 1612 that Roos, Matthew, Robert Cansfield, and George Gage are all in Venice on their way to Naples.[49] Clearly, their movements aroused suspicions on the part of the English and hopes on the part of Rome. However, after travelling through Italy over the next year and a half, Lord Roos "made haste from Florence to be present with us at our Communion [in Venice] on Christmas day" of 1614; such a gesture confirmed his allegiance to the Church of England at that time, and Carleton notes that it would frustrate Rome, who had "long had this young lord in their catalogue as one of their converts".[50] Doubts remained, however, and from this point Roos' life deteriorated into scandal, which served only to accelerate his movement toward Rome. After a failed diplomatic expedition to Spain on the king's behalf in early 1617, Roos' family affairs pulled him under. His wife, the daughter of Sir Thomas Lake, from whom he had long lived separately, brought a range of charges against him, including adultery with his grandfather's young wife. As this turmoil raged in 1617 he fled to Rome in what Gardiner calls "the character of a convert".[51] The king sent letters to him at Paris, commanding his return, but without success.[52] His actions from this point confirmed the suspicions aroused by his earlier sojourns on the continent and his association with Matthew and Gage. James offered a pardon to him in 1619 and invited his return, but he had already died at Naples, with attendant rumours that he had been poisoned.[53]

Such an end seems to have been typical of public converts to the Church of Rome in James' reign. Most frequently they lost all possible standing in England, with no guarantee of security on the continent. Seldom wholly trusted by either side, they were left in a no-man's land to fend for themselves. The success of figures like Tobie Matthew was rare in comparison to the ill fortunes of those like Croft and Roos who lost a great deal in their flight to Rome.

In the same period, a corresponding number of high-born Englishmen left their family roots in the Church of Rome for full communion with the Church of England.[54] With these figures the process was often more gradual

---

[49] Letter to Chamberlain, 14 August 1612, *Dudley Carleton to John Chamberlain*, ed. Maurice Lee, Jr. (New Brunswick, N. J.: Rutgers UP, 1972), pp. 132–3.

[50] Letter to Chamberlain, 24 December 1613/3 January 1614, *Dudley Carleton to John Chamberlain*, pp. 154–5.

[51] Gardiner, *History of England, 1603–1642*, vol. 3, p. 191.

[52] John Castle to Trumbull, 18 September 1617, *HMC 75* (Downshire), vol. 6, p. 292. Cf. Lorkin to Puckering, 14 July 1618, *Court and Times*, vol. 2, p. 81.

[53] Gardiner, *History of England, 1603–1642*, vol. 3, pp. 190–2. Later in the 1620s rumours were to surface that he was in fact still alive on the continent.

[54] Aveling, *The Handle and the Axe*, p. 122, stresses the "rapid and dramatic growth of Catholicism among the upper classes, both at court and in the country", but makes no statistically based claims, nor are any likely possible, given the fuzzy boundaries between conformity and recusancy, and that only notable conversions were remarked upon by

and less easy to discern. The various anti-recusancy laws of both Elizabeth's and James' reigns had been more directed toward outward conformity than inner conviction, and this outward conformity took different forms at different times. Some laws prohibited participation in illegal Catholic celebrations of the mass, others required participation in the services of the Church of England. The laws under Elizabeth had proscribed attendance at Church of England services, later enactments included the taking of communion.[55] Breaking of these laws most often involved a fine, which was not always collected. Compliance or conformity could thus be gradual and relatively unmarked, in a way that a new Catholic's flight to the continent would not be. Only in the case of a few notable figures was there a public acknowledgement of first attendance at an English service, or participation in English communion of a former non-communicant. Complicating the matter is the widespread belief at the time on the part of Protestants that there were many "Church-Papists", who outwardly conformed but maintained an inner allegiance to the Church of Rome.[56] After the Gunpowder Plot it became increasingly imperative for Roman Catholic Englishmen to demonstrate their allegiance, either through publicly affirming the Oath of Allegiance, while maintaining spiritual loyalty to Rome, or by taking the complete move of participation in the Church of England.[57] The actions of Pope Paul, especially his *muto proprio* of 1606 also diminished the opportunity for ambiguous compromise on the part of English Catholics.[58] A generational factor was also at work, for, as John Bossy has suggested, church-papacy "could hardly be maintained for longer than a single generation"; as a situation of compromise, it could hardly be held up as an ideal for offspring to follow.[59] The children of upper-class Catholics were frequently educated and raised in the homes of Protestant relatives; as Bossy suggests, "it is not surprising that some grew up extremely confused about which religion they belonged to".[60]

The highest born of those moving from the Church of Rome to that of England was Thomas Howard, second earl of Arundel, whose family had long suffered for the faith; his grandfather, Thomas Howard, the fourth duke of Norfolk, had been executed in 1572 for his connection with Mary, Queen of Scots; and his father, Philip, first earl of Arundel, who converted to the Roman Church in the 1580s, was imprisoned in the Tower, and was not allowed to see his son unless he renounced Rome and took communion in the Church of

contemporaries. It is fair to say, however, that at various points in both the reign of James and Charles, English Protestants were alarmed at the seeming preponderance of "papists" at court.

[55] See Rose, *Cases of Conscience*, pp. 11–22, for a discussion of the recusancy laws both "on paper" and "in practice". Rose's focus, however, is more largely on the Elizabethan situation.

[56] The most famous description of this type of figure is found in John Earle's *Microcosmography* (1628).

[57] Rose, *Cases of Conscience* p. 106.

[58] Ibid., p. 242.

[59] Bossy, *English Catholic Community, 1570–1850*, pp. 158–9.

[60] Ibid., p. 161.

England. His refusal meant that Thomas Howard never saw his father.[61] Thus, the younger man's movement to the English church, culminating in the taking of communion at Christmas 1616, was particularly noteworthy. His movement to the Church of England may have been a gradual one, and clearly one in which the king took an active part: in 1607 King James served as godfather to his son (Lord Maltravers) at his christening.[62] In these years, while his faith hung in uncertainty, he became an intimate of the young Prince Henry. The years from 1610 to 1614 were spent largely travelling on the continent, including time in Rome, building the art collection for which he would become famous. He returned to England in 1614, seemingly prompted by the death of his great-uncle, the earl of Northampton. However, his travels on the continent, along with the long-standing Catholicism of his family, had raised suspicions that needed to be cleared.[63]

David Howarth's *Lord Arundel and his Circle* markedly downplays the religious dimension of Arundel's life and his place in the religious and political struggles of the time. He sees Arundel's journey to Rome in 1613–14 simply as the artistic expedition or pilgrimage of an Italophile.[64] However, the symbolic religious significance of a trip to Florence and Rome at that time was not lost on contemporaries. Not only was controversy stirred by the travels of Matthew and Roos, but in that same year it was rumoured, because of his sojourn in Italy, that Sir Thomas Puckering had "grown a very hot and zealous Catholic".[65] Moreover, the letters of Dudley Carleton, ambassador in Venice at the time, express concern about Arundel's movements, which were kept quite well hidden. Arundel's mother, the dowager countess, sent letters pleading with her son to return home and put an end to the scandal. She was not advising him to join the English church – a step she warned him against in spiritual terms immediately before his taking of communion – but to avoid the seeming treason of visiting Rome. When such a figure was raised to the Privy Council in the summer of 1616, before his final conversion, it aroused resentment. André Paul, a member of the Elector Palatine's privy council, wrote to William Trumbull, "We cannot understand how such an appointment could have been made, considering that his very religion makes him susceptible to the influence of the greatest enemies of the King of England, and that he has just returned from Rome where all the conspiracies directed against His Majesty are hatched."[66] A full clearing would not take place,

[61] David Howarth, *Lord Arundel and his Circle* (New Haven and London: Yale UP, 1985), p. 7.
[62] Mathew, *James I*, p. 254.
[63] Howarth, *Lord Arundel and his Circle*, p. 51.
[64] See especially p. 38, where he contrasts Arundel's embracing of all things Italian with Wotton's attitude toward the Church of Rome. Ultimately, Arundel could not be as oblivious of the political ramifications of a trip to Rome as Howarth is.
[65] Lorkin to Puckering, 30 June 1613, *Court and Times*, vol. 1, p. 253; and Carleton to Chamberlain, 9 July 1613, *Court and Times*, vol. 1, p. 255.
[66] 3 August 1616, *HMC* (75) Downshire, vol. 5, p. 569.

however, until that Christmas Day in 1616, when Arundel knelt to receive holy communion in the Chapel Royal, an event widely noted at the time.[67]

The religious views of Arundel, and the significance of his conversion, have long been a matter of debate. Clarendon depicts him as unconcerned with religious commitment of any nature: "He was rather thought to be without religion than to incline to this or that party of any", and that he died "under the same doubtful character of religion in which he lived".[68] While Clarendon's comments might be dismissed as part of his overall negative portrait of Arundel, the sympathetic account by Sir Edward Walker presents a similar ambivalence about religion, but in more positive terms: "He was in Religion no Bigot or Puritan, and professed more to affect moral Vertues than nice Questions and Controversies."[69] His most significant modern biographer, Mary Hervey, presents his conversion as a heartfelt one of reaction against the Roman church as he had seen it on the continent, and a direct result of his relationship with the king. While a Protestant bias and a desire to see Howard in the best possible light seem to be at work in Hervey, her account is at least consistent with Howard's family history. Would he convert so lightly as Clarendon suggests given his father's suffering? However, like Howarth, Hervey's account has the effect of minimizing the religious and political significance of his earlier trips to Rome.

Some contemporary accounts of his conversion note that he became "sharp agaynst the Papists" and "in detestation of pope and al poperie".[70] When his house at Greenwich was destroyed by fire just over a week after his taking of English communion, Chamberlain speculated that "No doubt the Papests will ascribe and publish it as a punishment for dissembling or falling from them."[71] A few years after his conversion James was to describe him as one "who, through being a faithful servant, has earned the hatred of many papists".[72]

The doubts about Arundel's religion were magnified by his friendship with Tobie Matthew, one that had begun on the continent but resumed when Matthew returned to England in 1617.[73] Archbishop Matthew hoped that the

---

[67] See Mary Hervey, *The Life, Correspondence and Collections of Thomas Howard, Earl of Arundel* (Cambridge: CUP, 1921), pp. 115–16. Taking of communion in the Chapel Royal at Christmas seems to have been a highly symbolic way of demonstrating acceptance of the Church of England; Isaac Casaubon is described as doing the same upon his arrival in England (John Packer to Sir Thomas Edmondes, 17 January 1610/11, *Court and Times of James I*, vol. 1, p. 104).

[68] Edward, earl of Clarendon, *History of the Rebellion and Civil Wars in England*, ed. W. Dunn Macray, 6 vols (Oxford, 1888), vol. 1, p. 171.

[69] *A Short View of the Life of . . . Earl of Arundel*, in his *Historical Discourses upon Several Occasions* (London, 1705), qtd. Howarth, p. 220.

[70] Sir Horace Vere to Sherburn quoted by Hervey, p. 116.

[71] Chamberlain to Carleton, 4 Jan. 1617, *Chamberlain Letters*, vol. 2, p. 47.

[72] James' speech to parliament, 30 Jan. 1621, *CSPV, 1619–21*, p. 581.

[73] Howarth, *Lord Arundel and his Circle*, p. 66.

newly converted Arundel would succeed, where many bishops had failed, in persuading his son to reconvert.[74] However, from this point in his life Howard seems to have avoided religious controversy.

SCHOLARS AND CHURCHMEN

Being a "Church-Papist" was not possible for a priest during James' reign, nor was there opportunity for the gradual movement to conformity that we see among laymen. Instead, a clear breaking with the Church of Rome and full participation in the rites of the Church of England was necessary. Contemporaries carefully gauged the rewards, usually in the form of church livings, that accrued to those making such a move, and frequently conversions were derided as being born simply of ambition.[75] A list of clerics moving from the Church of Rome to the Church of England would include William Alabaster, Theophilus Higgons, John Salkeld, Richard Sheldon, John Copley, Leonard Rountree, Griffin Floyd, Anthony Clarke, and William Warmington. Notable among those moving the other way were Frances Walsingham, Humphrey Leech, James Waddesworth and Benjamin Carier. This study will take the two most notable converts, Higgons and Carier, as its focus.

Unlike the conversions of gentlemen and nobility, those of clerics generated a great deal of attendant written material. Sermons of recantation were common, and frequently published. The convertite often went on to further publication explaining his move and the errors of the church he had left. In response, defenders of the abandoned church would step forward, criticizing the argument, and unveiling the personal sins and shortcomings (often sexual) of the convertite. Clergy on both sides might be charged with homosexual desires; Roman clergy entering the Church of England and subsequently marrying might be dismissed by their former co-religionists as simply desiring sexual fulfilment.[76]

Reconversions were also possible with clergy: William Alabaster, best known today for his devotional poems of the 1590s, seems to have wavered between Rome and England for the better part of twenty years, and ultimately his theological positions corresponded neatly with neither.[77] He took Anglican orders early in the 1590s, but then bolted for Rome in 1598. Pardoned by James at his accession, he was imprisoned around 1606, left England once again, but ran afoul of Rome for his cabalistic *Apparatus in Revelationem Jesu Christi*. In 1610 he attempted a return to England; however, the authorities in Amsterdam, through which he passed on his way home, were suspicious of his claims and imprisoned him.[78] "The double or treble

---

[74] *DNB*, T. Matthew.

[75] Questier, *Conversion, Politics and Religion*, p. 42.

[76] Ibid., p. 44.

[77] Ibid., p. 55.

[78] *Memorials of Affairs of State*, vol. 3, pp. 210–11.

turncoat" as Chamberlain calls him finally seemed to have fixed his spiritual home in 1614. John Donne reports on his success in the church, and in January of 1615 he preached at Whitehall; however, as so often with these figures he was much resented by the unprodigal: "there were many clergiemen that do not greatly applaud him, but say he made a curious fantasticall peece of worke".[79] Any converted clergy faced suspicions because of men like Alabaster and their tendencies to reconversion. From a Catholic point of view, ordination in the Church of England tainted a man to the point that he might be expected even to reapostasise.[80]

Theophilus Higgons followed a similar wavering path, and attracted great attention in the process. Beginning as a much-admired Puritan-leaning preacher at St Dunstan's-in-the-West,[81] he left for the Roman church in 1608, and spent a number of years in French seminaries during which time he wrote a treatise explaining his move.[82] Thomas Morton, dean of Winchester, and a zealous participant in these controversies, responded with *A Direct Answer unto the Scandalous exceptions, which Theophilus Higgons hath lately objected* (1609), and Higgons was answered by Sir Edward Hoby as well. It was the intensity of these disputes and his earlier London fame that seem to have attracted such interest in his later reconversion. Upon his return to England in 1610 he was imprisoned, and then reconverted by Morton and Bishop Overall. Pardoned by the king, his recantation sermon at Paul's Cross on 3 March 1611 attracted widespread attention; numerous newsletters of the time mention that many of the nobility and privy councillors were present, and one notes that "The like audience was never seen in that place."[83] One newswriter reports that "The papists, of whom many were present, were scandalized, and had a purpose to have scattered divers of his books (which contain an answer to Sir Edward Hoby) among the people at the Cross."[84] Shortly afterwards the sermon was printed. A thoroughly Calvinist treatment of the theme of Grace, in its latter third the sermon turns to his personal situation, acknowledging his apostasy and remembering those churchmen who had helped him overcome his errors. He also alludes to James' interest in his situation, but praises the king for his refraining from coercive measures: the king ensured that he would be neither "allured, nor pressed".[85] Such

---

[79] Chamberlain to Carleton, 5 January 1615, *Chamberlain Letters*, vol. 1, p. 568.

[80] Aveling, *The Handle and the Axe*, p. 64.

[81] Questier, *Conversion, Politics and Religion*, p. 80.

[82] *The First Motive of T. H. Maister of Arts and lately minister, to suspect the integrity of his religions ... [with] an appendix intituled, Try before you trust, wherein some notable untruths of D. Field, and D. Morton are discovered* (1609).

[83] See *HMC* (75) Downshire, vol. 3, pp. 31, 33 and 56.

[84] Rev. John Sanford to Sir Thomas Edmondes, 6 March 1610/11, *Court and Times*, vol. 1, p. 108.

[85] Theophilus Higgons, *A Sermon Preached at Pauls Crosse* (1611), p. 49.

sermons of recantation were common, although none seems to have attracted as much attention as Higgons.

Appended to Higgons' sermon was Richard Sheldon's book *Certain General Reasons*, in which the former student at the Jesuit College at Rome writes in defence of the Oath of Allegiance. Soon after Sheldon proclaimed himself a Protestant, he was made a royal chaplain, and granted the degree of Doctor of Divinity (honorary) from Cambridge.[86] The publication of the two works together is an indication of how these conversions were presented as part of a broader phenomenon. John Chamberlain's letters of early 1612 are full of news describing Roman Catholic priests recanting their faith, and supporting James in his writing against Vorstius. Among these was John Copley, son of Sir Thomas Copley, one of the better known recusants of the Elizabethan age, who had himself converted from Protestantism early in Elizabeth's reign. The younger Copley was educated at Douai and came into England as a Jesuit in the 1590s. After frequent imprisonments he was converted to the Church of England in 1611, and in 1612 published *Doctrinall and Morall Observations concerning Religion*, wherein he explains his decision.[87] Also converting in these years was John Salkeld, with whom James seems to have taken a very personal role. From a Cumberland family, Salkeld had studied with the Jesuits in Spain and Portugal before accepting a mission to England. Captured by 1612, he eventually embraced the Church of England, reportedly after several conferences with the king.[88]

While James and his bishops might celebrate such figures as Higgons and Sheldon, the reality was that such conversions were offset by a significant number of English clergy leaving for Rome during these same years. The case of Benjamin Carier is particularly noteworthy because of his high position in the church and relative closeness to the king. In 1602 he had been created doctor of divinity, and in the following year appointed one of James' royal chaplains; in addition to later becoming a canon of Canterbury Cathedral, he was also named one of the original fellows of James' planned Chelsea College. Thus, when his desire for rapprochement with the Church of Rome was taken one step further by his abandoning the Church of England, it was a major blow for King James. In 1613 Carier journeyed to Spa, a popular resort for ill English folk, but also suspected as a major centre for Roman Catholic conversion.[89] From there rumours began to circulate that Carier was joining

---

[86] Sheldon was eventually to fall from royal grace in 1622, with an ill-timed sermon attacking the papacy.

[87] Davie, "Prêtre et Pasteur", pp. 403–21.

[88] *DNB.* Joseph Hall suggests that it was through reading the king's writings (*A Holy Panegyrick* [1613], p. 64).

[89] See Abbot to Trumbull, 10 March 1613/4, *HMC* (75) Downshire, vol. 4, p. 379. Joseph Hall, *Quo Vadis?* (1617), describes it as a place where men "can freely quaffe of the puddle of popish superstition" (sig. A4v). The earl of Argyll had also used a trip to Spa as an opportunity for his flight to the Church of Rome.

the Roman church; James ordered him to return to England, but in response received a letter from Carier, later printed, that acknowledged his acceptance of the Roman Church as the true church.[90] Carier's treatise not only defends his own move but encourages James to separate himself from the Calvinists and Puritans, and bring the Church of England into reconciliation with Rome. Carier had made similar, if more modest, arguments in a 1612 sermon, and throughout the treatise he presents his conversion as a gradual one.

Before sending his letter to James, Carier had written to Isaac Casaubon, a most respected French theologian, then living under James' patronage in England, enquiring about the possibility of reconciliation; it seems that Casaubon did not inform the king of this letter, but warned Carier that James "was resolved to have noe societie with the Church of Rome uppon any condition whatsoever".[91] Casaubon did attempt to intercede with James on Carier's behalf, but seemingly without success.[92] While Carier's argument to James is chiefly in reference to the theology and liturgy of the Church of England, he also appeals to James on a more personal level. He suggests that James' mother, Queen Mary, is praying with others in heaven for his conversion, and he reminds James that unlike Elizabeth he is not dependent on the Protestant settlement for his position as king.[93] Like later ecumenists such as de Dominis, Carier calls upon James to play a leading role by overseeing "a conference of learned and moderate men on eather side".[94] However, Carier's hopes of joining James in ecumenical mediation were quickly dashed.

Carier's conversion has far more credibility than many others; while the royal chaplain George Hakewill charged that his fellow cleric had been motivated by career disappointments,[95] Carier left behind a secure position in England for no clear rewards on the continent.[96] His claim that his illness forced him to consider last things and ultimately accept Roman claims is substantiated by his death less than nine months later. Carier's then is nearly a

[90] Benjamin Carier, *A Treatise Written by Mr. Doctour Carier* [1614?]. In 1615, another work of Carier's appeared, *A Copy of a Letter, written by M. Doctour Carier beyond Seas, to some particular friends in England* (*STC* 4621), this seems to have been published by those friends of Carier in England, and it also included "certaine collections found in his Closet". When Grey Brydges, fifth Lord Chandos, travelled to Spa in the summer of 1612, Chamberlain ironically commented "that yt is like to prove, and serve a turne hereafter for a holy as well as a healthfull pilgrimage".
[91] *A Treatise*, p. 18.
[92] Casaubon to Carier, 11 Nov. 1613, *Epistolae* (1709), pp. 547–8.
[93] *A Treatise*, p. 20.
[94] *A Treatise*, p. 33.
[95] Questier, *Conversion, Politics and Religion*, p. 43.
[96] Questier, p. 49, cites Carier as an example of the complexities of motivation behind conversion. See also his "Crypto-Catholicism, Anti-Calvinism and Conversion at the Jacobean Court: The Enigma of Benjamin Carier", *Journal of Ecclesiastical History* 47 (1996): 45–64.

death-bed conversion, but one where there is the hard evidence of his writings explaining and substantiating the move. Archbishop Abbot's letters to William Trumbull are heavy with disdain for the recent apostate; he was quick to downplay the significance of the event: "This dr. for many years hath not been held sound, so that we shall lose nothing by his departure."[97] However, his delight at the conversion of Anthony Clarke, canon of Ghent Cathedral, and comment that they now "had one come that would answer D. Carier", indicates that the defection was a major blow.[98] In a later letter Abbot suggests that "He [Carier] hoped to have been wooed to return, but we hold him a faithless hypocrite", and predicts "it will not be long before he pours out all the venom he can against this church and state".[99] However, Carier's *Treatise* is only venomous against what he calls the Calvinist and Puritan schismatics who are attempting to lead the church away from its theological roots. The work was responded to by George Hakewill.[100] Carier's *Treatise* was reprinted a number of times, including as late as 1649 and 1687, where appended to it was a list of converts to Roman Catholicism. Thus, it would seem that Carier's conversion continued to have a symbolic force within the struggle between Rome and Canterbury long after the death of both "Carrier and King".

Also worth considering in this context is the case of John Donne, who famously moved from being a gentleman Roman Catholic to a successful priest and then dean within the Church of England. Many biographers, including R. C. Bald, have assumed that Donne was unquestionably participating in the Church of England from early on. For biographers the years leading up to 1615 involve a struggle between a court career and a church one. Bald also seems to recognize Donne's questioning of his spiritual worthiness, but leaves this relatively unexplored. The recent work of Dennis Flynn suggests that Donne maintained his Roman Catholic allegiances far longer. Even Bald's account, however, recognizes that there was considerable surprise and suspicion over his taking of orders in 1615. For example, Donne notes in a letter that the countess of Bedford "had more suspicion of my calling, a better memory of my past life, then I had thought her nobility could have admitted".[101] Donne on a number of occasions makes reference to his "infirmity" as a barrier to ordination. Could this be in reference to his lingering Roman leanings? Also striking is the favour granted Donne upon his ordination, and the resentment and suspicion of this on the part of some others. In the year following his ordination he was made a royal chaplain and

---

[97] 9 September 1613, *HMC* (75) Downshire, vol. 4, p. 194. See Fincham and Lake, "The Ecclesiastical Policy of James I" for the suggestion that Carier was driven from England by Abbot and John King, bishop of London.

[98] Questier, *Conversion, Politics and Religion*, p. 350.

[99] 10 March 1613/14, *HMC* (75) Downshire, vol. 4, pp. 331–2.

[100] *An Answere to a Treatise Written by Dr. Carier* (1616), STC 12610.

[101] Donne to Sir H[enry] G[oodyer], *Life and Letters*, vol. 2, p. 73.

a doctor of divinity, at King James' insistence, and despite Cambridge's resistance. There were also rumours that Donne had been granted by James the reversion of the deanery of Canterbury.[102] Such success and resentment is similar to that experienced by Alabaster, whom Donne had noted in that letter of 1614. Future biographical work on Donne should consider him within this broader context of conversion.

FEMALE CONVERTS

To this point, all the converts I have discussed were male, but the terms of religious allegiance were markedly different for the women of the time. Restricted to a more private domain, women of James' reign had less political incentive to convert – they could not expect positions in church or state for their actions, and this same private realm seems to have left them freer to make the decision to convert. It was well known that in many families the husband conformed to the Church of England, while the wife remained recusant. Enforcement of the recusancy laws against women was possible but frequently not pursued.[103] James as king was notoriously uninterested in women; his wife Queen Anne was long known to harbour an inner allegiance to the Church of Rome, and James did relatively little in response. However, James recognized the role of women in propagating Roman Catholicism, lashing out at them as "the nourishers of papistry in this kingdom".[104]

Ironically, it was the female relatives of the duke of Buckingham whose religious commitment most interested the king. Buckingham's mother, styled the duchess of Buckingham, was a famous convert to Rome, and his wife Katherine Manners had been converted to Protestantism by Abbot before her marriage, but was to return to the ancient faith upon his death. According to Aveling, Buckingham "also had a sister, sister-in-law and niece who were all converts".[105] The duchess of Buckingham announced in 1622 her intention of joining the Church of Rome. A series of Protestant-Catholic debates were held in response to this, in which James played a personal role by disputing with the Jesuit, John Percy, better known as Fisher.[106] Her reconversion in response to

---

[102] R. C. Bald, *John Donne, A Life* (New York: OUP, 1970), pp. 307–9.

[103] A 1606 statute against recusancy had included a special section on female recusants (Questier, *Conversion, Politics and Religion*, p. 105).

[104] Sir Thomas Wynne to Carleton, 14 February 1618/19, *Court and Times*, vol. 2, p. 135. Cf. Lorkin to Puckering, 16 February 1618/19, *Court and Times*, vol. 2, p. 138.

[105] *The Handle and the Axe*, p. 124.

[106] See Timothy Wadkins, "King James I Meets John Percy, S. J. (25 May 1622)", *Recusant History* 19 (1988): 146. This event should be compared with the debate staged in June 1623 at the house of Sir Humphrey Linde to convince Edward Buggs to remain Protestant. Participating in this were John Percy, John Sweet, Daniel Featley and Francis White (Questier, *Conversion, Politics and Religion*, p. 28).

these debates was widely noted, and her motives held up to question: "The countesse of Buckingham hath recanted again and is come home to her mother church, and goes duly to the sermons in the chappell. Goode Dr. White our lecturer at Paules and the bishop of St. Davids Dr. Laud have the honor of reducing her, but the world sayes the daunger of leaving the court was the greatest and most pregnant motive."[107] As with Arundel, her taking of communion in the King's Chapel was a highly symbolic act: "The Countess of Buckingham received, on Sunday, in the King's Chapel, with both her daughters (though they had received before) and some others; and, for reward of her devotion and conformity, some say, she had a present of £2000."[108]

CONTINENTAL CHURCHMEN AND SCHOLARS

In addition to internal convertites, there was in James' reign an ongoing struggle for the allegiance of continental churchmen and scholars. Venice proved a particularly rich fishing ground for the English: because of its struggles with the Vatican in the period 1606–10 and the resulting papal interdict, Venice and its churchmen were more open to Protestant contact and influence than most Roman Catholic nations. Both Henry Wotton, the English ambassador in Venice for most of James' reign, and his chaplain, William Bedell, cultivated contacts among Venetian churchmen, encouraging them in their quarrel against the pope. In a 1619 letter to James, Wotton describes himself as taking the particular role of "secret semination" in the Protestant struggle to win converts in Italy.[109] Such negotiations were fraught with danger: in 1610, a Venetian Franciscan named Fulgentio was executed in Rome, the chief charge against him being that he had negotiated with the English ambassador, Wotton, to find Protestant sanctuary in England, a negotiation that Wotton denied.[110] Bedell translated the Book of Common Prayer into Italian, as well as James' *Apologie* and *Premonition*,[111] and through his influence such scholars as Paolo Sarpi – widely celebrated in Protestant Europe for his resistance to the Pope – became familiar with the chief works

---

[107] Chamberlain to Carleton, 8 June 1622, *Chamberlain Letters*, vol. 2, p. 439. Another writer notes that she is "said to be reclaimed", from being a "flat Papist" (Letter to Mead, 31 May 1622, *Court and Times*, vol. 2, p. 312).

[108] Chamberlain to Carleton, 22 June 1622, *Chamberlain Letters*, vol. 2, p. 441.

[109] *Life and Letters*, vol. 2, p. 178.

[110] Thomas Wharton Jones, *A True Relation of the Life and Death of . . . William Bedell*, Camden Society, new series, no. 4 (rpt. New York: Johnson, 1965), pp. 112–13. This Fulgentio should not be confused with Fulgentio the Servite, friend of Paolo Sarpi, who spent considerable time with Wotton and his chaplain, William Bedell.

[111] Bedell also mentions Sir Edwin Sandys' *Speculum Europae*, and "the third Homily of Chrysostome touching Lazarus" among the works he translated while in Venice (Letter to Samuel Ward, 30 November, 1613, in *Two Biographies of William Bedell*, ed. E. S. Shuckburgh [Cambridge: CUP, 1902], p. 254).

of English religious controversy.[112] A later letter from Wotton to Charles suggests that James was kept closely informed of the chaplain's contact with Sarpi.[113] Sarpi himself would have been the greatest catch, but while he became friend and correspondent to a wide range of significant Protestant controversialists, he never made the hoped-for final break with Rome.[114] During the Venetian Interdict Wotton claimed that Sarpi was Protestant at heart, and sending a portrait of the Venetian father to James, wrote "it may be likewise some pleasure unto his Majesty to behold a sound Protestant, as yet in the habit of a friar; which I affirm unto Lordship, not out of that vanity (which maketh Jesuits register every great wit in their catalogue), but upon assurance thereof given me by my chaplain, who hath sounded him in the principal points of our religion".[115] The English embassy in Venice also played an important role in channelling books on the Venetian situation, particularly those of Sarpi, to England for translation and publication there.[116] Even the Venetian ambassador in England, Giovanbattista Foscarini, was suspected by some, including James, to be secretly Protestant.[117] Writing in 1613, Bedell suggested that there were those who if they could expect reward in England would "transport their bodyes as their minds already, into these parts".[118]

Among the earliest Venetians who converted outright and successfully went to England was Giovanni Francesco Biondi.[119] While his conversion may have come about prior to contact with Wotton and Bedell, they certainly assisted in his eventual seeking of refuge in England in 1609.[120] James bestowed on him a pension of one hundred pounds a year, and made significant use of him as a diplomat on the continent. Unlike some other *convertitos* he seems to have been unwavering in his commitment to England and Protestantism, and proved of real use to King James. Of most significance for our purposes was his attendance as a representative of James at the Huguenot Assembly at Grenoble in 1615.

Not all *convertitos* worked out as well as Biondi for the Church of England. In the summer of 1612 two Carmelite friars, Giovanni Maria de Franchis (also Genochi)and Guilio Cesare Vandoni (also de Vinnes and Vanini), proclaimed

---

[112] John Leon Lievsay, *Venetian Phoenix: Paolo Sarpi and Some of his English Friends (1606–1700)* (Lawrence, Kan.: UP of Kansas, 1973), p. 21. See also Jones, *A True Relation*, p. 25.

[113] This letter is reproduced, without date, in Jones, *A True Relation*, p. 25.

[114] See David Wootton, *Paolo Sarpi: between Renaissance and Enlightenment* for the most recent and thorough consideration of Sarpi's beliefs and commitments.

[115] Wotton to the earl of Salisbury, 13 September 1607 [Ven. Style], *Life and Letters*, vol. 1, p. 299

[116] Lievsay, *Venetian Phoenix*, p. 22.

[117] Biondi to Carleton, 17 March 1612/13, *CSPD, 1611–18*, p. 176.

[118] Letter to Samuel Ward, 30 November 1613, in *Two Biographies of William Bedell*, ed. E. S. Shuckburgh, p. 254.

[119] Pearsall Smith, in his *Sir Henry Wotton, Life and Letters*, vol. 2, pp. 463–4 gives a short biography of Biondi.

[120] Wotton introduces him to James in a letter of 16 January 1609, *Life and Letters*, vol. 1, pp. 446–7.

conversion. Assisted in escaping by Carleton, ambassador in Venice at the time, in England they were "extraordinarily entertained so that they wanted nothing".[121] Vandoni was hosted by the archbishop of Canterbury, de Franchis by the archbishop of York.[122] A few months later Abbot reported that "The two honest men sent over by Carleton do very well", and that the one had presented to the king an Italian treatise against Rome.[123] Their sermons of recantation, like that of Higgons, attracted a great audience, including Francis Bacon.[124] De Franchis offered an epithalamium on the marriage of Princess Elizabeth and Count Frederick, which attacked the pope as the Antichrist.[125] However, less than two years later the two recanted of their conversion; Vandoni was taken into custody, and proclaimed hopes for a martyrdom, but regretted that King James was "rather religious than fanatical";[126] later he managed to escape, like de Franchis, and fled for the continent. The English response was largely one of disdain and dismissal. Thomas Lake commented that "I never had anie grate confidence in renegados",[127] and Dudley Carleton speculated that "they have been practiced withal and regained by great promises, since their conversion was held no small disgrace to their monastical orders".[128] Calvin F. Senning has shown that the Spanish embassy played a leading role in the reconciliation of the two with Rome.[129] Abbot ends his description of the affair by writing that "It will make us hereafter not too hastily to give trust to such hypocrites."[130] Abbot's enthusiasm may have been dampened, but the exodus continued, encouraged both by the zeal of Henry Wotton, who returned as ambassador to Venice in 1616, and by James' generous, if sporadic, response.

Some Italian churchmen who came to England – or desired to come – were more equivocal about their ecclesiastical allegiance. The Neapolitan Jacopo Marta received some pension or support from England while remaining in Italy as a Professor at Padua. In 1616 he promulgated a bizarre plan to have James foster a council of Greek bishops, and perhaps even grant sanctuary to them – all this in an attempt to undermine the authority of the Roman church. Wotton respectfully points out in a letter to James that "if your

[121] Abbot to Trumbull, 10 March 1613/14, *HMC* (75) Downshire, vol. 4, p. 331. This is the fullest account of the story of the two Carmelites, but is written from after their return to Rome. The correspondence between Carleton and Chamberlain shows the events unfolding.
[122] Giulio Cesare Vandoni to Carleton, 9 October 1612, *CSPD, 1611–18*, p. 151. Vandoni to Isaac Wake, 9 October 1612, *CSPD, 1611–18*, p. 151.
[123] Abbot to Carleton, 24 February 1612/13, *CSPD, 1611–18*, p. 171.
[124] Chamberlain to Carleton, 2 July 1612, *Chamberlain Letters*, vol. 1, p. 363.
[125] Senning, "Vanini and the Diplomats", p. 226.
[126] Biondi to Carleton, 18 Feb. 1614/15, *CSPD, 1611–18*, p. 274. This letter is erroneously dated 1614/15 in the calendar.
[127] Lake to Carleton, 27 January 1613/14, SP 14/76/9.
[128] Carleton to Chamberlain, 25 Feb. 1613/14, *Dudley Carleton to John Chamberlain*, p. 158.
[129] "Vanini and the Diplomats", pp. 228–9.
[130] *HMC* (75) Downshire, vol. 4, p. 331.

Majesty shall but once open your arm of protection, I must crave the liberty to think that all the colleges and hospitals of your kingdoms will not hold them". Wotton hoped to find means to "employ him in some things of more use and possibility".[131]

Some time before, one Ascanio Balliano left the Capuchins, and took a living in the Church of England, and an English wife.[132] Like the two Carmelites, his new allegiance did not last long: in January 1617, John Chamberlain reported that "Here is a rumor that the Italian preacher Ascanio is run away beeing as is saide enticed by one Grimaldi kinsman of Spinolas whom he accompanied on his way as far as Dover, and since his wife nor frends have no newes of him."[133] A few months later, in the summer of 1617, Tomasso Cerronio (also known as Letonio and Stanislao Ferrerio) convinced Wotton that he had learned of important details of a Jesuit plot to assassinate King James, which he must deliver in person to the king. The events leading to his flight to England are described by Wotton in a letter to the Privy Council from 30 May 1617.[134] Cerronio was a big fish, the Jesuit provost, or *praepositus*, of San Fedele in Milan. Wotton seems to have been of two minds about the affair, calling it a subject "as high as ever befell any foreign minister",[135] but also admitting that he finds himself "diversely distracted in mine own conceit touching the event".[136] However, he put his misgivings aside, perhaps desperate for some success to overcome his ill repute at the English court,[137] and allowed Cerronio to continue. Rumours of the Italian's endeavour spread quickly, breeding much speculation. Carleton, now ambassador at The Hague, reports that "The world is full of casting and inquiring touching Fabritio's [Wotton's] great affair",[138] but is his usual dismissive self in reference to Wotton: "I believe the issue will be some speculative Italian project about religion."[139] When Cerronio finally arrived in England in the late summer of 1617, James was in Scotland, and refused to see the Jesuit. Instead, the king insisted that Cerronio be interviewed by a small part of the Privy Council, including Abbot and Sir Ralph Winwood, one of the secretaries of state. Winwood reports that James refused personal access "first because the discourse which he had made (as we say in our proverb) had neither head nor tayle; secondly because I [Winwood] had discovered . . . that he was a man of a filthy and unclean life, defiling himself

---

[131] Wotton to James I, 30 July 1616, *Life and Letters*, vol. 2, p. 99. Cf. also "Il Dottor Marta" to Winwood [26 February] 1617, *HMC* 45 (duke of Buccleuch and Queensbury), vol. 1, p. 182. Earlier in 1613 Marta had published a letter calling for a general council of the church; see Patterson, *King James VI and I and the Reunion of Christendom*, pp. 119–20.

[132] Lionello to the Doge and Senate, 27 January 1616/17, *CSPV, 1615–17*, p. 421.

[133] Chamberlain to Carleton, 18 January 1617, *Chamberlain Letters*, vol. 2, p. 50.

[134] For the account by the Venetian ambassador, see *CSPV*, vol. 14, pp. 530–3 and 537–8.

[135] Recipient unknown, 30 May 1617, *Life and Letters*, vol. 2, p. 119.

[136] Wotton to Sir Ralph Winwood, 14 July 1617, *Life and Letters*, vol. 2, p. 120.

[137] *CSPV*, 14, p. 574.

[138] Carleton to Chamberlain, 18/28 July 1617, *Court and Times*, vol. 1, p. 22.

[139] Carleton to Trumbull, 10/20 June 1617, *HMC* 75 (Downshire), vol. 6, p. 201.

with such boyes as he could procure to satisfie his lustfull appetite".[140] While waiting for some resolution Cerronio was reported to spend his time reading Calvin's *Institutes* at Lambeth.[141] However, the Venetian ambassador reported that he intended to stay in England without changing his religion,[142] and it seems likely that at this point Cerronio was keeping his options open. When he finally revealed the details of the plot, they were dismissed by the English as groundless, and the praepositus sent on his way with a hundred pounds.[143]

Wotton continued his dogged pursuit of Italian churchmen in spite of such setbacks; in November of 1617 he wrote to Sir Thomas Lake, secretary of state that "an Italian bishop, and of another person of great learning (as yet both unnominated), who as they say, *di puro zelo* and *di certa scienze*, are resolved to leave this Church, and would retire into his Majesty's protection".[144] Nothing more seems to come of this *convertine*.

The fervour of Wotton and Carleton is clear, as is the suspicion of Abbot, but what of James' role in these attempts to lure Italian churchmen? The best indication of his stance is to be gained from a letter of Winwood to Wotton, possibly concerning an attempt to procure Paolo Sarpi. Winwood presents a careful openness on James' part; at this time at least (23 January 1617) he does not want to be perceived as encouraging *convertitos*, but he also wants to accept those who make the move of their own accord:

> [his Majesty] hath taken this resolution, not to write until he shall understand how those parties stand resolved, either to continue there where now they live, or to repair into England; wherein his Majesty's pleasure is that you carry yourself with that moderation, that neither by encouragement they be disheartened, if out of their own free motion, for the discharge of their consciences, they shall resolve to retire themselves under the safeguard of his Majesty's protection. For whensoever they shall come, his Majesty will be pleased to see them furnished with that complete provision which may give them cause of satisfaction, and make them acknowledge themselves perpetually beholding both to his goodness and God's providence.[145]

James' caution was likely both political and economic in nature. One or two notable churchmen had great symbolic value; a host of minor Italian priests and monks demonstrated the reality of declining marginal utility, and could prove expensive. In a time when emigration was exceptional, there were limits to the ability of any country to accept religious refugees. This was particularly the case with churchmen, who would be reliant on the public

[140] Winwood to Trumbull, 14 September 1617, *HMC 75* (Downshire), vol. 6, p. 284.
[141] Winwood to Wotton, 14 August 1617, quoted in *Life and Letters*, vol. 2, p. 123.
[142] 11 August 1617, *CSPV*, 14, p. 573.
[143] *Sir Henry Wotton: Life and Letters*, vol. 2, p. 123n. The judgement of Chamberlain is that the whole affair simply made Wotton look foolish; see his letter to Carleton, 11 Oct. 1617, *Chamberlain Letters*, vol. 2, pp. 101–11.
[144] 10 November 1617, *Life and Letters*, vol. 2, p. 124.
[145] From *SP Ven*, quoted in *Life and Letters*, vol. 2, p. 100n.

purse, and, as additional competitors for positions, liable to arouse resentment and envy. Biondi might bring real diplomatic abilities; Jaspar Despotine, an early convert of Wotton and Bedell, could pay his own way as a practising physician – but a host of minor Italian friars could become burdensome. Already with the arrival of the two Carmelites in 1612, Chamberlain warned Carleton of the lack of enthusiasm in England:

> I doubt you will reap no great thanks on either side. For, I find our bishops here not very fond of such guests, and think they might have enough of them, if they could provide them maintenance; so that unless they be very eminent, and men of mark, they shall find little regard after a short time.[146]

When some of those friars proved less than loyal or constant, it threw the whole phenomenon into disrepute.

The case of Marco Antonio de Dominis, archbishop of Spalato, deserves special attention, for he was the most noteworthy of the Italian *convertitos*, and his fate, which is still not clear, involved King James to a significant measure. Above all, his case demonstrates how the business of *convertitos* was not a static one in James' reign, but an ever-shifting attempt to find a solid place to stand in response to changing religious and political circumstances.

Analysis of de Dominis' story is complicated by his later English reputation; the *DNB* summary is typical: "His whole life, indeed, seems to have been one of dishonesty." These English accounts read his early actions all in the light of his later return to Rome, seeing every step as a matter of opportunism. However, this negative view of him did not appear until 1621, even in private letters. Thus, a bare outlining of de Dominis' movements is a worthwhile way to begin. After repeated disputes with the papacy over advancement and jurisdiction, de Dominis sought refuge in England in 1616, publishing major works explaining his departure and recounting the ways in which the Court of Rome was overstepping its jurisdiction. After four and a half years of moderate success in England, de Dominis returned to the continent in 1622, was imprisoned by the Inquisition the following year, and died in a Roman prison in 1624.[147]

Such a bare outline belies the questions surrounding de Dominis' career; for each movement was variously interpreted. Already in December of 1614 de Dominis was considering leaving his post for England; a letter of Abbot to

---

[146] 17 June 1612, *Chamberlain Letters*, vol. 1, p. 357.

[147] The best English studies of de Dominis are David L. Clark, "Marco Antonio de Dominis and James I: The Influence of a Venetian Reformer on the Church of England", *Papers of the Michigan Academy of Science, Arts and Letters* 53 (1968): 219–30; Noel Malcolm, *De Dominis (1560–1624): Venetian, Anglican, Ecumenist and Relapsed Heretic* (London: Strickland and Scott, 1984); W. B. Patterson, *King James VI and I and the Reunion of Christendom* (Cambridge: CUP, 1997), pp. 220–59. My concern is primarily with the evolving English response to him.

Carleton warns that the bishop cannot expect a similarly high-ranking position in England.[148] Both Carleton and Wotton, as English ambassadors to Venice, worked closely with de Dominis to bring him to England. In letters to Carleton, John Chamberlain always refers to him as "your archbishop", suggesting that Carleton had some association or friendship with him. Carleton also mentions that "Fabritio [Wotton] gives this good old man the title of my spiritual son, and I shall be glad he may so prove that I may own him."[149] Wotton, upon taking over the ambassadorship at Venice, continued to court de Dominis. In July 1616 he writes to King James "The Archbishop of Spalatro is resolved to endure no longer the idolatrous fooleries of this Church, but will within a week or such a matter begin his journey towards your Majesty; of whose favour I have given him fresh assurance."[150]

After his flight to England, de Dominis was immediately attacked by Roman Catholic writers. According to Wotton, his "desertion the Jesuits take much to the heart",[151] and

> the Pope is extremely nettled with the Archbishop of Spalatroe's defection, of whom I must needs say somewhat for his Majesty's entertainment. They know not how to blemish the matter seriously, and therefore I think they study how to make it ridiculous . . . To which purpose they have cast out a voice (spread farther than a man would imagine) that the King intendeth to make him a Pope, and to erect about him a College of Cardinals.[152]

Dudley Carleton reports that "The papists in this place [The Hague] (whereof here are some very passionate) have raised many scandalous reports against him, some saying that he had a wife and children at Venice", and that "Others charge the poor old man with an Italian peccadillo and will have it that he forsook his country for the love of Robin Barnes, who they saw here so diligent and serviceable about him."[153]

De Dominis arrived in England in early December of 1616: within a month churchmen were being shuffled to make room for him as dean of Windsor, and King James was typically lavish in his gift-giving, presenting him "with a fayre basen and ewre with a paire of liverie pots worth 140[li]".[154] De Dominis responded appropriately: drawing on what he must have known was the traditional iconography favoured by James, he wrote to Carleton that he found "like the Queen of Sheba, the greatness of Solomon more than ever it

---

[148] *CSPD, 1611–18*, p. 262.

[149] 17/27 December 1616, *Carleton to Chamberlain*, p. 229.

[150] 30 July 1616, *Life and Letters*, vol. 2, p. 100.

[151] Wotton to Sir Ralph Winwood, *Life and Letters*, vol. 2, p. 120. He speculates here as well that Cerronio might be intending to "revoke" de Dominis.

[152] Wotton to Sir Ralph Winwood, 16/26 January 1617, *Life and Letters*, vol. 2, p. 110. Cf. his letter to Sir Robert Naunton, 2 May 1619, *Life and Letters*, vol. 2, p. 171.

[153] 26 November to 2 December 1616, *Carleton to Chamberlain*, p. 226.

[154] Chamberlain to Carleton, 4 January 1617, *Chamberlain Letters*, vol. 2, p. 47. See also Fuller, *Church History*, vol. 5, p. 510.

was ever reported".[155] Both his books and person attracted a great deal of attention and admiration in England; his *Profectionis consilium*, an explanation of his motivation in leaving the Church of Rome, was published in both English and Latin shortly after his arrival, and his major work, *De Republica Ecclesiastica*, was widely anticipated.[156] Carleton reports in December 1616 that while the bishop's "Manifests" [*Profectionis consilium*] are being burned in Rome, they are "here [the Hague] translated into all languages".[157] Overall, the English response to de Dominis at the time of his coming over was unfailingly positive, both in public and private commentary: the worst that was said of him was the Roman Catholic Tobie Matthew's comment that "He is very fatt, but otherwise I have not in my life seene a more gallante presence of man."[158] George Carew described him as "a reverend and learnd Bishoppe" and "a man of great estimation".[159] Archbishop Abbot expressed clearly the significance of de Dominis' conversion for the English: "It is indeed a greate example that a learned man of his age, who hath been a Bishop twenty yeares, and for many of them an Archbishop who in Dalmatia had nine Suffragens under him, should by the instinct of Gods spiritt without perswasion of any man, attaine to the knowledge of Gods truth, and so resolvedly come out of Babilon."[160] The English also anticipated that de Dominis would prove useful in the ongoing war of the pen with the supporters of the papacy: Abbot anticipates a major work of de Dominis "which shall give the Pope a blow of extraordinary nature",[161] and Carleton suggests that de Dominis also will be effective in inter-Protestant disputes "wherein he doth use arguments of temper and moderation".[162]

A letter from de Dominis to Carleton suggests that James was taking a personal interest in having the *Manifesto* printed in English, as well "as his work on an ecclesiastical republic", which would share James' vision of reuniting Christendom.[163] In spite of this enthusiasm for the advent of the archbishop, David L. Clark's suggestion that de Dominis' arrival led to the development of a more high-church liturgy in the royal chapels and cathedrals rests on very slender evidence.[164] However, the Venetian ambassador did report that under de Dominis' encouragement, James

---

[155] De Dominis to Carleton, 31 December 1616, *CSPD, 1611–18*, p. 417.
[156] Lievsay, *Venetian Phoenix*, p. 30.
[157] 17/27 December 1616, *Dudley Carleton to John Chamberlain*, p. 229. Wotton also reports on Italian interest in the writings of de Dominis. Letter to James I (?) June 1619, *Life and Letters*, vol. 2, p. 178.
[158] Tobie Matthew to George Gage, 21 August 1617, *HMC* 75 (Downshire), vol. 6, p. 262.
[159] Letter to Sir Thomas Roe, 18 January 1616/7, SP 14/90/48v.
[160] Abbot to Trumbull, 19 December 1616, *HMC* 75 (Downshire), vol. 6, p. 71.
[161] Abbot to Trumbull, 26 June 1617, *HMC* 75 (Downshire), vol. 6, p. 211.
[162] 17/27 December 1616, *Carleton to Chamberlain*, p. 229.
[163] De Dominis to Carleton, 31 December 1616, *CSPD, 1611–18*, p. 417.
[164] "Marco Antonio de Dominis and James I", pp. 222–3.

was considering the introduction of auricular confession, "as a thing that would prove very advantageous politically".[165]

The first notes of tension between de Dominis and his hosts emerge early in 1617; Chamberlain reports that de Dominis is eager to have his books printed, but that they were "stayed by the greatest authoritie for that they do not in all points jumpe with our Tenets in matters of jurisdiction".[166] The difficulties between de Dominis and the English authorities developed for a variety of reasons: first, James' slowness in providing a living satisfactory to the former archbishop; secondly, envy towards de Dominis once that place was found; and finally an emerging recognition that de Dominis was not the Calvinist Protestant that they had originally thought.

On a number of occasions in mid-1617 Chamberlain laments the slowness with which de Dominis is being rewarded in England: he holds him up as an example of how Roman Catholics might be lured over by "fayre wordes",[167] and wishes that "he had some more certaintie of provision, but I heare (how truly I know not) that we are likely to have him preach shortly in the Italian church at Mercers chappell, which were too much abasing to do yt ordinarilie unles he desire yt".[168] Just over one year after his arrival, he presented a petition to the king, "wherin he complained that he was driven to live *alieno quadro*, and that in a countrie and place of such abundance [132] he should be *omnium egentissimus*".[169] In March of 1618 he finally received the long-promised mastership of the Savoy. However, de Dominis' pursuing of English offices began to arouse resentment in this year as well; Chamberlain reports that he "hath lost somwhat in the opinion of the world, by intruding himself into a parsonage that was in the guift of the Dean and Chapter of Windsor".[170] However, through 1619 the Venetian ambassador is still commenting on the prestige and power of the former archbishop.[171] By 1620 most of Chamberlain's comments on de Dominis are negative ones; he no longer refers to him as the "poor man" or "your archbishop" in his letters to Carleton. Some of this may have been a personal conflict: Chamberlain had been angered by the former archbishop's rude treatment of Lady Carleton.

Of greater significance than either de Dominis' disappointment at the rewards offered or the resentment of various English figures was a deep-lying discrepancy between the theological and ecclesiastical views of de Dominis and a major segment of the English church authorities. De Dominis' quarrel

---

[165] 7 June 1619, *CSPV, 1617–19*, p. 557.
[166] Chamberlain to Carleton, 8 February 1617, *Chamberlain Letters*, vol. 2, p, 51. In the next sentence Chamberlain mentions the publication of the king's works.
[167] 21 June 1617, *Chamberlain Letters*, vol. 2, p. 82.
[168] Vol. 2, p. 90. De Dominis did preach at Mercers Chapel on 30 Nov. 1617, if not earlier, printed as *STC* 7005.
[169] 17 January 1617/8, *Chamberlain Letters*, vol. 2, p. 132.
[170] 14 November 1618, *Chamberlain Letters*, vol. 2, p. 184.
[171] 18 April 1619, *CSPV, 1617–19*, p. 524; 7 June 1619, *CSPV, 1617–19*, p. 557.

had always been with the *Court* of Rome rather than the *Church* of Rome; like many Venetians he objected to the extension of papal authority at the expense of both bishops and states. Thus, his "Protestantism" was not that of such Calvinists as Archbishop Abbot; in fact de Dominis is best seen as an ecumenicist, whose hope was for a coming together of moderate Protestants with those Catholics who shared his concerns about papal powers. This vision is outlined in volume three of his *De Republica Ecclesiastica*.[172] De Dominis suggests that James must play a key role in convening a general council of the churches, one that would include not just Protestants, but also Orthodox and moderate Roman Catholics, a plan already put forward by Marta.[173] Given all this, conflict with Archbishop Abbot and other English churchmen who supported international Calvinism was inevitable.[174]

Eventually, these conflicts became public: "The archbishop of Spalato hath geven over preaching and taken his leave of the pulpit for broching straunge doctrine in seeking to prove in three or fowre sermons that the papists held no heresie, maintaining that he came not away from them to save his soule, but only that he might speake freely against their abuses."[175] Through the latter part of 1621 and the first part of 1622 these conflicts came to a head. On 16 January 1622 de Dominis expressed to James his intention to return to Rome, and in a sermon the next month at Mercers' Chapel he was noted to seem "well inclined towards the Roman Church".[176] There were soon rumours across Europe about his intentions: his old friend Carleton feared that the steps he was about to take amounted to suicide. In early February 1622 he was being kept prisoner in his own house in the Savoy, and there were rumours in March that he was to be sent to the Tower.[177] Wotton, in Venice, heard that the king of Spain had requested of the pope a safe conduct for de Dominis, with the promise that the king would make him bishop of Salerno. The pope had assented, but suggested a written safe conduct was unnecessary; both Wotton and Carleton were suspicious that it might be a ruse to lure him back.[178]

Whatever de Dominis' intentions and the reasons behind them, there was clearly enough substance for him to be convented before a group led by the

---

[172] Patterson, "The Peregrinations of Marco Antonio de Dominis", pp. 247–8.
[173] Patterson, "The Peregrinations of Marco Antonio de Dominis", p. 248.
[174] Clark, "Marco Antonio de Dominis and James I", p. 221, suggests that it was also inevitable that there be a conflict between de Dominis and James in the matter of church-state relations, as the theologian was concerned with "defend[ing] a constitutional republic and not the royal absolutism James was emulating".
[175] 6 June 1621, *Chamberlain Letters*, vol. 2, p. 379.
[176] Gardiner, *History of England, 1603–1642*, vol. 4, pp. 286–7; Thomas Locke to Carleton, 4 February 1621–2, *Court and Times*, vol. 2, p. 291.
[177] Letter to Rev. Joseph Mead, 2 February 1622, *Court and Times*, vol. 2, p. 295; letter to Mead, 1 March 1621/2, *Court and Times*, vol. 2, p. 233 [misdated in *Court and Times* as March 1622/23].
[178] Carleton to Chamberlain, 9 March 1622, *Court and Times*, vol. 2, p. 299; Wotton to Sir George Calvert, 6/16 March 1622.

archbishop of Canterbury on 30 March 1622. Two weeks later Chamberlain acknowledges that he does not have a great deal of information about the "conventing", but that de Dominis

> acknowledg[ed] that the generall tenets of our church are true and orthodox, but the practise and severall opinions of our private divines are not aunswerable, but rather savour of schisme; that his comming hither was for his safetie and to avoide the Popes indignation, whereas now there is a goode Pope whose eares are open to heare and redresse what is amisse.[179]

By mid-April, de Dominis had left England in the company of the emperor's ambassador, and headed for Rome. He was returning to the Rome of his friend Pope Gregory XV, not Pope Paul V, with whom he had his previous quarrel. Still there was widespread uncertainty about how he would be received there. Wotton provides an extended discussion on the various ideas about why he fled to Rome, and the use that was to be made of him:

> the question is, what use the Pope aims at of this man, that should thus increase his cherishments? Awhile there was a conceit (as I say in my letter) that he came with business from England; but that is absolutely vanished. The next was, that by his observations taken there of persons and humours, he might serve to direct well the young Roman emissaries. And this opinion increased by his going to the English College immediately after his having been with the Pope; but that was but to borrow a book . . . A third plainer sort of men there are, that think he shall only be employed in writing, and that therein both his use and himself shall end. For if they put him not only to a general *palinodia*, but to a punctual refutation of his own works, he will sink under that labour. Lastly, there is a conjecture made (and in this I dare concur upon the wager of my life, by circumstances nicely examined) that the scope of the Roman Court is, by his good treatment, and by his former familiarity with Maestro Paolo and Fulgentio, to bring them likewise into the net.[180]

While it is clear from this passage that de Dominis received some welcome in Rome, there are no clear answers about his role there. It was rumoured in London in March 1622/23 that "Our Archbishop of Spalato being heard by a consistory held for that purpose, is confined to a monastary at Monte Cassino, a day's journey from Rome."[181] The *Palinodia* mentioned by Wotton, entitled *M. A. de D. Sui Reditus ex Anglia consilium exponit*, was in circulation by April 1623, at which time Wotton sent a copy of it to Calvert. An English translation was produced at Douai in the same year.[182] In January 1623 he requested a better living in Rome,[183] but whatever success he was

---

[179] 13 April 1622, *Chamberlain Letters*, vol. 2, p. 431.
[180] To Sir George Calvert, 2/12 December 1622, *Life and Letters*, vol. 2, p. 252.
[181] Mead to Stuteville, 15 March 1622/23, *Court and Times*, vol. 2, p. 374.
[182] *Life and Letters*, vol. 2, p. 268.
[183] Patterson, "The Peregrinations of Marco Antonio de Dominis", p. 255.

enjoying ended with the death of Gregory XV in the summer of 1623. "By 17 April 1624, he was under suspicion of heresy" and imprisoned.[184]

W. B. Patterson's chapter on de Dominis in *King James VI and I and the Reunion of Christendom*, is the most insightful discussion of de Dominis' actions.[185] While recognizing the role of ambition in the cleric's career, he also highlights his commitment to a broad Christianity that quarrelled with Rome largely over matters of jurisdiction rather than theology or liturgy. His quarrel with Rome was that it trampled both on the rights of states as well as the rights of bishops. His taking up of residence in England was not so much a conversion as a translation to a nation free of the pope's interference. In England he had hoped for a climate of free inquiry that would lead to the eventual reunion of the Christian churches. This dream was eroded by the Roman Catholic-Protestant conflicts of the early 1620s, and he returned to Rome in a desperate hope that his old friend, now Pope Gregory XV, might pursue a more conciliatory papal policy. Such a step in 1617 might have been tolerated in England, but by 1622 the dividing lines were once again being more firmly drawn. By 1624 there was really no place for de Dominis anywhere in Europe, and Patterson suggests that ultimately he "died for an ecumenical ideal".[186]

At the time of de Dominis' departure there were whisperings that he had been tricked by the Spanish ambassador at London, Gondomar, into trusting the promises of Spain. However, it is also possible that de Dominis' flight was partially based on fear of growing Spanish influence in England. As a Spanish match for Prince Charles gathered momentum in the early 1620s de Dominis may have recognized the ramifications of such a marriage for him. *Détente* between the two powers would make such propagandists in England far less valuable. Rumours that Charles might himself adopt Catholicism at the marriage would certainly have concerned de Dominis. Thus, the churchman may have found himself stranded in the chasm between the two main forces in England at the time: the militant Protestants, who vehemently opposed the Spanish match, but whose theology repelled the ecumenism of de Dominis, and the supporters of a Spanish match who seemed willing to tolerate the Church of Rome, Jesuits, papal power and all.

While there were a few notable international converts to the English church after de Dominis, the dynamics of conversion had changed as the negotiations for the Spanish match went forward, and the conflict of the Thirty Years' War increased the chasm on the continent between Catholics and Protestants. This polarized situation made less likely the movement to a moderate anti-papal position by Catholic clerics. In England, until the collapse of the Spanish match in 1623, politically a movement toward Rome seemed more promising

---

[184] Ibid.
[185] pp. 220–59.
[186] p. 252.

than a movement in the other direction.[187] In his speech to parliament in January 1621, James assured the commons that he had "not grown cold" in his attitude toward papism, but his statement that his preachers "set a good example by their lives and win those whom they can",[188] seems rather mild. At the same time, the increasing marginalization of Archbishop Abbot meant that converts such as John Gee were at the service of a particular faction attempting to influence official behaviour rather than converting to a well-established centre of power.[189]

By late in his reign James' influence on the dynamics of conversion had come to an end, with Buckingham and Charles taking over control. The end of the proposed Spanish match seemed to promise a more militantly anti-Catholicism, but countering this was the personal sympathy of Buckingham for a wide range of members of the Church of Rome. With the marriage of Charles to the Roman Catholic Henrietta Maria a scant two months after his father's death, and the advent of her Roman priests and servants in England, conversion to the Church of Rome received a new impetus. James at least was not alive to watch this, and no rumours of a death-bed conversion plagued his reputation.

[187] Cogswell, *The Blessed Revolution*, p. 45, suggests that "the Catholic revival of 1622–23 remained one of the great taboo subjects for public discourse".
[188] *CSPV, 1619–21*, p. 581.
[189] Questier, *Conversion, Politics and Religion*, p. 357.

Chapter 7

THE SONGS OF DAVID:
KING JAMES AND THE PSALTER

AMONG James' earliest poetic endeavours was a versification of Psalm 104, which appeared in *Essayes of a Prentise* (1584). This psalm is described as "translated out of Tremellius", and being composed in an eight-line stanza would not have matched any of the common meter tunes then in use with the Psalms:

> To Jehova I all my lyfe shall sing,
> To sound his Name I ever still shall cair:
> It shall be sweit my thinking on that King:
> In him I shall be glaid for ever mair:
> O let the wicked be into no whair
> In earth. O let the sinfull be destroyde.
> Blesse him my soule who name Jehova bair:
> O blesse him now with notts that are enjoyde.

With this publication James began his life-long interest in psalm versification and the reform of the metrical Psalter used in the churches of England and Scotland. This chapter will consider the attempts, by both James and others, to fashion a new Psalter, and the attempt after his death to promote his version of the Psalms for use in the churches.

Psalm versification was a fairly common poetic exercise at the time, and the 104th, being rich in natural imagery, was a popular choice. James' tutor, George Buchanan, had produced a Latin version of it that had become famous across Europe. Thus, the publication of James' translation of this single psalm was by no means a signal that he intended a complete versification of the Psalter. Such an inclination was first hinted at only in his next collection of poetry, *His Maiesties Poeticall Exercises* (1591); if that collection were well received James would be moved "to haste the presenting unto thee, of my APOCALYPS, and also such nomber of the Psalmes as I have perfited: & incourage mee to the ending out of the rest".[1] How far James advanced in these efforts during his Scottish reign is unclear but in 1591 he

---

[1] *His Maiesties Poeticall Exercises at Vacant Houres* (Edinburgh, 1591), p. 3.

would complain that "scarslie but at stollen moments have I the leasure to blenk upon any paper, and yet not that, with free and unvexed spirit".[2] A surviving manuscript, with certain of his psalms in Scottish dialect and the signature "J. D. R. S.", meaning "Jacobus Dominus Rex Scotia", seems to indicate that he had completed at least twenty-eight of them while still in Scotland.[3] These versions are completely different from those that were finally published under James' name in 1631, and like Psalm 104 from *Essayes of a Prentise* do not conform to the meters usually found in the English and Scottish Psalter. They are most likely early Scottish experiments, which were then abandoned as James turned to forms more appropriate for congregational singing. Unfortunately, no other manuscript with a significant number of his psalms has come to light, and this has encouraged some scholars to conclude that the 1631 and 1636 publications were completely the work of Sir William Alexander, who, after James' death, was appointed to revise the king's psalms and prepare them for publication. While James' attempts at psalm versification were sporadic, he maintained throughout both his reigns the ideal of producing a new metrical version of the Psalter, that would be his legacy for the churches.

PSALMODY IN THE PROTESTANT TRADITION

The English and Scottish psalters were part of a movement throughout the Calvinist churches to render the Psalms in a metrical form appropriate for congregational song.[4] On the continent the Genevan psalter with texts translated by Clément Marot in a variety of meters was the best known and most celebrated of these. The Protestant exiles who returned to England with Elizabeth's accession promoted a similar use of the Psalms, and versifications largely by Thomas Sternhold and John Hopkins became the basis for the English psalter. In Scotland a psalter, also based partly on the work of Sternhold and Hopkins, appeared in 1564, and became the standard in the Scottish church until 1650. These psalms, while based on the work of a number of versifiers, became traditionally known as "Sternhold and Hopkins". They relied heavily on common meter (alternating tetrameter and

---

[2] Ibid.

[3] BL Old Royal MS 18B. XVI; it includes Psalms 1–7, 9–21, 29, 47, 100, 125, 128, 133, 148 and 150; and versifications of Ecclesiastes 12, the Lord's Prayer and Deuteronomy 32 (the Song of Moses). The manuscript is in a number of different hands, one probably of James and two others of scribes; see Westcott, *New Poems by James I of England*, p. lxxxviii. MS Bodl. 165, fol. 58b also includes Psalm 101 as translated by King James. It too is in Scots, and different from those appearing in the 1631 and 1636 editions. It is printed by Robert Rait in *Lusus Regius* (London: A. Constable, 1901).

[4] See W. S. Reid, "The Battle Hymns of the Lord: Calvinist Psalmody of the Sixteenth Century", *Sixteenth-Century Essays and Studies* 2 (1971): 43–53. On the widespread tradition of versifying the Psalms, see Rivkah Zim, *English metrical psalms: poetry as praise and prayer, 1535–1601* (Cambridge: CUP, 1987).

trimeter lines rhyming abcb) or long meter (tetrameter lines, abcb). The uniformity of meter made it possible for a limited number of familiar tunes to be used for all the psalms. With hymns playing no part in English or Scottish worship in the sixteenth and seventeenth centuries, these psalms were a central feature of lay participation in the worship service.[5] Certain psalms became strongly associated with militant protestantism; in James' own reign Psalm 124, which expressed defiant strength in the Lord in the face of persecution, was frequently used in Scotland at events of national signific-ance. Congregational, as opposed to choral, singing of the Psalms was a symbolic part of the Calvinist movement, one which joined the Scots and the English Puritans with their brethren in the Low Countries and Switzerland.

In both England and Scotland a consensus emerged in the early part of the seventeenth century that the "Sternhold and Hopkins" versions of the Psalms were not satisfactory. Even their defenders admitted that as translations they had their defects, and those with an interest in poetry frequently derided them for their barbarous language and "galloping" rhythm. George Wither, for example, lamented "that we make use of the most excelent expressions of the holy ghost in rude, and barbarous Numbers, whilst our own wanton fancies were paynted, & trymed out in the most mooving languag".[6] James found the Scottish psalter of 1564 unsatisfactory both poetically and biblically; at the Scottish General Assembly of 1601 he "did recite whole verses of the same, showing both the faults of the metre and the discrepance from the text".[7] At that assembly Robert Pont, minister at St Cuthbert's, was appointed to revise the Psalter, but nothing more is heard of his work.[8] In spite of James' objections to the old version, he was to draw on it to a limited extent in his own work, at least as it appears in the published versions.[9] Numerous early seventeenth-century poets attempted to supplant this old version; by includ-ing himself in these attempts, James hoped to fill a role consistent with his larger vision of the king as leader of the church.

A complete versification of the Psalms is a daunting task, one in which the writer is limited not only by his source, but also by the metrical forms established for psalmody in the church. Such versification must also be self-effacing: the goal of the versifier is to provide a clear glass through which the

---

[5] There seems to be some disagreement about the significance of psalm-singing in the Scottish church of the early seventeenth century. Millar Patrick, *Four Centuries of Scottish Psalmody* (London, New York: OUP, 1949), suggests that the "1564 Psalter cannot at any time have had more than a very restricted use" (p. 79). However, the references collected in Neil Livingston, *The Scottish Metrical Psalter of AD 1635* (London: Novello, 1935), seem to tell a different story.

[6] *Schollers Purgatory* (1624); *Works*, Spenser Society Reprint (New York: Burt Franklin, 1871–2, rpt. 1867), vol. 1, pp. 37–8.

[7] John Spottiswoode, *History of the Church of Scotland* (Edinburgh, 1851), vol. 3, p. 98. Spottiswoode's history was first published in 1655.

[8] *Acts and Proceedings of the General Assembly of the Kirk of Scotland*, ed. T. Thomson, 3 vols (Edinburgh, 1845), 6 May 1601, p. 970.

[9] William H. McMillan, "The Metrical Psalter of James VI", *RCHS* 8 (1944): 193.

Divine Word may be seen. Anything which attracts attention to the versifier is a sort of failure: the preface to the English bible of 1611 criticized earlier versions in that they had not opened the window, but replaced it with a variety of other windows – ornate, stained ones with varying degrees of transparency.[10] More than other biblical books, the Psalms presented special challenges because of the variety of versifications available, and the important place in Protestant worship and identity that they had achieved in the previous half century.

While the English psalter was largely in common meter, the Scottish psalter used a wider variety of verse forms; this meant that a single psalter to replace both would have to also introduce some new tunes.[11] Common meter was to become the standard form for most attempted replacements, including James'. However, the best-known Renaissance versification of the Psalms today is that of Mary and Philip Sidney; which used a variety of relatively complex verse forms that rendered it relatively unsuited to church use.[12] This collection remained unpublished in its own time, but circulated widely in manuscript.

JAMES' ACCESSION AND THE PSALTER

As James' interest in du Bartas sparked a number of translations dedicated to him, so did his well-known interest in psalm versification help fill the royal library with a variety of attempts, both manuscript and printed. While James seems to have been primarily interested himself in an English or Scots psalter, verse translations of the Psalms in neo-Latin were also directed towards him through both his reigns. His tutor Buchanan's elegant neo-Latin versification had become the benchmark for many later attempts. That James became increasingly hostile toward Buchanan as he matured only served to encourage those poets who wanted to outdo him. The most noteworthy of these was George Eglishem, a royal physician, who challenged both the psalms of Buchanan and the satiric epigrams of Melville in a 1619 collection. Among the other gifts James received were fifty psalms in Spanish verse by one P. Coster van der Ven,[13] and Esther Inglis' French versification of the Psalms, presented to James at New Year 1615.[14]

Such gifts were tangential to James' chief concern with English psalmody. His accession to the English throne presented the possibility of a broader scope for his psalter: it could be a unifying element in all the British churches,

---

[10] Preface to AV, 1611, A. W. Pollard, *Records of the English Bible 1525–1611* (Oxford: OUP, 1911), p. 349.

[11] However, McMillan, "The Metrical Psalter of James VI" notes that the most popular of the Psalms in Scotland used the common meter (p. 120).

[12] A number of the Sidney psalms were set to the music of the Genevan psalter and published in *All the French Psalm Tunes with English Words* (1632). See my note, "A Seventeenth-Century Publication of Three of Sir Philip Sidney's Psalms", *Notes and Queries* n.s. 38 (1991): 162–3.

[13] BL MS Old Royal 14 A.xxii.

[14] National Library of Scotland, MS 8874.

or what James hoped would ultimately be a single British church. Like his sponsorship of a new translation of the Bible, James' work on the Psalms confirmed his role as leader of his churches. Because of their dual biblical and royal origin James' translation of the Psalms would hold a special place. He felt that ordinary procedures of literary criticism did not apply: William Drummond of Hawthornden might think his psalm superior, but the king was to play both poet and critic. At the same time, the work in question was no ordinary work – as that part of scripture most used in worship, it had a status beyond even that of the king's work. In this situation, unlike, for instance, his translation of du Bartas, James was subordinate to his material. Readers might feel justified in using the source against James' treatment of it.

While there was widespread dissatisfaction with both the English and Scottish psalters, few attempts to replace them actually reached print in the first quarter of the century. Two factors are responsible for this: first, the desire of James himself to be the author of a new version, and secondly, the monopoly that the Stationers' Company enjoyed for the printing of metrical psalters in England.[15] James had made publicly known his intention, and any attempt at the same task might be perceived as disrespectful. At least until 1620 James seems to have made clear that composition of a new psalter was his prerogative. James was still active as a poet in the years leading up to his death, but it is not clear if he continued work on the Psalms at this time.[16] Nevertheless, the public knowledge, or semi-knowledge, that he contemplated such a work cast a shadow over any other endeavours. When a king himself is a poet, his role as a patron may be diminished. Joseph Hall noted in 1608 that "Many great wits have undertaken this taske; which yet have either not effected it, or have smothered it in their private desks, and denied it the common light."[17] William Alexander, who was later to complete the king's psalms, explicitly warned William Drummond of James's jealousy in the area of the Psalms:

> Brother, I received your last letter, with the Psalm you sent, which I think very well done; I had done the same long before it came; but He [King James] prefers his own to all else; tho' perchance, when you see it, you will think it the worst of the three [Alexander's, Drummond's, and the King's?]. No men must meddle with that subject, and, therefore, I advise you to take no more pains therein.[18]

15 On the Stationers' Company protection of this monopoly, see James Doelman, "George Wither, the Stationers Company and the English Psalter", *SP* 90 (1993): 74–82.
16 See "Poems of King James I of England and VI of Scotland", *Bodleian Library Record* (Supplement), vol. 3, pp. 1–7; and James Craigie, "Last Poems of James VI", *Scottish Historical Review* (1951): 134–42.
17 "To M. Hugh Cholmley. Ep. V. Concerning the Metaphrase of the Psalms", in *Poems*, ed. Davenport, p. 271.
18 18 April 1620, Drummond, *Works* (1711), p. 151. Drummond also sent one of his metrical psalms to Robert Kerr, earl of Ancrum. See *Correspondence of Kerr*, 2 vols (Edinburgh, 1875), vol. 2, pp. 520–1.

Further illustration of the caution exercised by those versifying psalms is shown by a letter of Sir Robert Kerr, earl of Ancrum, to his son, accompanying a psalm versified for the Genevan tunes:

> I began thereupon to trye if I could fit them [the Psalms] to their measure, that whilst I was there [in the Low Countries] I might doe as they did, not presuming to introduce them to be used in this Isle, well knowing how they are undertaken to the measure of our own tunes by those that can doe them farre better.[19]

If the psalm translations of James' courtiers were being rejected in such a fashion, it is not surprising that others held back from publication.

James' work was not the only obstacle to other new versions of the Psalms. The Stationers' Company's patent on the printing of psalters, which it had purchased in 1603, led the company to challenge any new versification, which found itself in a legal grey area: was it covered by the Stationers' monopoly? They claimed that it extended to "all manner of books of that nature", that is, any collection of psalms, even if incomplete, in English.[20] As will be explored below, this patent might very well have impeded the establishment of James' psalter itself. That authorization, either from James or the Stationers' Company, was necessary to proceed with such a publication is clear from the letter of an anonymous respondent to George Wither, perhaps the most dogged versifier of the Psalms in the period:

> there are soe many Reverend and learned Men, that have desired to doe the same thing that you doe; but out of respect they had to authoritie would not proceed, except they had bene imployed by publique Commaund.[21]

Of the major English versifiers of psalms in James' reign, Joseph Hall, Sir John Harington, Henry Dod, and George Wither, only Dod and Wither produced complete versions that reached print, and both of these had to have their work printed in Amsterdam to overcome the monopoly of the Stationers' Company.

The fate of Henry Dod's versification illustrates the difficulties faced by any new English psalter. His first publication, *Certain Psalmes of David* (1603) was merely a sample of a later promised work that was not to appear until 1620. Dod explains that the seventeen-year gap between his initial sample and his complete psalter is due to his waiting "for the performance of this worthie

---

[19] 24 April 1624, *Correspondence*, vol. 2, p. 488. At the time, Kerr was a gentleman of James' bedchamber.

[20] *Records of the Court of the Stationers Company*, eds W. W. Greg *et al.* (London: Bibliographical Society, 1930), 5 September 1631, p. 231.

[21] BL MS Add. 18648, fol. 19r. Rptd. by Allen Pritchard, "George Wither's Quarrel with the Stationers: An Anonymous Reply to *The Schollers Purgatory*", *SB* 16 (1963): 27–42.

worke, by some godly learned, whom I hoped wold have donne it in manner better beseemeing the same".[22] Upon publication, Dod's full psalter was publicly burned, likely due to its infringement of the Stationers' patent, although it is possible that James' attempt made such enforcement of the patent all the more possible.

In his 1598 collection of satires, *Virgidemiarum*, Joseph Hall had ridiculed the practitioners of biblical verse paraphrase; John Marston, responding to Hall in Satire IV *Reactio*, suggests that Hall's criticism in *Virgidemiarum* went beyond sacred poetry in general and did "raile impudent/ At *Hopkins*, *Sternhold*, and the *Scottish* King,/ At all Translators that doe strive to bring/ That stranger language to our vulgar tongue".[23] By 1607, Hall was attempting to make amends, with a sample of versified psalms, tentatively offered to the king. Ronald Corthell suggests that "Hall's attraction to Proverbial models was also, perhaps primarily, motivated by his 'almost sycophantic admiration' of the learning and sententious style of the English Solomon",[24] and this was manifest in such works as *Salomons Divine Arts* (1609), which included a prose paraphrase of the Song of Songs. Hall's nine psalms were published at the end of his *Holy Observations* (1607), under the tentative title *Some Few of Davids Psalms Metaphrased for a Taste of the Rest*. Hall claims in his dedicatory epistle that he has "been solicited by som revered friends to undertake this taske; as that which seemed well to accord with the former exercises of my youth, and my present profession", and that he is willing to continue if he "shall be imployed by authoritie".[25] At the beginning of the dedicatory epistle Hall claims for himself the conventional conversion to higher endeavours: "Indeed, my Poetrie was sithence out of date, yielded her place to graver studies: but whose vaine would it not revive to looke into these heavenly songs?"[26] Being a David-like poet and a Divine are compatible, and the Psalms fit in well with Hall's new career that began with his ordination in 1600.

The preface to Hall's psalms and an epistle to Hugh Cholmley, published in 1608, show his concern for fidelity to the original, and an admiration for the French and Dutch psalms. He found the long and common meters of Sternhold and Hopkins and most other English psalms unworkable: "I never could see good verse written in the wonted measures. I ever thought

---

[22] *All the Psalmes of David* (1620), sig. 6r.

[23] John Marston, *Poems*, ed. Arnold Davenport (Liverpool, 1961), ll. 40–3, p. 82. Marston's satire goes on to become a defense of sacred verse. Huntley, *Bishop Joseph Hall*, suggests that Marston was responding not only to *Virgidemiarum*, but to the comments in *Return to Parnassus*, a satirical play to which Hall might have contributed (pp. 37–8).

[24] Ronald Corthell, "Joseph Hall and Seventeenth-Century Literature", *John Donne Journal* 3 (1984): 258.

[25] "To my Loving and learned Cosen, Mr. Samuel Burton, Archdeacon of Glocester", *Collected Poems*, p. 128.

[26] *Collected Poems*, p. 127.

them most easie, and least Poeticall."[27] In his own version of the Psalms Hall, like the Sidneys, attempted a variety of verse forms.

The ten psalms published in 1607 remained simply a "taste" of a full meal which was never served. Hall would have been well-qualified to compose a new psalter, and those presented in the volume of 1607 are better than most attempts of the time. In the "Epistle to Cholmley", Hall recognizes the public nature of the task, and the need for the poet to aim neither too high nor too low, "with numbers neither lofty, nor slubbred". A "higher straine" is inappropriate not only because its readers will include the simple, but also because of "the grave majestie of the subject". This aesthetic was consistent with Hall's other work. For him plainness was essential for literary art: above all he detested affectation. Hall was to achieve great repute in the reigns of both James and Charles, but it was not to be for his psalms.

From George Wither's attempts to publish his psalter in the 1620s we get the best sense of the combined effect of James' personal desire to compose the Psalter, and the Stationers' Company's monopoly. In 1619 Wither published, in lavish form, *A Preparation to the Psalter* as the harbinger of the Psalms themselves. However, Wither's psalter was not to appear until 1632, when a cheap version was printed in Holland. Wither describes his change of plans in *The Schollers Purgatory* (1624):

> But before I had halfe ended them [the Psalms] I heard that one of much better sufficiency had made a long, and happy progresse into that worke: and thereupon in expectation of his more able performance delayed to proceed with what I had begunne, untill such tyme as I was informed that the other was by the multiplicity of weighty Affayres compelled to give over his laborious Attempt. And then, I thought my selfe engaged agayne, to proceed.[28]

Nowhere in this work does he make explicit the reference to the king, but the details of the latter part of the passage and the date confirm that he is the one referred to.

Wither's psalter was only part of his larger endeavour to contribute to the worship service of the Church of England, as he wrote a large collection of other biblical songs as well as original hymns. Wither may have first turned to this task because of the difficulties of publishing the Psalms. Between *A Preparation to the Psalter* and the publication of *The Psalmes of David*, Wither published a number of collections of other hymns and biblical paraphrases,

---

[27] Letter to Hugh Cholmley, *Collected Poems*, ed. Davenport, p. 271. His disdain for common meter may be part of a larger antipathy toward English poetry. He found rhyme to be an obstacle in the writing of satire, and challenges others to attempt a translation of Persius' satires without it. He holds up the example of Ariosto's satires, in which the rhyming "maie well afford a pleasing harmony to the eare, so can it yeeld nothing but a flashy and loose conceyt to the judgement" ("A Post-script to the Reader", *Virgidemiarum* in *Collected Poems*, p. 99).

[28] pp. 12–13.

culminating in *Hymnes and Songs of the Church* (1623). This work was granted a special patent by the king, giving Wither "during the Terme of 51. yeares, full License and Authoritie to imprint the said Booke, either with, or without Arguments and Musicall notes (and to utter and sell the same in any of His Dominions)", and also requiring "that no English *Psalme-Booke* in Meeter, shall be bound up alone, or with any other Booke or Bookes, unlesse the said *Hymnes* and *Songs* of the *Church* be annexed thereunto".[29] That Wither, who two years earlier had been imprisoned for his *Motto*, should now enjoy such an exceptional privilege from the king, was later explained by the poet himself as due to the intervention of William Herbert, earl of Pembroke.[30] This was an astonishingly lucrative patent, if it could be enforced, and one of the few examples of James' direct patronage of religious verse. However, it began a long feud between Wither and the Stationers' Company, who especially resented Wither's authority to seize any psalter published without his hymns. In spite of the bookbinders' protests, parliament allowed the patent to stand. Nevertheless, such hostility from the Stationers' made the work difficult to publish and distribute.[31] From our viewpoint the most interesting fruit of this dispute was Wither's 1624 work *Schollers Purgatorie* where he defended himself against the charges of the Stationers, who had not only objected to the infringement of their rights, but had accused Wither of a variety of sins ranging from blasphemy to popery to incompetence.[32] Throughout his response Wither tries to show that it is his opponents who are schismatics, and that both the crown and church hierarchy approve of his work:

> Now, that they have abused my Lo: Grace of Canterburye, by pretendinge his dislike of my booke (to the disparagement thereof) I shal make yt very apparant. For, his Grace tooke notise that my booke was perused and allowed by his Majestie himselfe; and worthily approved his Royall judgement both in Divinity and Poetry, the Stationers beeing present: he was informed likewise, concerning every perticuler circumstance in the Grant, and how it was his Majesties pleasure my book should be anexed to the metricall Psalmes; and

---

[29] *An Abstract of His Maiesties Royall Priviledge*, STC 8704.5. Rptd. in W. W. Greg, *Companion to Arber*, pp. 212–13.
[30] "To the Right Honourable Phillip, Earle of Pembroke", *A Collection of Emblems* (1635). This appears before the fourth section of the book on an unnumbered page. William Herbert died in 1630, at which time his brother Philip became the fourth earl of Pembroke.
[31] Pritchard, "George Wither's Quarrel with the Printers", p. 29.
[32] Concerning the broader conflict between Wither and the Stationers' Company there is a fair amount of primary material. We have Wither's lengthy defense in *The Schollers Purgatory*, an unpublished response to this defense (printed and discussed by Pritchard in "George Wither's Quarrel with the Stationers") a preface to the Psalms by Wither, written about 1625 and never published (BL MS Egerton 2404), and various official documents, including the patent given to Wither by King James (collected in Greg's *Companion to Arber*, pp. 212–17). See also Norman E. Carlson, "Wither and the Stationers", *SB* 19 (1966): 210–15, for a succinct account of the feud.

thereupon both illustrated the reasonablenesse thereof to the sayd stationers, and gave them and me incouragment to proceed to composition touching the same.[33]

Further on in the same passage he claims that the archbishop himself has perused the entire work, "and, giving me order to alter one word only, hath permitted al the rest to have free passage without controwle".[34] The anonymous reply to Wither confirms that in late 1623 four clergymen were appointed to review Wither's work.[35] That Wither's patent was upheld suggests that they found it acceptable. It cannot be asserted that the dispute was solely between the Stationers' and Wither; the Stationers' also resented the king's intrusion into what they considered their jurisdiction.

> For, some of them [the stationers] dare already tell me to my face, that if the King had not peremptorely commanded the addition of my Hymns to the metricall Psalmbooke, they would have the sooner anexed them; but by compulsion they will not.[36]

The Stationers' eventually turned to parliament for help in re-establishing their rights. In turn Wither made a number of appeals to the Privy Council for help to support his patent: a 1626 entry in the Record of the Stationers' Court suggests that they were complying.[37]

Wither's hymns deserve some comment in their own right. As with the Psalms, Wither proceeded cautiously. The preface to *Songs of the Old Testament* (1621) is addressed to George Abbot, the archbishop of Canterbury, in particular, and the clergy of the Church of England in general. His appeals to the clergy show a desire for church approval not found with earlier paraphrasers. Wither seems to be seeking approval, although he claims that "this Booke hath already the allowance appointed by Authority, and so much the approbation of many other good men, as that they desire it generally published (at least) for their private devotions".[38] However, Wither clearly intends that his songs serve public worship as well, that the Old Testament songs be part of worship as they were in the early church. Like *A Preparation, Songs of the Old Testament* seems to be a testing of the waters; Wither has had it printed only "to be distributed among your RR^ces [Right Reverences] and other speciall friends" in order that they might correct it and make suggestions.[39] In "The Epistle to the Cleargie" that precedes the fourteen songs in *Songs of the Old Testament*, Wither suggests that his approach to

---

[33] *Schollers Purgatory*, p. 46.
[34] p. 47.
[35] Pritchard, "Wither's Quarrel", p. 28.
[36] *Schollers Purgatory*, p. 65.
[37] *Records of the Court of the Stationers Company*, p. 112.
[38] sig. A4v.
[39] sig. A4r.

them has been in keeping with that outlined in *A Preparation to the Psalter*, Wither sees no distinction between psalms and other Old Testament songs: all were used in worship by the primitive church and are applicable to the present situation of the church.[40] To illustrate this Wither includes a brief prologue to each song, wherein he establishes the original context of the song, and also how it is applicable in his own time. Thus, the Song of Moses may be sung since the exodus out of Egypt "was a tipe of our deliverance from the bondage of our Spirituall Adversaries".[41] Wither's next publication, *Cantica Sacra* (1623?), contained the fourteen songs of the previous work as well as twenty-seven new ones, including the Song of Songs. These songs were then published along with hymns for the church calendar in the 1623 volume *Hymnes and Songs of the Church*, with tunes provided by Orlando Gibbons. The most recent study of the English hymn, by J. R. Watson, recognizes the significance of this volume as that "which first challenged the domination of psalmody" in Protestant England.[42]

The patent given to Wither by James for this work, along with the injunction that it be appended to the Psalter, would seem to have bode well for Wither. However, at this late stage of his reign, James' support could have limited effect, and Wither's hymns found no place in the congregational worship of the church, either in his own or later times. Ultimately, the Stationers' Company's resistance proved superior. The failure of Wither's hymns also stemmed from the unassailable position of the Psalter as the basis of congregational worship; freely composed hymns were not to figure largely in English worship until the introduction of Watts's hymns in the early eighteenth century. As Louis Benson notes, Calvin's injunction to sing the songs of scripture rather than those of man's making still held sway. This and the problems of publication, rather than any defect in the hymns themselves, explain their failure. They consist of acceptable, if not particularly noteworthy poetry, and the accompanying tunes by Gibbons have since found their way into other hymnals.[43] Wither finally fulfilled his ambition of publishing his psalms in 1632, but this poorly printed work fell far short of the expectations presented thirteen years earlier in *A Preparation to the Psalter*. Unlike most of Wither's work this publication does not seem to have attracted much attention in England.

The best efforts of Harington, Dod, Hall and Wither found little success in England, and while the situation in Scotland was somewhat different, there too James' reign saw no successful challenge to the traditional versification of the Psalms. In the northern kingdom, the privilege of publishing psalms belonged to the king's printer, rather than the Stationers' Company, and

---

[40] "Epistle", *Songs of the Old Testament* (1621), sig. A2v.

[41] p. 2.

[42] *The English Hymn: A Critical and Historical Study* (Oxford: Clarendon Press, 1997), p. 57.

[43] See P. Vining, "Wither and Gibbons: A Prelude to the First English Hymn Book", *Musical Times* 120 (1979): 245–6.

James allowed and even encouraged a number of new partial versions of the Psalms early in the century. Henry Dod published *Certaine Psalmes of David* in 1603, "Cum Privilegio Regiae Majestatis". Two years later Alexander Montgomerie, a member of James' poetic circle, put forward his *The Mindes Melodie. Contayning Certayne Psalmes of the Kinglie Prophete David*, again "Cum Privilegio Regali". Later, some Scottish opponents of James' version would refer back to Montgomerie's psalms as a more suitable revision.

In the last few years of his life James' attitude toward other attempts at psalm versification seems to have changed as he recognized his own inability to finish the task. The most explicit assertion of this is by Wither in his prefatory letter "To the Reader" in MS Eg. 2404, where he refers to

> ye late Soveraigne of happie memory: who having worthely begunn ye same taske himself and finding that the multitude of his royall and waightie affaires threatned to prevent his p[er]sonall performance thereof, was lately mooved, through an earnest desire of adding a reformed version of ye metricall Psalmes unto ye translation of ye Bible to hearten on many of those in this undertaking, who had discovered themselves voluntarily enclined thereunto.[44]

Wither visited James a few months before the king's death in 1625, and in the preface to his 1632 publication he claims that it was specifically he himself who was thus encouraged by James: "I was commanded to perfect a *Translation* of the *Psalmes*, which he understood I had begunn; & by his encouragment, I finished the same about the tyme of his *Translation* to a better Kingdome."

His claim is substantiated by a letter of Joseph Mead from 23 April 1625: "Mr. Withers is come to Cambridge to print his psalms, whereof he showed the old king an hundred in Christmas time, who then told him himself had done fifty, but meant not now to go on."[45] In the preface to the 1632 *Psalms*, Wither once again makes reference to James' work on the Psalms:

> I waited long, to see a more exact *performance*: But, none appearing, answerable to the dignitie of our *English-Muses*, I have sent forth my *Essay*, to provoke others, to discover their endeavours, on this *subject*; the best might receive the best Approbation.[46]

It would seem that about 1624 James recognized that he himself would not complete a psalter, and became more open to others, like Wither, attempting

---

[44] "To the Reader", sig. 4r. This manuscript of Wither's psalms is in a scribe's hand and contains a version different from those in the final printed version of 1632. The preface was also replaced in the printed work. The manuscript likely dates from 1625 when Wither attempted to have the psalms printed at Cambridge. See Allan Pritchard, "A Manuscript of George Wither's *Psalms*", *MP* 77 (1980): 370–81.

[45] Rev. Joseph Mead to Sir Martin Stuteville, in Thomas Birch, *Court and Times of Charles I* (1848), pp. 12–13.

[46] sig. A6r.

to do so. That Francis Bacon and Sir John Davies both published versions of some of the Psalms in that year would support this as well. His encouragement of others also suggests that he did not foresee that his translations would form any part of a new psalter after his death.

Just how many psalms James had completed at the time of his death is unclear. John Williams, bishop of Lincoln, in his sermon for James' funeral notes that

> This translation he was in hand with, when God called him to sing Psalms with the angels. He intended to have finished and dedicated it to the only saint of his devotion – the Church of Great Britain and that of Ireland. This worke was staied in the one and thirty Psalme, Blessed is he whose unrighteousnesse is forgiven, and whose sinne is covered.[47]

Whether James completed this number of psalms, or the fifty mentioned by Mede, it is clear that he was far from having produced a complete psalter. It is not surprising that the king failed to complete his translation: James' interest in poetry waned during his English reign, and was replaced by an increasing interest in theology. His final years were also marked by failing health.

While many knew of James' psalms during his lifetime they seem to have circulated very little. A few years after his death Henry Wotton procured some of them as a gift for James' grandson, the prince of Bohemia, but notes that he was able to do so only "with much adoe".[48] This limited circulation is in contrast to the majority of James' works, which were frequently republished and provoked response both in England and abroad. The idea of them, rather than their substance, had the larger effect. Ironically, in the 1630s they became the most public and controversial of his works, at a time when his other works faded into the background.

THE RECEPTION OF JAMES' PSALTER

In reference to the biblical translation of 1611 James wrote, "Whosoever attempteth any thing for the publike (specially if it pertaine to Religion, and to the opening and clearing of the word of God) the same setteth himselfe upon a stage to be glouted upon by every evil eye, yea, he casteth himself headlong upon pikes, to be gored by every sharpe tongue."[49] James never took that final step of setting his psalms upon a stage, and only a few of his contemporaries had any first-hand acquaintance with them. In his own time

---

[47] *Great Britains Salomon* (1625), p. 42. The passage that Williams quotes is actually from Psalm 32.

[48] "To my most dear and worthy friend, Mr. John Dinely, at the Hague", 12 August 1628, *Reliquiae Wottoniae* (1685), p. 558.

[49] Preface to AV, 1611, rptd. Pollard, p. 344.

they lived a ghost-like existence, known only by reputation and rumour. After James' death, Charles attempted to give the work – as amended by Sir William Alexander – a public existence, but the role it eventually played was far from what either the royal father or son had hoped. Scholars of the present have also found James' psalms to be something of a phantom work. The greatest problem is that we do not have a static or definitive text to work with: none of the existing manuscripts or the published versions likely represent James' work as he left it at his death.

In his epistle dedicating James' *Works* to Charles, James Montague describes the young prince as "the trew Heire and Inheritor of them".[50] It was certainly in this spirit that Charles accepted his father's psalms, regardless of how incomplete they stood. While James had recognized his work on the Psalms as insufficient, Charles took it upon himself to bring that work upon the public stage, to present it as his father's final legacy for the "British Church". The problem of the Psalter in the 1630s seems to have been created by Charles, rather than bequeathed to him by his father. His motivation in this is far from clear.

The question of authorship would loom over the work as Charles promoted it through the late 1620s and 1630s: were these the psalms of King David, King James or William Alexander? With a king's work generally, public reception is of great import, but as a volume that could form a central part in the worship of the Scottish and English churches, the Psalms attracted special attention. The Psalms required a far more involved public response than any other work of James: a new Psalter would entail the participation of every voice in every parish of the church.

Charles began the institution of his father's psalms in 1626 by dividing the labour of reviewing them into two parts: the Scottish archbishop John Spottiswoode was to appoint churchmen who were to "confer them [the Psalms] with the originall text and with the most exact translations", and Sir William Alexander, the long-time courtier of James and Charles' secretary for Scotland, was "to consider and revew the meeter and poesie".[51] Not mentioned in this letter is any indication of how large Alexander's role in this would need to be. The work was to be done "for the good of all the Churches within his dominions", which clearly suggests that Charles was contemplating James' work as a new Psalter for England, Scotland and Ireland. John Spottiswoode suggests that James himself had commissioned Alexander to complete the work: "The revising of the Psalms he made his own labour; and, at such hours as he might spare from the public cares, went

[50] *The Workes* (1616) [sig. a3v].
[51] Letter of Charles to the Archbishop of St Andrews, 25 August 1626, *Earl of Stirling's Register of Royal Letters Relative to the Affairs of Scotland and Nova Scotia from 1615 to 1635*, 2 vols (Edinburgh, 1885), p. 73. Calderwood, "Reasons against the reception of King James's metaphrase of the Psalms", p. 237, suggests that "another, if not others, also hath had ane hand in them".

through a number of them, commending the rest to a faithful and learned servant, who hath therein answered his Majestie's expectation",[52] but there is no other evidence for this. In January of 1628 Alexander was granted a 21-year patent on the work.[53] This patent would have proven very lucrative if the Psalter had been successfully established. However, it also raised a potential conflict with the Stationers' Company and their patent on the existing Psalter. The archbishops and bishops clearly found themselves in a difficult situation: they had to review the work of the late king in light of the original texts. At the same time Charles was promoting the work not just on the basis of its quality, but as "a perpetuall monument to his [James'] memorie", a phrase that was to recur throughout his correspondence promoting the use of the Psalter.[54] No response from the bishops seems to survive.

The joint work finally appeared in 1631 as *The Psalms of King David, translated by King James*, printed by W. Turner at Oxford. The title-page shows Kings David and James standing as parallel figures on either side of a psalter, a reflection of James' lifelong desire to be the godly poet-king in the tradition of David. Alexander's name appears nowhere in the volume. In a preface Charles makes clear his intention that this psalter become the standard one for church use:

> CHARLES R. Haveing caused this Translation of the Psalmes (whereof oure late deare Father was Author) to be perused, and it being found to be exactly and truely done wee doe hereby authorize the same to be Imprinted according to the Patent graunted thereupon: and doe allow them to be song in all the Churches of our Dominiones, recommending them to all oure goode Subjects for that effect.[55]

Charles was to find that introducing a new psalter required more than publication and a printed authorization. A year after the publication he wrote again to the archbishop of Canterbury, encouraging him to promote the use of the psalter, leaving the means up to Abbot, in consultation with other English bishops. The two possibilities are for them to "be receaved by a generall ordour, or to beginn in some Churches by the particular recommendatioun of everie bischop within his owin dyocie".[56] Neither happened, and from this point Charles seems to have silently abandoned his plans for

---

[52] *History of the Church of Scotland* (1851), vol. 3, p. 99.

[53] "To our right trustie and weelbeloved Cousen and Counseller the Erle of Marleburh, our Thesaurer of England", 28 December 1627, *Earl of Stirling's Register of Royal Letters*, pp. 240–1. In this letter Charles asks the earl to make arrangements for the patent. It was actually granted on 21 January 1628 (*CSPD, 1627–28*, p. 524). In this letter Charles also calls for a bill to be drawn up for Ireland.

[54] Letter to the Archbishops and Bishops, 14 June 1631, *Earl of Stirling's Register of Royal Letters*, vol. 2, p. 538.

[55] Opposite title-page in *The Psalmes of King David, Translated by King James* (Oxford: W. Turner, 1631), STC 2732. The same authorization was included with the 1636 edition.

[56] 13 March 1632, *Earl of Stirling's Register of Royal Letters*, p. 581.

James' psalter in England. David Calderwood, in his argument against James' version, suggests that the English bishops had rejected the work, but no other evidence has been found to confirm this.[57] I would suggest that the Stationers' Company's tight monopoly on the printing of the Sternhold and Hopkins psalter discouraged Charles from attempting to introduce the widespread use of his father's psalter in England. Without their full co-operation the distribution of enough psalters to the English parishes would have been impossible. That Charles had the first edition of his father's psalter printed at Oxford, which was to a certain degree beyond the reach of the Stationers' Company, suggests that they would not co-operate in his plans.[58] From 1631 Charles' efforts with the psalter shifted to Scotland. Ironically, that Charles turned his attention to establishing the new psalter in Scotland while abandoning the project in England breaks with his usual pattern of moving toward uniformity between the two national churches.

Charles' attempts in Scotland were to be stymied for close to six years by the slow response of the bishops and clergy. The many delays in the publication and distribution of the psalter may have reflected the bishops' uncertainty about how to promote a work they knew would arouse the hostility of many within the Scottish church, and make the already distrusted bishops even less popular.[59] This is just one instance of Charles' tendency to conduct his Scottish affairs without a full understanding of the complexities of the situation.[60] Shortly before the book went to press Charles wrote to his Scottish privy council and the archbishop of St Andrews, expressing the hope that "the first beginning [of instituting the Psalter in all his churches] may be made in that our ancient kingdome, wher our said dear father, the Authour, was borne".[61] In May of 1631 he called a meeting of the bishops and archbishops to consider not only the introduction of the new psalter, but also the place of organ music, surplices and a potential new service book.[62]

---

[57] David Calderwood, *Bannatyne Miscellany* (Edinburgh, 1827), vol. 1, p. 238. The manuscript in the Advocates Library in which this appears is undated; however, Calderwood's comment that the present Psalms had been in use "thriescoir and eight yeirs" would suggest that he wrote it in 1632.

[58] The 1631 edition likely did contravene the Stationers' patent, and to correct this before the edition of 1636 an Order of the King in Council was passed on 9 March 1636, granting Oxford printers limited rights to print psalters outside the Stationers' Company's domain (*CSPD, Charles I, 1636*, p. 281).

[59] Since 1625 Charles had appointed a number of new Scottish bishops perceived by their countrymen as the creations of the king, and little connected to the clergy. See Henry Guthry, *Bp. Of Dunkeld. Memoires* (Glasgow, 1747), p. 16.

[60] Kevin Sharpe, *The Personal Rule of Charles I* (New Haven: Yale UP, 1982), pp. 774–7.

[61] *Earl of Stirling's Register of Royal Letters*, p. 815. These letters are undated, but his comment "sieing we have alreadie gevin ordour for ane Impression of that Translatioun" indicates that he is writing just before the 1631 or 1636 edition. The overall tone of the letter is more like that of the others from 1631.

[62] Alexander Peterkin, *Records of the Kirk of Scotland* (Edinburgh: John Sutherland, 1838), vol. 1, p. 50n.

John Row reports that in 1631 "There was also brute that the King wold have the Psalmes translated by his father to be receaved in the Kirk of Scotland; and some of the books wer delyvered to Presbyteries, that Ministers might advyse concerning the goodnes of the translation, or badness, and report their iudgments to the Diocesian Assemblies; but that lay over for a while."[63] On 2 June 1631, Samuel Rutherford, minister at Anwoth in Galloway, wrote to his godly friend Marion McNaught the recent news:

> I have received a letter from Edinburgh, certainly informing me that the English service, and the organs, and King James' Psalms, are to be imposed upon our Kirk; and that the bishops are dealing for a General Assembly.[64]

He perceives the new psalter as part of a broader program of English change to the kirk, and from this letter it is possible to see organized opposition to the changes developing.

The fullest surviving expression of Scottish opposition is that of the anti-episcopal David Calderwood.[65] He rehearses a large number of reasons for maintaining the present Psalter despite some minor imperfections. While this Scottish divine seems to have been most strongly motivated by a loyalty to the Scottish psalter and antagonism towards any changes not initiated by the kirk itself, he gives some further objections to "James"' psalter.[66] Unlike Charles he attempts to distance the former king from the work, and asserts that Alexander was responsible for much of it. He argues that such work should be done by clergy rather than "a courteour or commone poet", and notes that "the people call them Menstries Psalmes", after Alexander's manor house, Menstrie.[67] That Alexander stands to gain so substantially from the psalter also attracts Calderwood's notice, and he suggests that earlier poets, like Alexander Montgomerie, had "offered to translate the whole book frielie without anie pryce for their paines, ather frae the public state or privat mens purses".[68] He also objects that the "metaphrase", as he calls it, is full of "heathenish libertie and poeticall conceats" and uses too many hard and foreign words. Scottish psalm versifiers of the later 1630s and 1640s were to

---

[63] *Historie of the Kirk of Scotland, 1558–1637*, 2 vols (Edinburgh: Maitland Club, 1842, rpt., New York: AMS, 1973), vol. 1, p. 144.

[64] *Letters of Samuel Rutherford*, ed. Andrew Bonar, 4th edn (Edinburgh, 1891), p. 60.

[65] "Reasons against the reception of King James's metaphrase of the Psalms". This attack on James' psalter was not published in the seventeenth century, but survives in a number of different versions in manuscript. Calderwood and the king had clashed as early as James' visit to Scotland in 1617, with the result that Calderwood was imprisoned and then exiled. He returned to Scotland in 1625.

[66] In the late 1640s the revised psalter was brought in with seemingly few objections; this would suggest that Calderwood and the other Presbyterians were most opposed to what James' psalter represented, rather than a deep-seated loyalty to the old Psalter.

[67] p. 237.

[68] p. 236.

stress the simplicity of their translations. Calderwood also fears that to change will make the Scottish church seem "inconstand and unsetled in our orders". He not only objected to the church use of James' psalter, but also to its private use, largely because of fear that this might lead to later public use.[69]

In spite of such opposition, Charles broadened his attempt in the spring of the next year, calling on the archbishop of St Andrews, and "the ministerie and burgh of Edinburgh", to assist in seeing that his father's psalter "might be receaved and sung in the Churches thereof".[70] In a general letter "To the Clergie" from 6 July 1632 Charles urges them "at last to effectuat that which we so much desyre".[71] Between that letter and one written on 13 September to the archbishop of St Andrews, the clergy responded by arguing that there were not enough copies available.[72] While the bishops may have been prevaricating over a move they were unsure of, it is reasonable that there were legitimate problems with distributing the work. After all, it was only being printed at Oxford, and from there sent to Scotland, and the numbers required to supply the churches of Scotland would be very high.[73] His patience obviously wearing thin, Charles expressed the hope "that the work may be found setled at our comeing, God willing, at the nixt spring of the yeir to that our kingdome".[74] At the same time, Charles does give indications in this letter that he is willing to consider changes to the work, possibly in response to objections raised: he will order the "reformeing or adding to that work what shalbe fund necessarie".

Resistance to the psalter was part of a broader fear of "innovation" in the Church of Scotland sponsored by Charles or the bishops appointed by him.[75] Calderwood in 1632 feared that if the new Psalter was accepted, "Then may they luik for the new service to be recommended to them, the nixt day the organes, &c."[76] Calderwood was not simply engaging in a slippery slope argument: he feared that the usual forms for worship and discipline in the Scottish church, which had always been printed with the Psalter, would be lost.[77] The new

[69] p. 241.
[70] All letters, 5 May 1632, *Earl of Stirling's Register of Royal Letters*, pp. 591–2. On this same day Charles also wrote to James Ussher, the archbishop of Armagh in Ireland, urging the same.
[71] *Earl of Stirling's Register of Royal Letters*, vol. 2, p. 605.
[72] *Earl of Stirling's Register of Royal Letter*, vol. 2, p. 621.
[73] Calderwood estimated that it would take six hundred thousand psalters to fulfill the need (p. 245); this figure is rightly challenged as ridiculous by McMillan, "The Metrical Psalter of James VI", pp. 127–8.
[74] *Earl of Stirling's Register of Royal Letters*, vol. 2, p. 621.
[75] On Charles and the Scottish church, see Gordon Donaldson, *The Making of the Scottish Prayer Book of 1637* (Edinburgh: Edinburgh UP, 1954); and Maurice Lee, Jr., *The Road to Revolution: Scotland under Charles I, 1625–37* (Urbana: U of Illinois P, 1985). For a more particular study of his relations with the Covenanters, see Allan I. MacInnes, *Charles I and the Making of the Covenanting Movement, 1625–1641* (Edinburgh: J. Donald, 1991).
[76] Calderwood, p. 242.
[77] *STC*, vol. 2, pp. 106–7. The Psalter was always far more than a collection of psalms: it included prayers, forms for communion, baptism, excommunication, ordination, etc. Some editions also included an almanac and a calendar of Scottish fairs.

Psalter would, in effect, make necessary the introduction of a new Service Book and Book of Canons as well. That psalter revision could have this effect was clear to those at the General Assembly of 1601, who had specified that any such revision must not include an altering or deletion of the prayers printed with it.[78] If Charles were not aware of these ramifications of replacing the old Psalter with his father's, his bishops certainly were. Suspicion of innovation was to increase over the next few years, as Charles added a Book of Canons and Prayer Book to the Psalter, and culminate in the riots of 1637. However, by that point the Service Book as a whole had replaced James' psalter as the focus of opposition.

Charles misjudged if he believed that the connection of James' name with the Psalter would endear it to the people of Scotland. James had alienated the more Presbyterian members of the clergy by pushing through the Five Articles of Perth in 1621, which many had attacked for their Roman tendencies. While James had never enforced the articles, Charles seemed to go beyond them in his attempts to change the Scottish liturgy.[79] Where James had been content with words, Charles insisted that reform be taken one step further to the active changing of Scottish church life.[80] Ultimately, the different treatments of the Psalter by James and Charles is a further example of this.

In May 1635 Charles approved the revised Book of Common Prayer for Scotland and ordered that James' psalms be printed with it, to be "receaved and used togidder in the Church of that our Kingdome".[81] An undated letter to the Privy Council of Scotland orders "that no other Psalmes of aney edition whatsoever be aither printed heirafter within that our kingdome, or imported thither, aither bund by themselffs or otherwayes from any forrayne port."[82] Charles' injunction against the publishing in Scotland of the traditional Psalter seems to have been ineffective, and even a full suppression of new editions would not have had any effect on the great supply of them already established.

James' psalms reached their final form in 1636, when an edition in two different forms appeared.[83] The octavo has the prose version of the Psalms appearing in the margins, and includes the music of thirty-six tunes. For those Psalms without a tune, one elsewhere in the Psalter is suggested. This

---

[78] *Acts and Proceedings of the General Assembly*, vol. 3, p. 970; Calderwood, *Historie of the Kirk of Scotland* (1845), vol. 6, p. 124.

[79] See I. B. Cowan, "The Five Articles of Perth", *Reformation and Revolution*, ed. D. Shaw (Edinburgh, Saint Andrew Press, 1967), pp. 160–77.

[80] On the differences between James' and Charles' style in treating Scotland, see Sharpe, *The Personal Rule of Charles I*, p. 773.

[81] *Earl of Stirling's Register of Royal Letters*, vol. 2, p. 855.

[82] *Earl of Stirling's Register of Royal Letters*, vol. 2, p. 815. A similar letter to the archbishop of St Andrews appears on the next page. See also *Register of the Privy Council of Scotland, 1635–37*, 2nd ser., ed. P. H. Brown (Edinburgh, 1905), pp. 409–10.

[83] *STC* 2736 (folio) was printed in England by Thomas Harper; *STC* 2736.5 (octavo) has no printer identified; *STC* suggests that Harper may have printed this as well, but it seems more likely that it was produced in Scotland.

1636 edition was significantly different from that of 1631. These differences were noticed by at least one contemporary, John Row, the Presbyterian historian: "In the first impression, thair were some expressions so poeticall, and so farre from the language of Canaan, that all quho had any Religion did dislyke them; as, calling the Sunne 'the Lord of light,' and the Moone 'the pale Ladie of the night', etc."[84] McMillan, in his thorough comparison of the two published versions, finds that the majority of terms and phrases objected to by Calderwood were amended in the 1636 edition.[85] Psalm 148: 3–4 from the two versions illustrates the extent of the changes:

> His praise at length dilate
> You flaming Lord of light
> And with the starres in state
> Pale Lady of the night.
>
> Heavens, heavens him praise
> And all you floods;
> Enclos'd in cloudes;
> His glory raise.
>   (1631)
>
> His praise at length dilate,
> Thow Sun that shin'st so bright,
> Praise him with stars in state,
> Thou moon the lesser light.
>
> Heavens, heavens him praise,
> Ye flouds that move,
> The heavens above,
> His glory raise.
>   (1636)

That the revised Psalter attracted less direct negative comment than the 1631 edition may have been due to these changes, or to the fact that the new Book of Canons and the Service Book became the foci of opposition. However, as the Psalter was nearly always bound with the new Service Book – in Charles' own words they were to be "receaved and used togidder in the Church" – it had no chance of independent acceptance. Frequently, Scottish opponents of the changes referred simply to the "Service Books", by which they likely meant all three of the Book of Canons, the Prayer Book, and the Psalter. That in Scottish tradition these had always been a unit likely encouraged such perception of the new works.

The controversy came to a crisis in 1637, as Charles became more aggressive in his attempts. On 3 February, he sent a letter to the Privy Council of Scotland:

---

[84] These phrases were also among those which Calderwood had ridiculed.
[85] "The Metrical Psalter of James VI", p. 125.

Whereas the late psalmes have by auctoritie frome ws and clergie of both kingdoms been exactlie revised and approved, we now (according to our pleasure formerlie signified for receaving thame in the church of that kingdome) being fullie resolved to have that worke goe on for the churches good and the authors memorie, it is our expresse will and pleasure that, according as yow sall thinke fitt, yow suffer no further impression to be made of the old psalmes, and that yow give suche order as yow sall find necessarie, and whiche is in your power, for printing and receaving of the new, to be generally receaved, and sung in all the churches of the said kingdome . . .[86]

The council responded on 14 March 1637 by encouraging the archbishop to sternly instruct the printers that no printing or importing of the old Psalters would be allowed.[87] Both the king and the official acts of the Privy Council associate the Psalms with the name of James, but Sir Thomas Hope recorded in a more personal account that Charles has sent an order to the Scottish privy council forbidding the use of the old Psalms, "and geving command to sing the new of the Erl Stirling".[88] Throughout the spring Charles urged the whole new liturgy, and the Scottish clergy resisted. Finally, on 23 July 1637 the new liturgy was used at a number of Edinburgh churches. The long delays in introducing the new Prayer Book and Psalter had given those opposed to it ample time to organize resistance. Thus, the uprisings at St Giles and other Edinburgh churches on 23 July were less than spontaneous events, but nevertheless reflected widespread opposition to the new liturgy. This was followed by further violent resistance to the new liturgical works on 17 October.[89] Eventually, the resistance led to the Scottish Covenant and the Bishops' War of 1638–39.

Ultimately the content of the psalter, like that of the Prayer Book, may have been less significant than the way it was introduced. Charles worked solely through the bishops, completely bypassing parliament and the Assembly of the Church.[90] The Prayer Book was, in Walter Makey's words, "merely the outward manifestation of the system which the bishops had created".[91] The bishops themselves were referred to as "Canterburians", for their close connections to Archbishop Laud and the English court in general.[92] Frequently, later popular history came to see the work as "Laud's Liturgy",

---

[86] *Register of the Privy Council of Scotland*, vol. 6, p. 409.
[87] Ibid.
[88] Sir Thomas Hope, *Diary of Correspondence*, ed. T. Thomson (Edinburgh: Bannatyne Club, 1843), p. 56. Hope was the king's advocate, but, according to Guthry, was a party to the opponents of the new liturgy (p. 23).
[89] Hope, p. 66.
[90] No General Assembly of the Church of Scotland was called between 1618 and 1638.
[91] *The Church of the Covenant, 1637–51: Revolution and Social Change in Scotland* (Edinburgh: John Donald, 1979), p. 16.
[92] Horton Davies, *Worship and Theology in England*, 5 vols (Princeton: Princeton UP, 1975), vol. 2, p. 341.

stemming from the archbishop's personal desires, but at the time, the Scots blamed their own bishops and archbishops.[93] Kevin Sharpe has shown that Charles himself was largely responsible for the religious policy of uniformity and order in the church.[94] The same is true of the Psalter: Laud makes no reference to it in his correspondence. Also, the attempted imposition of the Psalter and Prayer Book has the hallmarks of Charles' tendency to work by decree rather than consultation or persuasion.[95] According to Donaldson, "If the Scots suspected the truth – that the principal author and inspirer of the book, outside Scotland, was King Charles himself – they could not directly accuse him as long as the fiction was maintained that 'our sweet prince' had been acting under evil advice."[96] In the same way, the Psalter was attacked not as the work of James, but as the work of William Alexander, earl of Sterling. However, in this case the attribution of the work to a non-royal figure did have a strong basis. By 1637 Alexander's name was anathema to the people of Scotland: he had been responsible a few years earlier for the introduction of a new coin, the "Turner", which profited him, but played havoc with the Scottish economy. At the death of his son in 1638 the Presbyterian historian Robert Baillie commented:

> His father is old and extreamely hated of all the countrey for his alleged briberie, urgeing of the Psalmes and the Books [service-Books] for them [i.e. on account of the Psalms], overwhelming us with his Black money.[97]

With such a reputation, the derisive attacks on the Psalter as "Menstrie's Psalmes" had great effect. While James may not have been universally loved by the more radical Scottish Presbyterians for his insistence upon an episcopal system, his doctrinaire Calvinist theology was useful for the Scottish who accused the new liturgy of Arminianism. They could charge the bishops without rebelling against the sound orthodoxy of the former king. To treat it as Charles did, as a memorial to his father, would have made opposition all

---

[93] Donaldson, *The Making of the Scottish Prayer Book of 1637*, pp. 79–80.

[94] Sharpe, *Politics and Ideas in Early Stuart England: Essays and Studies*, pp. 108–9; Julian Davies, *The Caroline Captivity of the Church*, pp. 36–9.

[95] Sharpe, *The Personal Rule of Charles I*, has argued that Laud generally preferred to work through persuasion (p. 126).

[96] Donaldson, *The Making of the Scottish Prayer Book*, p. 80.

[97] Quoted in Charles Rogers, *Memorials of the Earl of Stirling*, 2 vols (Edinburgh: Paterson, 1877), vol. 1, p. 173. Rogers also quotes a manuscript satire by Sir James Balfour written shortly after Alexander's own death:

> Heir layes a farmer and a miller,
> A poet and a Psalme booke spiller,
> A purchaser by hoode and crooke,
> A forger of ye service booke,
> A copper smith who did much evill
> A friend to Bischopes and ye Devil.
> (p. 190)

but impossible. Later, in the 1640s, the Presbyterian historian John Row could take a more balanced view of the Psalter: "The worke wes comonlie thought to be rather Sir William Alexander's of Menstrie than the King's; howbeit, it is most probable that both hes had a hand in it."[98]

In the 1640s both the English and Scottish churches would consider more moderate emendations of the old Psalters. Charles' pressing of his father's psalter had cleared the field, and in the late 1630s and 1640s new versions by William Mure of Rowallan, Zachary Boyd, Francis Rous and William Barton appeared. Ultimately, through the deliberations of the Westminster Assembly, a new version based substantially on that of Francis Rous was instituted for both England and Scotland. In the Assembly of 1647 the Kirk of Scotland considered the new Psalter prepared in England. They recommended an examination of the work, and the examiners "to make use of the travels of Rowallen, Master Zachary Boyd, or any other on that subject, but especially of our own Paraphrase, that what they finde better in any of these Works may be chosen".[99] While it failed to take hold in England, from 1650 this work became the new standard Scottish psalter in the churches. Among those "other[s] on that subject" that were considered was James' work: William McMillan has demonstrated the great irony that his psalms were substantially drawn upon by those who put together the 1650 Psalter. He estimates that as many as 572 lines (of a total of 9,000) are taken directly from James' work, with a further 1400 lines that show some influence.[100] However, by the late 1640s all such indebtedness had to go unacknowledged: the reputation of James, Alexander and the coupling of their Psalter with the 1637 Prayer Book made it impossible for it to be publicly recognized as influencing the new version. Thus, James' ambitions in regards to the Psalms were ultimately partially fulfilled, but in a way that completely eclipsed his image as a latter-day David. Both in his own reign and that of his son James' "Psalms" were a sort of phantom work; the reality of them was inconsequential or elusive, while the idea of them played a major role. Subsequently in the Scottish church James' authorship has become the phantom, with his actual lines remaining as the real presence.

[98] *The Historie of the Kirk of Scotland, 1558–1637*, p. 492.

[99] 28 August 1647, Peterkin, *Records of the Kirk of Scotland*, vol. 1, p. 475. This same act also advises them to heed the "animadversions sent from Presbyteries".

[100] McMillan, "The Metrical Psalter of James VI", p. 192. McMillan also cites an independent study by a Dr Rorison who found 516 lines taken from James's psalter.

Chapter 8

THE DEATH OF SOLOMON

"His rest, no question, is in Abraham's bosom, and his crown changed into a crown of glory."[1]

AT the beginning of King James' reign, William Thorne had reminded him that while men might praise him as a God, he would "die like a man", an eminently safe, if unwelcome, prediction.[2] Daniel Price, dean of Hereford, in his sermon preached at Theobalds just hours before James' death, recalled that biblical verse as well.[3] The occasion of the king's death, in March 1625, provided the people of England with an opportunity to reconsider both the human and divine qualities of their monarch of twenty-two years. Some attention was also given to the mark he had left on religious life in England, but this aspect of his life received far less attention than at his accession. As at earlier times, biblical comparisons were common, with the peaceful King Solomon most often presented as the type of James. The most important of these works marking James' death was the funeral sermon preached by John Williams, bishop of Lincoln, entitled "The Death of Solomon". More so than most poems and speeches it surveyed James' life and reign, rather than looking forward to the possibilities his death opened up. Williams' sermon was a sort of lone light, in striking contrast to the general speed with which the late English king's life and death were forgotten, as attention turned to the immediate situation of a royal marriage and foreign conflicts.[4]

The latter years of James' reign found him in failing health, and much of the power and public attention devolving to Charles and Buckingham. As we saw above with his encouragement of George Wither, James seem to have recognized that his end was drawing near. G. P. V. Akrigg suggests that "The King's death was hardly unexpected" because of general failing

---

[1] Laud, "Memorables of King James", *Works*, vol. 6, p. 7.
[2] Fuller, *Church History of Britain* (1868), vol. 4, pp. 292–3, reports how Anthony Rudd, bishop of St Davids, offended Queen Elizabeth by preaching sermons on her aging and decay in 1596 and again in 1602.
[3] *A Heartie Prayer*, p. 9.
[4] The poetic response to James' death has been largely neglected by scholars; as with the transition from Elizabeth to James, this historical moment also produced some rich and ambivalent responses.

health over the previous years, and certainly at Christmas of 1624 his condition was known to be very poor.[5] It does seem, however, that few Englishmen were expecting his immediate death in March of 1625. At that time he had gone up to Theobalds in his usual fashion to hunt. The letters of Chamberlain in March of 1625 contain references to the king's ague, but reflect no widespread public concern that this might lead to the king's death. Given his isolation at Theobalds, it is possible that only those in his immediate company knew of the seriousness of the illness. Unlike that of Elizabeth, James' death was not widely anticipated or feared, largely because the accession of Charles was clear and uncontroversial. The death of the old monarch and accession of the new clearly would not lead to major, or at least immediate, disruption. The influence of Buckingham on both James and Charles also helped to guarantee continuity. The lack of upheaval is noted in a short poem by Sir Isaac Wake, which seems to have circulated fairly widely. The poem questions why no comet marked James' passing, but then concludes

> No innovation being to be heard,
> Why should Heaven summon men unto their guard?
> His spirit was redoubled on his son,
> And that was seen at his assumption.[6]

Scotland, like England, seems to have been little troubled by the death of its king; Calderwood reports

> Upon the Lord's day following [James' death] the ministers of Edinburgh commendit King James for the most religious and peacable prince that ever was in the world; yea, some of them said, that if he had not been a king, but a commoun man, he was the best man in the kingdom. Mr. John Adamsone said, King David had moe faults than he had; for he committed both adulterie and murther, whereof our king was not guiltie. Mr Struthers laboured with all the art he had to move the people; but they were not much moved with sorrow and greef for his death.[7]

The date of James' death, 27 March, offered an occasion for a number of clever conceits. Daniel Price cites a poem of William Goodwin, dean of Christ Church, crediting Mars, the god of war, with destroying the king of peace:

> Tu Marten odisti, Mars odit pacis amantem,
> Hinc tanta clades, hinc tot conamina Martis.[8]

---

[5] *Jacobean Pageant* (Cambridge: Harvard UP, 1962), p. 391.
[6] Chamberlain includes this poem in his letter to Carleton describing the funeral of James.
[7] Calderwood, *Historie of the Kirk of Scotland* (1845), vol. 7, p. 634. It seems that neither of these sermons survives.
[8] *A Heartie Prayer*, p. 33. [You have hated Mars, and Mars hated the lover of peace; hence all

The month of "Mars" had destroyed James, but in another sense the threat of war on the continent could be seen as his assailant. However, hope was found in the date as well. As with the death of Elizabeth, it fell near the beginning of the year (Lady's Day), thus presaging a new beginning, as well as an ending.

The king's body was brought from Theobalds to London on 4 April, and lay at Denmark House until burial on 7 May.[9] In the weeks following, James' death was overshadowed by other events and developments. Military preparations were at hand, including the mustering of soldiers; a parliament was pending, and there was much talk of the negotiations and preparations for Charles' wedding to the French princess, Henrietta Maria. In fact, the funeral was delayed by marriage preparations, and in this case a Hamlet might be justified in complaining that "the funeral baked meats did furnish forth the marriage table". However, few seemed concerned with the general neglect of the king's memory. The funeral was duly observed on 7 May, with over nine thousand black-clad mourners.

As six weeks passed between James' death and his funeral on 7 May, the public responses were stretched out over this period as well. The Daniel Price sermon quoted above was in many ways the first "funeral sermon" although it actually preceded James' death by a few hours. Price frequently draws attention to the dying king, and anticipates the reign of his son.[10] John Donne preached a scant few days after James' death on 3 April 1625 "to King Charles, at Saint James", on the text "If the foundations be destroyed, what can the righteous doe?" (Psalm 11:3). He glances at James' death at the beginning of the sermon:

> We are still in the season of *Mortification;* in *Lent*: But wee search no longer for *Texts* of *Mortification*; The Almightie hand of *God* hath shed and spred a *Text* of *Mortification* over all the land. The last *Sabboth* day, was his *Sabboth* who entred then into his everlasting *Rest*;[11]

The sermon is noteworthy in presenting a moment of transition for the church and England; it seems to point toward imminent change, but suggests that such change will not involve the foundations, and thus should be peaceably accepted:

> we must not too jealously suspect, not too bitterly condemne, not too peremptorily conclude, that what soever is not done, as wee would have it done, or as wee have seene it done in former times, is not well done: for there is

destruction, hence so many efforts of Mars.] Cf. a similar treatment of the month of James' death in Ed. Mottershed's poem "In Symbolum IACOBI, Beati Pacifici, & quod mense Marte obiit.", in the commemorative volume *Oxoniensis Academiae parentalia* (1625), sig. E1v.

[9] John Stow, *Annales, or General Chronicle of England* (1615), p. 1036.

[10] This sermon was printed sometime in May, with Price apologizing for bringing it out at the time of Charles and Henrietta Maria's wedding (sig. A2r).

[11] *Sermons*, vol. 6, p. 241.

a large Latitude, and, by necessitie of Circumstances, much may bee admitted, and yet no *Foundations destroyed*; and till *Foundations bee destroyed, the righteous should bee quiet.*[12]

The official funeral sermon by Williams some six weeks later was far gloomier in its anticipation of changing times. Among the higher clergy Williams was closest to the person and position of James. He had attended him during the final days of illness, and served him his final communion. By James' death Williams lost a great patron; he was one of the few prominent figures who still supported the policy of peace with Spain, and with the accession of Charles war became far more likely.[13] His seventeenth-century biographer, John Hacket, suggests that from the very beginning of Charles' reign Williams was being excluded from decision-making, and in danger of losing his office. His role in the spring of 1625 was not to look forward to the new reign, but to remember and bury the past. He diligently prepared for his role as preacher at the funeral:

> He enquired after the Sermon which Bishop Fisher made at the Funeral of King Henry the Seventh, and procur'd it; likewise for the Oration which Cardinal Peron made for King Henry the Fourth of France, and had by the hands of Dr. Peter Moulin the Father. These he laid before him to work by, and no common Patterns.[14]

The sermon he finally produced stands as a testament to the accomplishments of James. The response to it gives some indication of how things were changing, and the eventual fate of James' legacy, particularly in religious matters.

Williams took as the text for his sermon I Kings 11:41–43, describing the death of Solomon, and the work is largely a comparison of Solomon and James, particularly in their wisdom and peacefulness. In fact, Williams argued that James surpassed Solomon in that he shared his predecessor's virtues, but not his vices.[15] While the sermon proceeds by first outlining the words and deeds of Solomon, and then turning to James, there is a fair amount of slippage of identity between the two. We cannot always easily discern which of the two is being discussed, and, furthermore, Williams at times renders Solomon as a type of Christ as well. In this way James becomes a Christ-like king, standing in apposition to Christ as the antitype of Solomon.[16] Williams

---

[12] Ibid., p. 243.

[13] See Sharpe, "The Earl of Arundel, His Circle and the Opposition to the Duke of Buckingham, 1618–1628", *Faction and Parliament: Essays on Early Stuart History* (London and New York: Methuen, 1978), pp. 209–44.

[14] John Hacket, *Scrinia Reserata* (1693), pt. 1, p. 223.

[15] sig. A3r.

[16] Strangely, Goldberg concludes that "In Williams' sermon, the Biblical matrix is subordinated

also stresses the uniqueness of James, suggesting that he and Solomon are not only alike, but in a way that "they differ from all kings besides".[17]

Most significant are those points where Williams comments on James' role in the religious affairs of his nation: "Salomon was the greatest Patron we ever read of to Church and Churchmen, and yet no greater (let the house of Aaron now confesse) then King James."[18] Williams describes him as a greater founder of churches than Constantine, Charlemagne, or Alphonso of Spain. His support of the church, especially in terms of building new churches and restoring decayed ones, is a constant theme in other eulogies marking his death. His support of episcopacy is noted by Williams, who suggests that God "blessed" James with Presbyterianism in Scotland so that he might learn the dangers of it.[19] Williams also commemorates the new translation of the Bible, describing it as a work against the papists, and the Hampton Court Conference as a work against "Novellists".[20]

James' peacemaking is prominent in the sermon: it is the chief of James' work, and the most important way in which he is like Solomon. Like so many others, Williams puts forth the biblical image of prosperity-bearing peace: "Every man liv'd in peace under his vine, and his Figge-Tree in the daies of Salomon, I Kings 4:25 And so they did in the blessed daies of King James."[21] Once again, the rhetoric of peacemaking is contingent on the context: as it was no longer fashionable or official in May of 1625, Williams must struggle much harder than earlier writers to defend James' position. In fact, lamenting James' death might have been the only acceptable means of expression for those opposing the war party.[22] He presents James as one capable of military sternness when it was necessary to preserve peace, and he connects the actions of war with the result of peace: "The third sort of Actions, which are those of Warre, are also observable in the peaceable Raigne of our late Salomon."[23] However, the only active engagement of James that Williams can point to is his defeat of the earl of Argyle.[24] In the same passage he rebukes those who deny the gift of peace: "yet surely nothing, but the malice of some people, that would place their wheeles in Princes, as Daedalus did in his Statues, to pull to combustions at their

---

to Roman art" (p. 42). He seems to overlook the fact that the whole sermon's extended comparison of Solomon and James grows out of biblical typology, and that Christ, the other prince of peace, figures centrally in it as well.

[17] p. 37.

[18] p. 38.

[19] pp. 47ff.

[20] p. 46.

[21] p. 39.

[22] Cf. John Taylor, "A Living Sadnes in Duty Consecrated to the Immortall Memory of our Late Deceased all-beloved Soveraigne Lord, the Peerelesse Paragon of Princes, James", in *Works* (1630), pp. 322ff.

[23] p. 55.

[24] p. 56.

owne pleasure, can denie this Laurell to our late Soveraigne". James' active, defensive peacemaking is also presented in biblical terms – terms that associate England with the Garden of Eden:

> I say, beside these Adventures of his person, he was unto his people, to the houre of his death, another Cherubin with a flaming sword, to keepe out Enemies from this Paradise of ours; wherein, above al neighbouring Nations, grew in abundance those Apples of peace, which now I am to gather in the last place. And surely Actions of Peace (what ever debauched people say to the contrarie) set out a Prince in more orient colours then those of War, and great combustions.[25]

This final affirmation of James' peacemaking role overshadows the earlier section in the sermon where Williams had pointed out that Solomon and James were alike in having to face new enemies at their deaths.[26] The overall emphasis of the sermon is on James' capacity for peacemaking, and as such it stands apart from most of the literature of the spring of 1625.

While Germano may be right in suggesting "There is not a single idea in the sermon that has not appeared before in the literature addressed to King James I",[27] the sermon is significant in that it rehearses these concepts after his death, and the beginning of his son's quite different reign. Inevitably, the sermon stirred some controversy for its backward-looking stance: as Fuller reports, "Some conceived him too long in praising the past – too short in priming for the present – king, though saying much of him in a little; and of the bishop's adversaries, whereof then no want at court, some took distaste, others made advantage thereof."[28] Williams also seemed doubtful about the continuing effect of James' peaceful ways; in a striking passage near the end of the sermon he gloomily looked forward to James' pen being replaced once more by the sword:

> For although King James had no such Officers as Solomon had, a Commentar-iis, appointed of purpose to write his Actions; yet *Dulce est oculis videre Solem*, the Sunne cannot shine in such a brightnesse, but Eyes must behold it, nor set in so lasting night, but the world will misse it. Private Histories (as Adrian said of Apers accusations) are but Incke, and Paper, and may bee holpe in part with the golden pin-dust; whereas *Suffragia mundi nullus emit*, None can be honoured of all Europe, but he that held the Ballance of all Europe; and, for the space of twentie yeares at the least, preserved the peace of all Europe. Christendome therefore will be the Booke, Swords, I feare, will prove the

---

[25] p. 56.
[26] Cogswell, *The Blessed Revolution*, p. 298, suggests that Williams' reference to the military preparations of Solomon is often overlooked by scholars who have considered the sermon. He points to Trevelyan, *England under the Stuarts*, 1904 (Harmondsworth: Penguin, 1960), pp. 130–1 and Russell, *Parliaments*, p. 203, as among those who overlook this dimension.
[27] *The Literary Icon of James I*, p. 207.
[28] *Church History of Britain*, pp. 375–6.

Pennes, and the Remembrance of the times past, the Acts, and Monuments of our blessed Salomon.[29]

In addition to this emphasis on the lost legacy of Solomon/James, Williams also praised the dead king in ways felt by some to denigrate his son. The sermon's emphasis on James' eloquence seemed to reflect badly on Charles:

> Some auditors, who came thither rather to observe than edify, cavil than observe, found or made faults in the sermon; censuring him for touching too often and staying too long on a harsh string, three times straining the same, making eloquence too essential and so absolutely necessary in a king, "that the want thereof made Moses in a manner refuse all government, though offered by God;" "that no man ever got great power without eloquence; Nero being the first of the Caesars *qui alienae facundiae eguit,* 'who usurped another man's language to speak for him.'" Expressions which might be forborne in the presence of his son and successor, whose impediment in speech was known to be great, and mistaken to be greater.[30]

In his life of Williams, Hacket confirms Fuller's report.[31] Shortly afterwards the sermon was published, "which gave but the steadier mark to his enemies, noting the marginal notes thereof, and making all his sermon the text of their captious interpretation".[32] Fuller's account also suggests that Charles was less than zealous about the publication of the work, noting that it was "publicly set forth by the printer (but not the express command) of his Majesty".[33]

THE KING'S TUNE

Williams' voice was a solitary one, crying in the wilderness for the saviour who had been: far more writers and speakers celebrated the promise of the new reign. In Chapter 2, I noted the expectations aroused by the accession of James; at his death and the consequent accession of Charles we can hear echoes as poets once more betook themselves to the court in hope. Among these was Robert Aylett, formerly patronized by Williams; in 1625 he produced a further volume of his poetic meditations, *The Brides Ornaments.* Within this volume is a divine poem, *Urania,* that would not have been out of place in the 1603 response to James. *Urania*'s dedicatory poem to John Maynard, "one of the Gentlemen of his Majesties Privie Chamber in Ordinarie",[34] signals a shift in Aylett's interests and concerns; in it Aylett

---

[29] p. 60.
[30] Fuller, *Church History of Britain* (1868), p. 375.
[31] *Scrinia Reserata,* p. 41.
[32] Fuller, *Church History of Britain* (1868), p. 375.
[33] Ibid.
[34] According to the dedication Maynard himself has forsaken a promising career as a poet himself to serve the king: he "Who (had not his great Princes Love and Grace/Him brought from Muses Groves to's Royall place)/Might on his Front have worne thy Crowne of Bays,/

comments that his Urania, the divine muse, is now off to court. The poem becomes a celebration of the royal court and its relation to religious poetry. It is such a court where "Arts, and Learning so increase,/Hence followeth all our happinesse and Peace."[35] In the last two lines of the poem he establishes a hierarchy of fashion or influence: "The Muses needs must dance when Courtiers sing,/All follow the example of the King." The monarch is once again seen as the setter of literary fashions: the muses are not free, but compelled to dance to the tune sung by the courtiers and called by the king. But this tune was always one with which there might be a multitude of descants.

And beene the Prince of Poets in his dayes". However, he still would do all he could to "entertaine" the heav'nly Muse.
[35] [p. 108].

WORKS CITED

All biblical quotations are from the Authorized Version of 1611, unless otherwise noted.

MANUSCRIPT COLLECTIONS

Bodleian Library
MS Rawlinson poet. 246
British Library
MS Egerton 2404
MS Harl. 3496.2
MS Lansdowne 213, fol. 59ff.
MS Lansdowne 885
MS Old Royal 14A.xxii
MS Old Royal 18B. XVI
MS Royal 18 A. LVII
MS Royal 20 D.xiv–xix
National Library of Scotland
MS 8874
Public Record Office
SP 14/76/9
SP 14/90/48v

PRINTED PRIMARY SOURCES

Academiae Oxoniensis. Oxford, 1603.
Acts and Proceedings of the General Assembly of the Kirk of Scotland. Ed. T. Thomson. 3 Vols. Edinburgh, 1845.
Adams, Thomas. *Works.* Ed. Joseph Angus. 3 Vols. 1861–2.
Adamson, John. *Τα των μουσων εισωδια: the Muses Welcome.* Edinburgh, 1618.
Adamson, Patrick. *De Sacro Pastoris Munere.* [Ed. Thomas Wilson.] 1619.
Alexander, Sir William. *Earl of Stirling's Register of Royal Letters Relative to the Affairs of Scotland and Nova Scotia from 1615 to 1635.* 2 Vols. Edinburgh, 1885.
All the French Psalm Tunes with English Words. 1632.
The Answer of the Vice-Chancellor, the Doctors with the Proctors and other Heads of Houses in the University of Oxford. Oxford, 1603.
Ashton, Robert. *James I by his Contemporaries.* London: Hutchinson, 1969.
Athenae Oxonienses. Third edition. London, 1815.

Augustine. *On Christian Doctrine.* Trans. D. W. Robertson, Jr. Indianapolis: Bobbs-Merrill, 1958.

Aylett, Robert. *The Brides Ornaments.* 1625.

——. *Peace and her Foure Garders.* 1622.

Bacon, Francis. *The Advancement of Learning and The New Atlantis.* Ed. Arthur Johnston. Oxford: Clarendon Press, 1974.

——. *The Charge of Sir Francis Bacon Touching Duells.* 1614. Fasc. Amsterdam: Theatrum Orbis Terrarum, 1968.

——. *The Letters and Life of Francis Bacon.* Ed. James Spedding. London, 1861–74.

Bartas, Guillaume de Saluste Sieur du. *Divine Weeks and Works.* Ed. Susan Snyder. 2 Vols. Oxford: Clarendon Press, 1979.

Breton, Nicholas. *Works in Verse and Prose.* Ed. A. B. Grosart. 2 Vols. London, 1879.

Bridges, John. *Sacro-Sanctum Novum Testamentum.* 1604.

Browne, Sir Thomas. *Religio Medici and Other Works.* Ed. L. C. Martin. Oxford: Clarendon Press, 1964.

Browne, William. *Britannia's Pastorals. The Second Booke.* 1616.

Burton, Robert. *Anatomy of Melancholy.* 1621. Fasc. Amsterdam: Theatrum Orbis Terrarum, 1971.

Calderwood, David. *Altare Damascenum.* 1623.

——. *Historie of the Kirk of Scotland.* Ed. T. Thomson. Edinburgh, 1845.

——. *Parasynagma Perthense.* 1620.

——. "Reasons against the reception of King James's metaphrase of the Psalms", *Bannatyne Miscellany.* Vol. 1. Eds Sir Walter Scott and D. Laing. Edinburgh, 1827.

——. *The True History of the Church of Scotland.* Edinburgh, 1678.

Calvin, John. *Commentary on the Book of the Prophet Isaiah.* Trans. William Pringle. Edinburgh, 1850.

Carier, Benjamin. *A Copy of a Letter, written by M. Doctour beyond Seas, to some particular friends in England.* 1615.

——. *A Treatise Written by Mr. Doctour Carier.* [1614?]

Carleton, Dudley. *Dudley Carleton to John Chamberlain.* Ed. Maurice Lee, Jr. New Brunswick, NJ: Rutgers UP, 1972.

Casaubon, Isaac. *Epistolae.* 1709.

Chamberlain, John. *The Chamberlain Letters.* Ed. Norman Egbert McClure. 2 Vols. Philadelphia: American Philosophical Society, 1939.

Clapham, Henoch. *A Briefe of the Bible.* [Edinburgh, 1596].

——. *Doctor Andros his Prosopopeia Answered.* 1605.

——. *Epistle Discoursing upon the Present Pestilence.* 1603.

Clarendon, Edward, Earl of. *History of the Rebellion and Civil Wars in England.* Ed. W. Dunn Macray. 6 Vols. Oxford, 1888.

Court and Times of Charles I. Ed. Thomas Birch. 1848.

Court and Times of James I. Ed. Thomas Birch. 1848.

Crakanthorpe, Richard. *The Defense of Constantine.* 1621.

Damman, Adrian. *Schediasmata Hadrianus Dammanis A Bisterveld Gandavensis.* Edinburgh, 1590.

Daneau, Lambert. *A Fruitfull Commentary upon the Twelve Small Prophets.* Trans. John Stockwood. 1594.

Daniel, Samuel. *Panegyric Congratulatorie.* 1603. Fasc. Menston: Scolar Press, 1969.

Davies, Eleanor. *Eleanor Davies: Prophetic Tracts*. Ed. Esther Cope. Oxford: OUP, 1993.

Davies, John. *Poems*. Ed. Robert Krueger. Oxford: Clarendon Press, 1975.

Davies, John of Hereford. *Complete Works*. 2 Vols. Ed. A. B. Grosart. 1878. Rpt. New York: AMS Press, 1967.

Dekker, Thomas. *The Wonderfull Yeare*. 1603.

——. *Non-dramatic Works*. London, 1863.

Dempster, Thomas. *Historia Ecclesiastica*. Edinburgh: Andreas Balfour, 1829.

Denison, Stephen. *The White Wolf*. 1627.

Dod, Henry. *All the Psalmes of David*. 1620.

——. *Certain Psalmes of David*. 1603.

Donne, John. *Life and Letters*. Ed. Edmund Gosse. 2 Vols. 1899.

——. *Sermons*. Eds George R. Potter and Evelyn M. Simpson. 10 Vols. Berkeley: U of California P, 1953–62.

Drummond, William. *Works*. 1711.

du Moulin, Pierre. *The Accomplishment of Prophecies*. Oxford, 1611.

Earle, John. *Microcosmography*. 1628.

Eglishem, George. *Duellum Poeticum*. 1618.

Farley, Henry. *The Complaint of Paules to all Christian Soules*. London, 1616.

Fowler, William. *A True reportarie . . . of the Baptism of . . . Prince Henry*. Edinburgh, [1594].

Foxe, John. *Actes and Monuments*. 1570.

Fugitive Tracts Written in Verse. Ed. W. C. Hazlitt. 1875.

Fuller, Thomas. *Abel Redivivus*. 1651.

——. *Church History of Britain*. 1655.

——. *Church History of Britain*. London, 1868.

Gee, John. *The Foot out of the Snare*. 1624.

Greene, Thomas. *A Poets Vision and a Princes Glory*. 1603.

Greg, W. W. *Companion to Arber*. Oxford: Clarendon Press, 1967.

Grotius, Hugo. *Epistolae*. Amsterdam, 1687.

Guthry, Henry. *Bp. of Dunkeld. Memoires*. Glasgow, 1747.

Hacket, John. *Scrinia Reserata*. 1693.

Hakewill, George. *An Answere to a Treatise Written by Dr. Carier*. 1616.

Hall, Joseph. *The Best Bargaine*. 1623.

——. *Collected Poems*. Ed. Arnold Davenport. Liverpool: Liverpool UP, 1949.

——. *A Holy Panegyric*. 1613.

——. *Quo Vadis?* 1617.

——. *The True Peacemaker*. 1624.

——. *Works*. 1624.

——. *Works*. Ed. Philip Wynter. Oxford, 1863.

Harington, John. *Letters and Epigrams*. Ed. N. E. McClure. Philadelphia: U of Pennsylvania P, 1930.

——. *Nugae Antiquae*. Ed. T. Park. London, 1804.

Herbert, George. *The Latin Poetry of George Herbert: A Bilingual Edition*. Eds Mark McCloskey and Paul R. Murphy. Athens, Ohio: Ohio UP, 1965.

Higgons, Theophilus. *A Sermon Preached at Pauls Crosse*. 1611.

Hope, Sir Thomas. *Diary of the Correspondence*. Ed. T. Thomson. Edinburgh: Bannatyne Club, 1843.

Howson, John. *A Sermon Preached at St. Maries in Oxford*. 1603.

James I. *Essayes of a Prentise*. Edinburgh, 1584.

——. *His Majesties Poeticall Exercises at Vacant Houres*. Edinburgh, 1591.

——. *Lusus Regius*. Ed. Robert Rait. London: A. Constable, 1901.

——. *New Poems by James I of England*. Ed. Allan F. Westcott. New York: Columbia UP, 1911; Rpt. New York: AMS Press, 1966.

——. *Political Works*. Ed. Charles Howard McIlwain. New York: Russell & Russell, 1965.

——. *The Psalmes of King David, Translated by King James*. Oxford, 1631.

——. *The Psalmes of King David, Translated by King James*. Oxford, 1636.

——. *The True Law of Free Monarchies* and *Basilikon Doron*. Eds Daniel Fischlin and Mark Fortier. Toronto: CRRS, 1996.

——. *Workes*. London, 1616. Fasc. Rpt. New York: George Olms Verlag, 1971.

James I and the earl of Northampton. *A Publication of his Maties. Edict and Severe Censure against Private Combats and Combatants*. London, 1614.

Jones, Thomas Wharton. *A True Relation of the Life and Death of . . . William Bedell*. Camden Society, new series, no. 4. Rpt. New York: Johnson, 1965.

Jonson, Ben. *The Oxford Authors: Ben Jonson*. Ed. Ian Donaldson. Oxford: OUP, 1985.

Kerr, Robert, earl of Ancrum. *Correspondence*. 2 Vols. Edinburgh, 1875.

King, John. *A Sermon at Paules Crosse, on behalf of Paules Church*. 1620.

Laud, William. *Works*. Oxford, 1847–60.

Le Fevre de la Boderie, Antoine. *Ambassades de M. De la Boderie en Angleterre*. [Paris], 1750.

Leighton, William. *Vertue Triumphant, or a Lively Description of the Foure Vertues Cardinall*. 1603.

Marston, John. *Poems*. Ed. Arnold Davenport. Liverpool: Liverpool UP, 1961.

Matthew, Tobie. *A True Historical Relation of the Conversion of Tobie Matthew*. London, 1904.

Maxwell, James. *Admirable and Notable Prophecies*. London, 1614.

Melville, Andrew. *Principis Scoti-Britannorum Natalia*. Edinburgh, 1594.

——. *Στεφανισκιον*. Edinburgh, 1590.

Melville, Andrew and Patrick Adamson. *Viri Clarissimi A. M. Musae, et P. Adamsoni vita et Palindoia*. 1620.

Memorials of Affairs of State. London, 1725.

Middleton, Thomas. *The Peace-maker*. 1619.

Musica deo Sacra & Ecclesiae Anglicanae. 1666.

Nichols, John (ed.) *The Progresses of King James I*. 4 Vols. London, 1828. Rpt. New York: Burt Franklin, 1964.

Nixon, Anthony. *Eliziaes Memoriall; King James his Arrivall; and Romes Downefall*. 1603.

Northerne Poems Congratulating the Kings Majesties Entrance to the Crown. 1604.

Owen, John. *Ioannis Audoeni Epigrammatum*. 2 Vols. Ed. John R. C. Martyn. Leiden: E. J. Brill, 1978.

Oxoniensis Academiae Parentalia. 1625.

Peterkin, Alexander. *Records of the Kirk of Scotland*. Edinburgh, 1838.

Pollard, A. W. *Records of the English Bible 1525–1611*. Oxford: OUP, 1911.

Price, Daniel. *A Heartie Prayer*. 1625.

Records of the Court of the Stationers Company. Eds W. W. Greg *et al*. London: Bibliographical Society, 1930.

Register of the Privy Council of Scotland, 1635–37. 2nd Ser. Ed. P. Hume Brown. Edinburgh, 1905.

Rogers, Charles. *Memorials of the Earl of Stirling*. 2 Vols. Edinburgh: Paterson, 1877.

Row, John. *Historie of the Kirk of Scotland, 1558–1637, by John Row, minister at Carnock; with additions and illustrations by his sons*. Ed. David Laing. 2 Vols. Edinburgh: Maitland Club, 1842; rpt. New York: AMS Press, 1973.

Rutherford, Samuel. *Letters*. Ed. Andrew Bonar. 4th edn. Edinburgh, 1891.

Shuckburgh, E. S. (ed.) *Two Biographies of William Bedell*. Cambridge: CUP, 1902.

Source Book of Scottish History. Eds W. Croft Dickinson *et al*. 3 Vols. London: Nelson, [1952–4].

Speed, John. *History of Great Britain*. 1611.

Spottiswoode, John. *History of the Church and State of Scotland*. 4th edn. Edinburgh, 1677.

——. *History of the Church of Scotland*. Ed. M. Russell. Edinburgh: Oliver & Boyd, 1851.

Stow, John. *Annales, or, General Chronicle of England*. 1615.

Stradling, John. *Beati Pacifici*. 1623.

——. *Epigrammatum Libri Quatuor*. 1607.

Sylvester, Joshua. *Complete Works*. Ed. A. B. Grosart. 1877. Fasc. New York: AMS Press, 1967.

——. *The Divine Weeks and Works of Guillaume de Saluste du Bartas*. Ed. Susan Snyder. 2 Vols. Oxford: Clarendon Press, 1979.

Taylor, John. *Works*. 1630.

Thorne, William. Εσοπτρον Βασιλικον: or A Kenning-Glasse for a Christian King. 1603.

Tom Tell-Troath: or a Free Discourse Touching the Manners of the Time, Directed to His Majesty. [1622]

Wakeman, Robert. *Salomons Exaltation: A Sermon Preached Before the King's Majestie at Nonesuch, Apr. 30, 1605*. 1605.

Walton, Izaak. *Life of George Herbert*. 1670.

Walton, Izaak, *Lives*. Ed. Thomas Zouch. York, 1796.

Weldon, Anthony. *Court and Character of King James*. 1650.

Williams, John. *Great Britains Salomon*. 1625.

Wither, George. *Britains Remembrancer*. 1628.

——. *A Collection of Emblems*. 1635.

——. *Fidelia*. 1615.

——. *The History of the Pestilence*. Cambridge, Mass.: Harvard UP, 1932.

——. *Juvenilia*. 1626. Spenser Society, 1871. Rpt. New York: Burt Franklin, 1967.

——. *Miscellaneous Works of George Wither*. Publications of the Spenser Society, nos. 12–13, 16, 18, 22 and 24. Manchester: C. E. Simms, 1872–8; Rpt. New York: Burt Franklin, 1967.

——. *Songs of the Old Testament*. 1621.

Wotton, Henry. *Reliquiae Wottoniae*. 1685.

——. *Sir Henry Wotton, Life and Letters*. Ed. Logan Pearsall Smith. Oxford: Clarendon Press, 1907.

PRINTED SECONDARY SOURCES

Akrigg, G. P. V. *Jacobean Pageant.* Cambridge: Harvard UP, 1962.

Aveling, J. H. C. *The Handle and the Axe: The Catholic Recusants in England from Reformation to Emancipation.* London: Blond & Briggs, 1976.

Bald, R. C. *John Donne, A Life.* New York: OUP, 1970.

Barroll, Leeds. "A New History for Shakespeare and His Time", *SQ* 39 (1988): 441–64.

Bazerman, Charles. "Verses Occasioned by the Death of Queen Elizabeth I and the Accession of King James I." Ph. D., Brandeis, 1971.

Beal, Peter. *Index of English Literary Manuscripts.* 5 Vols. London: Mansell, 1980–

Bell, Sandra J. "Poetry and Politics in the Scottish Renaissance". Ph. D., Queens, 1995.

Benson, Louis F. *The English Hymn.* Philadelphia: Presbyterian Board of Publication, 1915.

Berg, Christine and Philippa Berry. "'Spiritual Whoredom': An Essay on Female Prophets in the Seventeenth Century", *Literature and Power in the Seventeenth Century*, eds Francis Barker *et al.* Colchester: U of Essex P, 1981.

Bingham, Caroline. *The Making of a King: the Early Years of James VI and I.* London: Collins, 1968.

Binns, J. W. *Intellectual Culture in Elizabethan and Jacobean England.* Leeds: Francis Cairns, 1990.

Bols, Laurens J. *Adriaen Pietersz. van de Venne: Painter and Draughtsman.* Doornspijk: Davaco, 1989.

Borris, Kenneth. *Spenser's Poetics of Prophecy in The Faerie Queene V.* Victoria: English Literary Studies, 1991.

Bossy, John. *The English Catholic Community, 1570–1850.* New York: OUP, 1976.

——. "The English Catholic Community 1603–1625", *The Reign of James VI and I*, ed. Alan G. R. Smith. New York: St Martin's Press, 1973.

Bradner, Leicester. *Musae Anglicanae.* New York: MLA, 1940; Rpt. New York: Kraus, 1966.

Burrage, Champlin. *The Early English Dissenters in the Light of Recent Research, 1550–1641.* Cambridge: CUP, 1912.

Bush, Christopher. *Constantine the Great and Christianity.* New York: Columbia, 1914.

Cameron, Euan. *The European Reformation.* Oxford: Clarendon Press, 1991.

Cameron, James K. "Some Continental Visitors to Scotland in the Late Sixteenth and Early Seventeenth Centuries", *Scotland and Europe, 1200–1850*, ed. T. C. Smout. Edinburgh: John Donald, 1986.

Carlson, Norman. "Wither and the Stationers", *SB* 19 (1966): 210–15.

Clark, David L. "Marco Antonio de Dominis and James I: The Influence of a Venetian Reformer on the Church of England", *Papers of the Michigan Academy of Science, Arts and Letters* 53 (1968): 219–30.

Cogswell, Thomas. *The Blessed Revolution: English Politics and the Coming of War 1621–1624.* Cambridge: CUP, 1989.

Collinson, Patrick. *Archbishop Grindal, 1519–1583: the Struggle for a Reformed Church.* London: Jonathan Cape, 1979.

Works Cited

——. *Birthpangs of Protestant England: Religion and Cultural Change in the Sixteenth and Seventeenth Centuries.* New York: St Martin's Press, 1988.

——. *The Religion of Protestants: the Church in English Society, 1559–1625.* Oxford: Clarendon Press, 1982.

Corthell, Ronald J. "Joseph Hall and Seventeenth-Century Literature", *John Donne Journal* 3 (1984): 249–68.

Cowan, I. B. "The Five Articles of Perth", *Reformation and Revolution*, ed. D. Shaw. Edinburgh: Saint Andrew Press, 1967.

Craig, D. H. *Sir John Harington.* Boston: Twayne, 1985.

Craigie, James. "Last Poems of James VI", *Scottish Historical Review* (1951): 134–42.

——. "Poems of King James I of England and VI of Scotland", *Bodleian Library Record* (Supplement) Vol. 3: 1–7.

Crane, Mary Thomas. "*Intret Cato*: Authority and the Epigram in Sixteenth-Century England", *Renaissance Genres: Essays on Theory, History, and Interpretation*, ed. Barbara Kiefer Lewalski. Cambridge, Mass.: Harvard UP, 1986.

Cressy, David. "Foucault, Stone, Shakespeare, and Social History", *ELR* 21 (1991): 121–133.

Cross, Claire. "Churchmen and the Royal Supremacy", *Church and Society in England*, eds Felicity Heal and Rosemary O'Day. Hamden, Conn.: Archon, 1977.

Curtis, Mark. "The Hampton Court Conference and its Aftermath", *History* 46 (1961): 1–16.

Daiches, David. *The King James Version of the English Bible.* Chicago: U of Chicago P, 1941.

Davie, Neil. "Prêtre et Pasteur en Angleterre aux XVI et XVII Siècles: La Carrière de John Copley (1577–1662)", *Revue d'histoire moderne et contemporaine* 43 (1996): 403–21.

Davies, Godfrey. *The Early Stuarts, 1603–1660.* 2nd ed. Oxford: Clarendon Press, 1959.

Davies, Horton. *Worship and Theology in England.* 5 Vols. Princeton: Princeton UP, 1975.

Davies, Julian. *The Caroline Captivity of the Church.* Oxford: OUP, 1992.

Diehl, Huston. *Staging Reform, Reforming the Stage: Protestantism and Popular Theater in Early Modern England.* Ithaca: Cornell UP, 1997.

Dinshaw, Fram. "Two New Epigrams by Joseph Hall", *Notes and Queries* 29 (1982): 422–3.

Doelman, James. "The Contexts of George Herbert's *Musae Responsoriae*", *George Herbert Journal* 2 (1992): 42–54.

——. "'The Fruit of Favour': The Dedicatory Sonnets to Henry Lok's *Ecclesiastes*", *ELH* 60 (1993): 1–15.

——. "George Wither, the Stationers Company and the English Psalter", *SP* 90 (1993): 74–82.

——. "'A King of Thine Own Heart': The English Reception of King James VI and I's *Basilikon Doron*", *Seventeenth Century* 9 (1994): 1–9.

——. "A Seventeenth-Century Publication of Three of Sir Philip Sidney's Psalms", *Notes and Queries* n.s. 38 (1991): 162–3.

Donaldson, Gordon. *Scottish Church History.* Edinburgh: Scottish Academic Press, 1985.

——. *The Making of the Scottish Prayer Book of 1637.* Edinburgh: Edinburgh UP, 1954.

——. *Scotland, James V to James VII.* Edinburgh and London: Oliver & Boyd, 1965.

Donaldson, Gordon. "The Scottish Church, 1567–1625", *The Reign of James VI and I*, ed. Alan G. R. Smith. New York: St Martin's Press, 1973.

——. "Scottish Presbyterian Exiles in England, 1584–8", *Scottish Church History*. Edinburgh: Scottish Academic Press, 1985.

Dubinski, Roman. *English Religious Poetry Printed 1477–1640*. Waterloo, Ont.: North Waterloo Academic Press, 1996.

Dunlap, Rhodes. "James I, Bacon, Middleton, and the Making of *The Peace-Maker*", *Studies in the English Renaissance Drama*, eds Josephine W. Bennett *et al*. New York: New York UP, 1959.

Elton, Geoffrey. *Reformation Europe, 1517–1589*. New York: Harper and Row, 1963.

Fincham, Kenneth. *Prelate as Pastor: the Episcopate of James I*. Oxford: Clarendon Press, 1990.

Fincham, Kenneth and Peter Lake. "The Ecclesiastical Policy of King James I", *Journal of British Studies* 24 (1985): 169–207.

Frontain, Raymond-Jean and Jan Wojcik. *Poetic Prophecy in Western Literature*. London and Toronto: Associated UP, 1984.

French, J. Milton. *The History of the Pestilence*. Cambridge, Mass.: Harvard UP, 1932.

Frost, Kate. *Holy Delight: Typology, Numerology, and Autobiography in Donne's Devotions Upon Emergent Occasions*. Princeton: Princeton UP, 1990.

Galloway, Bruce. *The Union of England and Scotland, 1603–1608*. Edinburgh: John Donald, 1986.

Gardiner, Samuel Rawson. *History of England, 1603–42*. 10 Vols. 1883–4.

Germano, William P. "The Literary Icon of James I". Ph. D., Indiana University, 1981.

Goldberg, Jonathan. *James I and the Politics of Literature*. Stanford: Stanford UP, 1989.

Hannay, Margaret P. *Philip's Phoenix: Mary Sidney, Countess of Pembroke*. Oxford: OUP, 1990.

Hasler, P. W. *The House of Commons, 1558–1603*. London: HMSO, 1981.

Heal, Felicity and Rosemary O'Day (eds). *Church and Society in England: Henry VIII to James I*. Hamden, Conn.: Archon, 1977.

Heinemann, Margot. *Puritanism and Theatre*. Cambridge: CUP, 1980.

Hervey, Mary. *The Life, Correspondence and Collections of Thomas Howard, Earl of Arundel*. Cambridge: CUP, 1921.

Hill, Christopher. *Collected Essays of Christopher Hill, vol. 1: Writing and Revolution in Seventeenth-Century England*. Amherst: U of Massachusetts P, 1985.

Holmes, Urban Tigner, Jr. (ed.) *Guillaume de Salluste Sieur du Bartas: A Biographical and Critical Study*. Vol. 1 in *The Works of du Bartas*, eds John Coriden Lyon Holmes and Robert White Linker. Chapel Hill: U of North Carolina P, 1935.

Howarth, David. *Lord Arundel and his Circle*. New Haven and London: Yale UP, 1985.

Huntley, Frank Livinston. *Bishop Joseph Hall: A Biographical and Critical Study*. Cambridge: D. S. Brewer, 1979.

——. *Essays in Persuasion*. Chicago: U of Chicago P, 1981.

Jack, R. D. S. "Poetry under King James VI", *The History of Scottish Literature. Volume I: Origins to 1660*, ed. R. D. S. Jack. Aberdeen: Aberdeen UP, 1988.

Jemielity, Thomas. *Satire and the Hebrew Prophets*. Louisville: Westminster/John Knox Press, 1992.

Kendall, Ritchie D. *The Drama of Dissent: The Radical Poetics of Nonconformity*. Chapel Hill, NC: U of North Carolina P, 1986.

Lake, Peter. "The Moderate and Irenic Case for Religious War, Joseph Hall's *Via*

Media in Context", *Political Cultural and Cultural Politics in Early Modern England*, eds Susan D. Amussen and Mark A. Kishlansky. Manchester: Manchester UP, 1995, pp. 55–83.

Lamont, William. *Godly Rule: Politics and Religion, 1603–60*. London: Macmillan, 1969.

Le Huray, Peter. *Music and the Reformation in England, 1549–1660*. New York: OUP, 1967.

Lee, Maurice, Jr. *Great Britain's Solomon: James VI and I in his Three Kingdoms*. Urbana and Chicago: U of Illinois P, 1990.

——. *James I and Henri IV: An Essay in English Foreign Policy, 1603–1610*. Urbana, Chicago and London: U of Illinois P, 1970.

——. *The Road to Revolution: Scotland under Charles I, 1625–37*. Urbana: U of Illinois P, 1985.

Lewalski, Barbara K. *Protestant Poetics and the Seventeenth-Century Religious Lyric*. Princeton: Princeton UP, 1979.

——. "Typology and Poetry: A consideration of Herbert, Vaughan and Marvell", *Illustrious Evidence: Approaches to English Literature of the Early Seventeenth Century*. Berkeley: U of California P, 1975.

Lievsay, John Leon. *Venetian Phoenix: Paolo Sarpi and Some of his English Friends (1606–1700)*. Lawrence, Kan.: UP of Kansas, 1973.

Livingston, Neil. *The Scottish Metrical Psalter of AD 1635*. London: Novello, 1935.

Luxton, Imogen. "The Reformation and Popular Culture", *Church and Society in England: Henry VIII to James I*, eds Felicity Heal and Rosemary O'Day. New York: Archon Press, 1977.

MacInnes, Allan I. *Charles I and the Making of the Covenanting Movement, 1625–1641*. Edinburgh: John Donald, 1991.

Maclure, M. *Register of Sermons Preached at Paul's Cross, 1534–1642*. Rev. P. Pauls and J. C. Boswell. Toronto: CRRS, 1989.

Makey, Walter. *The Church of the Covenant, 1637–51: Revolution and Social Change in Scotland*. Edinburgh: John Donald, 1979.

Malcolm, Noel. *De Dominis (1560–1624): Venetian, Anglican, Ecumenist and Relapsed Heretic*. London: Strickland and Scott, 1984.

Mason, Roger A. "George Buchanan, James VI and the Presbyterians", *Scots and Britons: Scottish Political Thought and the Union of 1603*, ed. Roger A. Mason. Cambridge: CUP, 1994.

Mathew, David. *James I*. London: Eyre & Spottiswoode, 1967.

McCullough, Peter. *Sermons at Court: Politics and Religion in Elizabethan and Jacobean Preaching*. Cambridge: CUP, 1998.

McFarlane, I. D. *Buchanan*. London: Duckworth, 1981.

McMillan, William H. "The Metrical Psalter of James VI", *RCHS* 8 (1944): 114–33, 184–208.

——. *The Worship of the Scottish Reformed Church, 1550–1638*. London: J. Clarke, 1931.

M'Crie, Thomas. *Life of Andrew Melville*. Edinburgh, 1824.

Milward, Peter. *Religious Controversies of the Jacobean Age: A Survey of Printed Sources*. Lincoln: U of Nebraska P, 1978.

Morrill, John *et al.* (eds). *Public Duty and Private Conscience in Seventeenth-Century England: Essays Presented to G. E. Aylmer*. Oxford: Clarendon Press, 1993.

Mulligan, Winifred Joy. "The British Constantine and English Historical Myth", *JMRS* 8 (1978): 257–79.

Neale, John. *Queen Elizabeth I*. New York: Doubleday, 1957.

Norbrook, David. *Poetry and Politics in the English Renaissance*. London: Routledge and Kegan Paul, 1984.

Ong, Walter. *The Presence of the Word*. Minneapolis: U of Minnesota P, 1981.

Opfell, Olga. *The King James Bible Translators*. Jefferson and London: McFarland, 1982.

Parry, Graham. *The Golden Age Restor'd*. Manchester: Manchester UP, 1981.

Patrick, Millar. *Four Centuries of Scottish Psalmody*. London, New York: OUP, 1949.

Patterson, Annabel. *Censorship and Interpretation: The Conditions of Writing and Reading in Early Modern England*. Madison: U of Wisconsin P, 1984.

Patterson, W. B. "King James I and the Protestant Cause in the Crisis of 1618–22", *Studies in Church History* 18, ed. S. Mews. Oxford: Basil Blackwell, 1982.

——. "King James I's Call for an Ecumenical Council", *Councils and Assemblies: Studies in Church History*, vol. 7, eds G. J. Cuming and D. Baker. Cambridge: CUP, 1971.

——. *King James VI and I and the Reunion of Christendom*. Cambridge: CUP, 1997.

——. "The Peregrinations of Marco Antonio de Dominis", *Religious Motivation: Biographical and Sociological Problems for the Church Historian*, ed. Derek Baker. Oxford: Basil Blackwell, 1978.

Peck, Linda Levy. *Court Patronage and Corruption in Early Stuart England*. Boston: Unwin Hyman, 1990.

Perry, Curtis. *The Making of Jacobean Culture: James I and the Renegotiation of Elizabethan Literary Practice*. Cambridge: CUP, 1997.

Peters, Robert. "The Notion of *the Church* in the Writings attributed to Kings James VI and I". *Studies in Church History* 3 (1966): 223–41.

Petersen, Rodney L. "Bullinger's Prophets of the '*Restitutio*'", *Biblical Hermeneutics in Historical Perspective*, eds Mark S. Burrows and Paul Rorem. Grand Rapids: William B. Eerdmans, 1991.

Pollard, A. W. *Records of the English Bible 1525–1611*. Oxford: OUP, 1911.

Prescott, Anne Lake. "English Writers and Beza's Latin Epigrams", *Studies in the Renaissance* 21 (1974): 83–117.

——. "Evil Tongues at the Court of Saul: The Renaissance David as a Slandered Courtier", *JMRS* 21 (1991): 163–86.

——. *French Poets and the English Renaissance*. New Haven and London: Yale UP, 1978.

Pritchard, Allen. "George Wither: the Poet as Prophet", *SP* 59 (1962): 211–30.

——. "George Wither's Quarrel with the Stationers: An Anonymous Reply to *The Schollers Purgatory*", *SB* 16 (1963): 27–42.

——. "A Manuscript of George Wither's Psalms", *MP* 77 (1980): 370–81.

Questier, Michael C. *Conversion, Politics and Religion in England, 1580–1625*. Cambridge: CUP, 1996.

——. "Crypto-Catholicism, Anti-Calvinism and Conversion at the Jacobean Court: The Enigma of Benjamin Carier", *Journal of Ecclesiastical History* 47 (1996): 45–64.

——. "John Gee, Archbishop Abbot, and the Use of Converts from Rome in Jacobean Anti-Catholicism", *Recusant History* 21 (1993): 347–60.

Reid, W. S. "The Battle Hymns of the Lord: Calvinist Psalmody of the Sixteenth Century", *Sixteenth-Century Essays and Studies* 2 (1971): 43–53.

Ridley, J. *John Knox*. Oxford: OUP, 1968.

Rose, Elliot. *Cases of Conscience*. Cambridge: CUP, 1975.

Ross, Ian. "Verse Translation at the Court of King James VI of Scotland", *Texas Studies in Language and Literature* 4 (1962/63): 252–67.

Russell, Conrad. *Parliaments and English Politics, 1621–1629*. Oxford: Clarendon Press, 1979.

Rypins, Stanley. "The Printing of *Basilion Doron*", *PBSA* 64 (1970): 393–417.

Salmon, J. H. M. "James I, the Oath of Allegiance, the Venetian Interdict, and the Reappearance of French Ultramontanism", *The Cambridge History of Political Thought, 1450–1700*, eds J. H. Burns and Mark Goldie. Cambridge: CUP, 1991.

Schmutzler, Karl E. "Harington's Metrical Paraphrases of the Seven Penitenial Psalms: Three Manuscript Versions", *PBSA* 53 (1959): 240–51.

Senning, Calvin F. "Vanini and the Diplomats, 1612–1614: Religion, Politics, and Defection in the Counter-Reformation Era", *Historical Magazine of the Protestant Episcopal Church*, 54 (1985): 219–39.

Shami, Jeanne. "The Absolutist Politics of Quotation", *John Donne's Religious Imagination*, eds Raymond-Jean Frontain and Frances M. Malpezzi. Conway, Ark.: UCAP, 1995.

Sharpe, Kevin. "The Earl of Arundel, His Circle and the Opposition to the Duke of Buckingham, 1618–1628", *Faction and Parliament: Essays on Early Stuart Political History*. London and New York: Methuen, 1978.

——. *The Personal Rule of Charles I*. New Haven: Yale UP, 1982.

——. *Politics and Ideas in Early Stuart England: Essays and Studies*. New York and London: Pinter, 1989.

Shriver, Frederick. "Hampton Court Re-visited: James I and the Puritans", *JEH* 33 (1982): 48–71.

——. "Orthodoxy and Diplomacy: James I and the Vorstius Affair", *English Historical Review* 85 (1970): 449–74.

Sinclair, William MacDonald. *Memorials of St. Paul's Cathedral*. Philadelphia: Jacobs, n.d.

Smuts, R. Malcolm. *Court Culture and the Origins of a Royalist Tradition in Early Stuart England*. Philadelphia: U of Pennsylvania P, 1987.

——. "Cultural Diversity and Cultural Change at the Court of James I", *The Mental World of the Jacobean Court*, ed. Linda Levy Peck. Cambridge: CUP, 1991.

——. "The Political Failure of Stuart Cultural Patronage", *Patronage in the Renaissance*, eds Guy F. Lytle and Stephen Orgel. Princeton: Princeton UP, 1981.

Solt, Leo F. *Church and State in Early Modern England*. Oxford: OUP, 1990.

Sommerville, Johann P. "Absolutism and Royalism", *The Cambridge History of Political Thought, 1450–1700*, eds J. H. Burns and Mark Goldie. Cambridge: CUP, 1991, pp. 347–73.

——. "James I and the Divine Right of Kings: English Politics and Continental Theory", *The Mental World of the Jacobean Court*, ed. Linda Levy Peck. Cambridge: CUP, 1991.

Steadman, John. "'Meaning' and 'Name': Some Renaissance Interpretations of Urania", *Neuphilologische mitteilungen* 64 (1963): 209–32.

Strong, Roy. *Britannia Triumphans: Inigo Jones, Rubens and Whitehall Palace.* London: Thames and Hudson, 1980.

——. *The Cult of Elizabeth.* London: Thames and Hudson, 1977.

——. *Henry, Prince of Wales and England's Lost Renaissance.* London: Thames & Hudson, 1986.

Tate, William. "King James I and the Queen of Sheba", *ELR* 26 (1996): 561–85.

Trevelyan, George Macauley. *England under the Stuarts* 1904. Harmondsworth: Penguin, 1960.

Tyacke, Nicholas. *Anti-Calvinists: the Rise of English Arminianism ca. 1590–1640.* Oxford: Clarendon Press, 1987.

Usher, Roland G. *The Reconstruction of the English Church.* 2 Vols. New York: D. Appleton, 1910.

Vining, P. "Wither and Gibbons: A Prelude to the First English Hymn Book", *Musical Times* 120 (1979): 245–6.

Wadkins, Timothy. "King James I Meets John Percy, S. J. (25 May, 1622)", *Recusant History* 19 (1988): 146–254.

Watson, J. R. *The English Hymn: A Critical and Historical Study.* Oxford: Clarendon Press, 1997.

Welsby, Paul. *George Abbot.* London: SPCK, 1962.

White, Peter O. G. *Predestination, Policy and Polemic: conflict and consensus in the English Church from the Reformation to the Civil War.* Cambridge and New York: CUP, 1992.

Williamson, Arthur H. "Scotland, Antichrist and the Invention of Great Britain", *New Perspectives on the Politics and Culture of Early Modern Scotland,* eds John Dwyer *et al.* Edinburgh: John Donald [1980–2], pp. 34–58.

——. *Scottish National Consciousness in the Age of James VI.* Edinburgh: John Donald, 1979.

Willson, David Harris. *King James VI and I.* London: Jonathan Cape, 1956.

——. "James I's Literary Assistants", *HLQ* 8 (1944–5): 35–57.

Wittreich, Joseph Anthony. *Milton and the Line of Vision.* Madison: U of Wisconsin P, 1978.

Wootton, David. *Paolo Sarpi: between Renaissance and Enlightenment.* Cambridge: CUP, 1983.

Wormald, Jenny. *Court, Kirk, and Community: Scotland 1470–1625.* Toronto: U of Toronto P, 1981.

——. "James VI and I: Two Kings or One?" *History* 68 (1983): 187–209.

——. "James VI, James I and the Identity of Britain", *The British Problem, c. 1534–1707,* eds B. Bradshaw and J. Morrill. New York: St Martin's Press, 1966.

Wright, Thomas. *Biographia Britannica Literaria.* 1842–6. Rpt. Detroit: Gale, 1968.

Zim, Rivkah. *English metrical psalms: poetry as praise and prayer, 1535–1601.* Cambridge: CUP, 1987.

INDEX

Index